MAKING CHILD PROTECTION WORK

Harry Ferguson

First published in Great Britain in 2026 by

Policy Press, an imprint of
Bristol University Press
University of Bristol
1–9 Old Park Hill
Bristol
BS2 8BB
UK
+44 (0)117 374 6645
bup-info@bristol.ac.uk

Details of international sales and distribution partners are available at
policy.bristoluniversitypress.co.uk

© Bristol University Press 2026

British Library Cataloguing in Publication Data
A catalogue record for this book is available from the British Library

ISBN 978-1-4473-7825-9 hardcover
ISBN 978-1-4473-7826-6 paperback
ISBN 978-1-4473-7827-3 ePub
ISBN 978-1-4473-7828-0 ePDF

The right of Harry Ferguson to be identified as author of this work has been asserted by him in accordance with the Copyright, Designs and Patents Act 1988.

All rights reserved: no part of this publication may be reproduced, stored in a retrieval system, or transmitted in any form or by any means, electronic, mechanical, photocopying, recording, or otherwise without the prior permission of Bristol University Press.

Every reasonable effort has been made to obtain permission to reproduce copyrighted material. If, however, anyone knows of an oversight, please contact the publisher.

The statements and opinions contained within this publication are solely those of the author and not of the University of Bristol or Bristol University Press. The University of Bristol and Bristol University Press disclaim responsibility for any injury to persons or property resulting from any material published in this publication.

Bristol University Press and Policy Press work to counter discrimination on grounds of gender, race, disability, age and sexuality.

Cover design: Nicky Borowiec
Cover image: Shutterstock/balenopix

Bristol University Press' authorised representative in the European Union is: Easy Access System Europe, Mustamäe tee 50, 10621 Tallinn, Estonia, Email: gpsr.requests@easproject.com

For Claire,
always and forever

Contents

Acknowledgements		viii
Introduction: Bringing child protection to life		**1**
	Stepping into another world …	1
	Thinking about practice and relationships	3
	Lifelessness and the neglect of practice	7
	Bringing child protection to life: a forward-facing approach	8
	Structure of the book	10
1	**The child protection system and the making of practice**	**13**
	In the office and beyond	13
	The child protection system	15
	Time management and organisational practices	16
	The Practice Cycle and spaces for creativity	20
	Improvising and making practice	22
	Conclusion	25
2	**Starting relationships: investigating and assessing child protection concerns**	**27**
	Routine everyday practices in duty and assessment work	27
	Into the unknown: drama, risk and inquisitiveness	33
	Courage and composure under pressure	37
	Conclusion	38
3	**Relationships over time: care, holding and reliability**	**41**
	Holding practices	41
	The contexts for long-term work	43
	Honesty, openness and building trust	44
	'Good enough' practice	46
	Empathy, compassion and endurance	47
	Sustaining care: being a reliable hate object	50
	Conclusion	52
4	**Automated practice: the invisible and unheld child**	**55**
	Thinking about invisible children	55
	A case of fully invisible and unheld children	57
	The process of detaching from children and losing sight of them	60
	Time and organisational culture	61
	The use of transitional space	63
	Emotional and interactional dynamics	64

	Reflection and decision-making	64
	Conclusion	65
5	**Disorganised practice: chaotically thought about and unsafe children**	**67**
	Stepping into fear and complexity	67
	Disgust and the smell of child protection	73
	Abjection, disorganised practice and chaotic thinking	74
	The making of disorganised practice and avoidance	76
	Conclusion	78
6	**The intimate pattern: seen, heard and held children**	**81**
	Intimate practice in initial encounters with children	82
	Responding to children's needs in the moment	86
	From engagement to immersion in children's lives	89
	The ethics of intimate practice	90
	Intimate practice with older children and teenagers	92
	Achieving intimate practice through the Practice Cycle	92
	Conclusion	94
7	**Hands-on practice: making relationships with babies and young children**	**97**
	The baby blind spot: in search of infant voice and experience	98
	How babies get overlooked in practice	100
	Developing relationships with babies and young children	101
	Thinking about the rights of babies and hands-on practice	104
	Conclusion	108
8	**Holding relationships: helping parents, families and enabling change**	**111**
	From the Practice Cycle to the seasons of child protection	112
	A case of holding relationships in practice	113
	Parental perspectives	117
	The components of therapeutic holding relationships	118
	Conclusion	122
9	**Hostile relationships: conflict and good authority in working with involuntary service users**	**125**
	Involuntary relationships	126
	Sustaining hostile relationships over time (or trying to)	128
	The relational dynamics of hostility	132
	Good authority in working with and beyond hostility	134
	Conclusion	138

10	**Close or distant? Relational styles in child protection work**	**141**
	The embodied self and relational vocabularies	142
	The relational continuum	144
	Relationships to the world: resonance and alienation	148
	Developing the professional self and relational styles	150
	Conclusion	153
11	**Crafting relational spaces: digital, outdoor and mobile practices**	**155**
	The home as a space for improvisation and mobile practice	155
	Screen relations: digital spaces	158
	Beyond the home: walking interviews and out and about practice	162
	Conclusion	165
12	**Beyond reflective practice: helping practitioners with thinking and non-thinking**	**169**
	Thinking about reflection	170
	Reflective practice, in practice	173
	Suspended self-preservation: the limits to reflection	175
	Towards analytical thinking	179
	Conclusion	180
13	**Holding environments: supervision and live organisational support for relational practice**	**183**
	More than formal support: 'live' supervision	184
	Spaces for organisational support	187
	Workplace defences against unbearable feelings	190
	Enhancing supervision and staff well-being	194
	Conclusion	195
14	**Making child protection work well**	**199**
	Putting life and practice first	199
	The Practice Cycle, presence and practising resonance	201
	New knowledge and skills for relationship-based practice	204
	Re-making systems and child protection work	206
	Child protection and a good life	207

Appendix: Methodology and the research studies	211
References	217
Index	239

Acknowledgements

This book has been a long time in the making, mainly because I planned it that way, but also because life had other ideas. In researching and writing it I have been incredibly fortunate to have had the support of many people.

Catherine Gray, my editor, deserves very special thanks. Catherine encouraged me to write this book in the first place and read and commented on multiple drafts, always pushing me to think harder, dig deeper and make it relevant to practice. I am so grateful for her wisdom, her patience, her friendship and for the huge amount she has put into trying to make the book as good as it could be. Her care and commitment have been extraordinary.

Isobel Bainton, Rupert Spurrier, Koel Mukherjee and Rich Kemp at Policy Press have been great to work with and I thank them for their enthusiastic support for the project and all kinds of intellectual and very practical help.

When I decided around 2010 that I wanted to learn about child protection and social work by getting as close as possible to practice by observing it, the entire project rested upon me being allowed to do it. My heartfelt thanks to all the social work managers, administrators, social workers, and family support workers who allowed me into their workplaces, gave me their time, and trusted me enough to let me shadow them everywhere they went, in their offices, cars, on walks, on screens, and to observe them in their practice with children and families and talk to me at length about it. And to the families who welcomed me into their homes and lives and consented to me observing their interactions with social workers, often at very vulnerable moments: thank you. I am sorry that I am not able to name them all here, or even where they are based, because all information that could possibly identify the participants has been changed to protect their anonymity. It takes enormous generosity and courage to allow yourself to be observed, especially at difficult times when the pressure is greatest. It has been a profound privilege to witness families' and professionals' experiences, and I hope that this book repays the trust that was placed in me.

I have been so lucky to spend most of my working life, 48 years of it to be precise, connected to social work and in universities, learning alongside and inspired by wonderful colleagues and students. I am grateful to the School of Social Policy and Society at the University of Birmingham for granting me a period of study leave, which gave me valuable time to immerse myself in writing the book. I am also thankful to my colleagues in the Department of Social Work and Social Care for the learning I have gained from the countless discussions we have had about many of the ideas contained here. I remain deeply grateful to Professor Fred Powell of University College Cork for the encouragement and support he has offered me from very early on in my career.

Some of the book draws on research I conducted in collaboration with Liz Beddoe, Tom Disney, Tarsem Singh Cooner, Matthew Gibson, Abby Gilsenan,

Acknowledgements

Laura Kelly, Jadwiga Leigh, Sarah Pink, Gillian Plumridge, Jason Schaub and Lisa Warwick. I thank them for their insights, contributions and support, which have been invaluable.

I have presented a lot of the ideas and arguments in this book to many hundreds of social workers at conferences and other events I have been invited to speak at over the years. I am very grateful for their critiques, challenges and support, which have helped deepen my understanding of day-to-day practice and relationships. This includes joint workshops I have conducted with the brilliant Geese Theatre Company about home visits to children and families. I am very grateful to Andy Watson, Louise Heywood and the rest of the team for the pleasure of working with them.

Charlotte von Bülow has been a great source of support over several years, initially as an executive coach and, more recently, as a close friend. I'm so thankful for her resonant presence, insight and kindness. Hartmut Rosa's book on 'resonance' and a lecture I attended in 2019 that he did on it, set me on a path that has deeply influenced both my thinking and this book. I'm very grateful for the kindness and encouragement he showed me.

Several people were good enough to take the time to read parts of the book and provide feedback. Sincere thanks to Karen Bateson, Marta Bolongnani, Charlotte von Bülow, Caroline Guard, Sally Hogg, Lucy Morton, Nicola O'Sullivan, Kelly Tighe and Andrew Turnell. This feedback and the many lively discussions helped me greatly to clarify and develop my thinking, and I alone am responsible for the views that remain.

For discussions and activities that have helped me to think, learn and supported my work in various ways, I am very grateful to Amy Adams, Fergus Anderson, Philip Archard, Andrew Arnold, Ann Arnold, Mary Ayim, Dave Barron, Safina Bi, Marta Bolognani, Stephen Briggs, Mark Campbell, Tarsem Singh Cooner, Andrew Cooper, Linda Cooper, Alison Davis, Steve Denton, Kim Detjen, John Devaney, Alison Ferguson, David Ferguson, Ian Ferguson, Yvon Guest, Simon Haworth, Steve Hennessy, Rianne Houghton, Steven Hudson, Jeewan Kala Gurung, Debbie Innis-Turnhill, Joel Kanter, Brett Kahr, Michelle Lefevre, Helen Lincoln, Steven Lucas, Christine McFarland, Lee Pardy-McLaughlin, Clare Parkinson, Ali Roy, Gillian Ruch, Liz Salter, Mike Snudden, Kelly Tighe, Pam Trevithick, Suzanne Triggs, Lisa Warwick, Andrew Whittaker, Helen Woods, and Peter Yates.

Social media – particularly Twitter (now X) between 2012 and 2023, and more recently, LinkedIn and Bluesky – has connected me with a large community of 'virtual friends' in social work, social care and the wider social sciences, from whom I've learned a great deal – and had some fun along the way.

I don't have the words to fully express the depth of my gratitude to my wife, Claire Mackinnon, for her unwavering love, care and support. She has quietly and steadfastly held things together during the most difficult times, especially when I was seriously ill and in recovery. Her resilience, compassion and loving presence have been a profound gift. In addition, Claire's wisdom as a psychotherapist and our many discussions about the ideas in the book have been enormously helpful.

I am deeply grateful to my daughter Ellen for all the love, learning, craic and everything else she has given me for 25 years and for her technical and artistic skills in producing the diagrams for the book. I am very thankful to my stepchildren, Marc, Katie, Ben and Susie, for all their, love, support and inspiration. Ronnie, Marnie, Arthur, Francesca, Sofia, Immie, Aleiya, Lila, Megan, Caitlin and Lottie keep me grounded in the joys of grandparenting and remind me constantly just how precious and remarkable children are. A special shout out to Claire Finlay and Victoria Crewes for keeping the family social work flag flying. Wishing you long, healthy and satisfying careers – may what I set out in Chapter 13, in particular, be achieved for you, and for everyone committed to making child protection work.

The reason the book has taken a bit longer to finish than I had planned is because at a point when an initial full draft was nearing completion in early 2023, I became seriously ill. This culminated in August 2023 with me having a liver transplant. This was exactly 19 years to the day after my first liver transplant. I owe my life to the doctors, nurses, healthcare assistants, transplant coordinators and social workers who provided me with excellent care and supported me to find my way back to health. I thank and love you all. I would not be alive now were it not for the enormous generosity of my liver donors and their families who supported their loved ones' wishes to donate. I waited five months for a donor for my first transplant in 2004, while for the second in 2023 I was very fortunate to get a donor quickly because I was so ill. Tragically, some patients don't get them on time. Not surprisingly, I am passionate about organ donation and due to the shortage of donors, I can't let any opportunity go by without trying to raise awareness of the need for it.

This experience has deepened my understanding of what generosity, skilled care and good relationship-based practice in health and social care look like. While I don't write about that personal experience directly, I hope its resonance can be felt throughout the vision of intimate child protection work I set out in what follows.

Harry Ferguson
Bristol, England
30 April 2025

Introduction: Bringing child protection to life

Stepping into another world ...

It is 3.30 on a warm summer afternoon and I am being driven by a social worker, who I will call Jenny, to a home visit to see two children aged six and ten regarding concerns about possible neglect and domestic abuse.[1] Jenny parks up and as we walk towards the home the closer we get to it the louder the sound of dogs barking gets and Jenny whispers, 'I do hate visiting families with dogs. It's my biggest bugbear. Why does everybody who's got a dog think that people like them?' Jenny adds: 'And remembering people's names is a challenge as well, especially if it's the first visit, like the first I've read about them.'

Mrs 'Nolan' opens the door while restraining her two large dogs. Jenny remembers her name and is invited in. The social worker manages to maintain her composure in the sitting room despite the dogs sniffing at and snuggling up beside her on the sofa. Six-year-old Bethany and ten-year-old James are present and Jenny takes control by initially asking to see their mother on her own and for the television to be turned down. The children leave the room, although Jenny said afterwards she suspected they were listening outside (I sat on an armchair to one side and could see that they were). The social worker put to Mrs Nolan the concerns the school have about her alcohol consumption and forgetting to pick the children up and that social care had received prior referrals suggesting she was a victim of domestic abuse. Mrs Nolan said she did not have a drink problem and that her abusive partner had now moved out. After 27 minutes of discussion Jenny gains Mrs Nolan's consent to see the children on their own separately in their bedrooms. Jenny goes upstairs into James' bedroom, without Bethany, and asks him if it is okay if she sits on his single bed (I sit on the floor in the corner). She places herself towards the top of the bed with her legs folded under her. James leans back against the end of the bed while remaining standing. Jenny introduces herself, explains her job and talks to James for 11 minutes, during which she leans towards him with an open stance, making eye contact and responding to him in a pleasant, animated manner. The child speaks quite openly, such as when the social worker asks: 'And do you ever worry when mum drinks?' and he replies, 'About 20 per cent I worry', and Jenny probes about 'what's that 20 per cent then?'

---

[1] While the case materials and examples used in the book reflect actual events and findings, all names and some other details have been changed to protect the anonymity of the families, professionals and research sites.

Her approach and manner is the same during the 12 minutes she spends with six-year-old Bethany in the same bedroom, without James being present. Jenny begins by seeking to put the child at ease, telling her she is not there to take them away but to find out more about their mother's care and drinking so she can support her to get help if this is needed. Jenny takes up the same position on the bed while Bethany stays further from it than her brother did and leans back against the radiator on the wall, taking support from it. Jenny adjusts her language to make it appropriate for the younger child and pays attention to the children's things – DVDs, toys, a musical instrument – and incorporates them in a playful way into her communication. Jenny then goes downstairs and the dogs continue their interest in her (and me). She shares her view with Mrs Nolan that there are possible family difficulties that she needs to explore further and may be able to help with and makes an appointment to see her again the following week when the children are not present. On the journey back to the office Jenny tells me how awkward she can feel about asking to see children alone and how she wants them and their mother to feel like she can help them.

This snapshot of a home visit to inquire into children's safety and well-being is one of several hundred practice encounters between children, families and social workers I have observed in recent years for my research. As a practitioner in another case put it when reflecting on how social workers routinely enter families' most private spaces, this kind of work is like 'stepping into another world'. This book is intended as a journey into that 'world' of child protection and what is, and is not, good practice in family homes and the other places it goes on. Journey, as the previous case illustration shows, is meant quite literally. The book travels alongside social workers on the journeys they undertake, exploring how they engage with children and families about child protection concerns. What do they do to prepare before leaving the office? What runs through their minds as they travel to see the child? How do they gain access to where the child is? What do they say, do and feel when face to face with parents and children – in their homes and elsewhere? And what support do they need afterwards from managers to help them make sense of the experience and guide their decisions?

In this book I shall refer to this activity as *making child protection work*. This is intended to capture two meanings: the sense of practice having to be made in how social workers have to be active in using their communication and improvisation skills, their authority and empathy, their bodies and the objects around them to try to understand and change children's and families' lives. And, second, *making child protection work* means ensuring that children are kept safe and that parents and other carers are worked with in ways that are fair, humane and helpful. A huge amount of research, academic literature, and government and other reports now exists about how child protection can and should be made to work. What is striking is the almost total absence of detailed, rich descriptions and analysis of the actual doing and experiencing of child protection work by practitioners and family members in real time, the kinds of relationships they forge and what is good, helpful practice. It is this big gap in knowledge and understanding of how child protection can be made to work that this book is seeking to fill.

This is the world of activity that in an earlier book I termed *Child Protection Practice* (Ferguson, 2011). This new book develops and deepens analysis of the themes I opened up in *Child Protection Practice*, while being different from it in several key respects. When I wrote *Child Protection Practice* some 14 years ago I had done some observations of practice that I was able to draw upon, but I have since been involved in several studies that have observed over 400 practice encounters between social workers and children and families. This has involved going on more than 600 car journeys with social workers to and from home visits and other meetings, spending lengthy periods observing in social work offices to learn about the interactions between staff and organisational culture, and doing hundreds of interviews with social work staff and many with family members (for a full account of the research, see the Appendix). Drawing on this wealth of experience, I intend to open up the world of practice and relationships in a systematic, rigorous and intensely close-up, intimate way that has never been done before and to provide new ways of understanding what is involved in making child protection work.

Thinking about practice and relationships

This experience of observing so many encounters has enabled me to see a whole variety of practice in which some children were not 'seen' and families superficially engaged with, while in others the practice was deeply relational, intimate and effective. Over the past two decades or so, 'relationship-based practice' has become a highly influential perspective through which what goes on between social workers and service users is theorised and analysed (Howe, 1998; Trevithick, 2003; Trevithick, 2012; Ruch, 2013; Bryan et al, 2016; Ruch et al, 2018; Ingram and Smith, 2018). This focus on relationships has arisen in part because of how the growth of computerisation, managerial oversight and audit culture has meant practitioners having to spend a great deal of time completing bureaucratic tasks. Since the 1990s, a significant body of research has addressed social workers' experiences of bureaucracy, the majority of which has been published since 2015, suggesting that the amount of such administrative activity has expanded across the sector (Pascoe et al, 2023). This, it is argued, has pushed social work towards becoming more about office activities like case recording, box-ticking and meeting timescales than relationship-based practice, squeezing the time available to spend with service users (Ingram and Smith, 2018). Research and writing has therefore sought to reclaim the importance of relationships and the emotional and unconscious components of people and practices (Ingram, 2013; Hood et al, 2019). Gillian Ruch (2018) shows how the concept of relationship-based practice has developed by integrating theory from psychoanalysis, attachment theory, systems theory, politics and sociology. The result is a concept of relational practice that incorporates awareness of the effects of power, inequalities, and emotions, internal life and unconscious processes.

Important work has also been done on different experiences of relationships that involve working with strong feelings like anger (Smith, 2018), hopelessness (Parkinson, 2018) and love (Turney, 2018). This work has been very helpful to reclaiming the vital importance of the relationship at the heart of practice and in the book I will build on it and refine it in at least three ways.

First, this book will show that different kinds of relationships between professionals and families exist in child protection and detailed attention will be given to the various forms they take. In some, meaningful connections are forged from the start and over time evolve into what I call 'holding relationships' that have positive therapeutic outcomes. Then there is relating that occurs with parents and sometimes children who are opposed to child protection involvement that become what I call 'hostile relationships' that are based on conflict and hate. The book also shows the range and complexity of relationships by being sensitive to children's ages and developmental stage and the types of needs and harms involved.

In recent years, the scope of what constitutes 'child abuse' has expanded significantly. While extreme cases of sadistic abuse that resulted in the deaths of children are given prominence in media coverage and political and public outcries (Leedham, 2022), neglect and emotional abuse remain the most recognised forms of harm, alongside growing awareness of sexual and criminal exploitation beyond the family (Pearce, 2014; Thomas and Darcy, 2017; Home Office, 2020). 'Child sexual exploitation' was formally introduced in UK policy in 2009 (DCSF, 2009). Firmin's (2020) ground-breaking work on 'Contextual Safeguarding' argues that the exclusive focus on the home and parental responsibility overlooks key public spaces where exploitation occurs and where safeguarding efforts are needed. Most known victims of child sexual exploitation are between 14 and 17 years old, with a peak at 15 (Gohir, 2013; Home Office, 2020), though younger children are also affected. This age profile has many implications that must be considered. In this book the focus is mainly on 'child protection' issues that relate to the needs and harms to children and young people *within* the family, which involves high numbers of young children and some who are unborn. A key issue is how relationship-based practice can extend beyond older children who can engage through speech, play or messaging, to pre-school children and babies who lack such capacities. There is an emerging argument that the needs of infants have been overlooked, even in early childhood studies (Guard, 2023) and the book will show how this gap in child protection with babies can be addressed.

A second way in which the book seeks to expand the concept of relationship-based practice is by including attention to the body. I will build on work that has begun to explore the vital issue of how the body is used and experienced in interactions in social work (Cameron and McDermott, 2007; van Rhyn et al, 2020; Kong et al, 2022; Bogue, 2025). I argue that child protection is practised through the use of all the senses – sight, smell, hearing and touch. It is an 'embodied self' (Bloom, 2006) that is at work at the heart of relational practice. Empathy, for example, as van Rhyn et al (2020) have shown, is communicated in non-verbal bodily ways by how people are, their posture and demeanour. Touch is the most neglected sense of all in analysis of social work and child protection (Green, 2017) and much more attention needs to be given to tactile engagement and questions such as where should picking up and holding infants and children fit into safeguarding practices? I will be using the concepts of 'intimate practice', 'holding' and 'visibility' to outline the nature of good practice and reveal some very significant differences between practitioners in how they use their bodies and their willingness to get close to children, or not. This will be explored in terms of what I call 'relational styles'.

This directly relates to a third way in which the book develops thinking about relationship-based practice, by giving attention to the 'energy' of encounters and spaces. In the practice encounters I have observed, commonly recognised aspects of interactions such as rapport building, empathy and active listening were often apparent. But there was something else too, where people and the encounters generated particular kinds of energy and atmospheres. They had a *feel* to them that was very significant in whether the participants gelled or not and the relationship worked. I argue that not nearly enough attention has been given to the uniqueness of social work and child protection as forms of practice, such as the fact that a great deal of this work happens on the move. As the book will show, social workers sometimes spend most of their time with service users on their feet and barely sit down. More commonly, they alternate between mobility and stillness, moving, standing or sitting as needed. This is evident in the way the social worker Jenny, discussed at the beginning of this chapter, drove to the home, walked and gained access to it, spent time sitting on the sofa talking to the family, moved around the home, got onto the bed to relate to the children, and off it to connect with them through their toys, and then went back downstairs and was seated again before leaving. This means child protection work takes energy in the literal sense of needing the vitality to do it in the ways required. This energy in motion, also known as kinetic energy, requires vigour and, over time, stamina. In the book, I characterise this as a state of 'aliveness', a term that seeks to capture the dynamic energy and vitality required and experienced through the full engagement of the senses, body and mind.

The energy required in the setting of the family home is very different to that in helping relationships that take place in offices, consulting rooms and clinics where the encounters are basically stationary and still. While creating calmness and space for thinking and meditative reflection can have value in child protection work, very often practitioners have to try to connect with parents and children and build rapport, trust and the relationship while on the move and by doing at least two things at once – such as talking to parents while playing with children. Of crucial importance here is the quality of *presence* that workers convey, the 'energy' or 'aura' they exude. When they are with children and families, sometimes I have seen (and sensed) practitioners who were emotionally flat, their energy was low and they gave off vibes of not really wanting to be there. Their communication lacked aliveness and the desire to connect and make a difference. The book will show how this kind of robotic 'automated' presence can have major consequences by leading to children becoming invisible and unsafe, and families not being helped.

On the other hand, there are encounters where practitioners are present with children and families in ways that are full of vitality, aliveness and purpose. Their energy, the way they hold themselves and the quality of attention they give, conveys that they are there to engage in meaningful, helpful ways. They are available to hear and accept whatever the service user needs to communicate. Bazzano (2013) explores the importance of 'presence' in therapy and argues that it is not just about technique, but practitioners needing to know 'how to be with a client, not just what to do'. Following the sociologist Hartmut Rosa (2019; 2023), I will call this quality of aliveness, presence and relating 'resonance'. Resonance occurs wherever people in the course of an interaction are touched by it, feeling moved and changed as a result (Rosa, 2019, p 179). Rosa likens the experience to a vibrating wire of connection between people, a fitting metaphor, as creating vibration requires energy. The encounter between Jenny, the two Nolan children and their mother had resonance. There was an aliveness, curiosity, playfulness and confidence in the social worker's capacity to move, attune and communicate, and in the family's response.

As the book will illustrate, I have been privileged to be present at many encounters where social workers engaged meaningfully with children and families in ways that fostered deep resonance. It has similarities to what Bloom (2005; 2006), a psychotherapist, refers to as 'energetic attunement' between therapist and client. Within humanistic counselling and psychotherapy the concept of 'relational depth' has been developed to try to capture what occurs in the 'moments of meeting' when change takes place (Murphy, 2012). The approach of 'motivational interviewing' refers to collaboration and 'evocation' being used to draw out the service user's own motivations to enable change (for examples, see Forrester et al, 2021). Such a 'working alliance' generates an emotional bond that helps to create change (Pérez-Rojas et al, 2019; Koprowska, 2020). While such theories are helpful, the conceptual framework and language we use to understand and describe the energetic qualities of encounters and relationship-based practice require further development. The book will do this by giving attention to negative as well as positive energies and advancing concepts such as 'automated' practice and 'resonance'.

The ways in which practitioners relate to children and families, the extent and quality of their energy and attention, is not merely determined by their individual capabilities. It is influenced by networks of power, resources and the organisational context and wider systems within which they and managers work. This includes the nature of supervision and the help and support they get to prepare and come alive, in the office and on journeys to see families. The concept of the 'Practice Cycle' will be developed to capture these linkages between organisations, journeys, practice encounters and what occurs when back at the office. The ways in which this Practice Cycle is navigated will be shown to be crucial in the making of different patterns of practice and relationships.

Introduction

Lifelessness and the neglect of practice

A huge problem with the ways in which child protection is written and talked about is its *lifelessness* and the distance it keeps from practice. This failure to get under the skin of real-life practice is most apparent in the highly influential discourse that concerns failures to protect children and young people at high risk of physical abuse, neglect and sexual abuse. In the UK, for five decades now, since the inquiry into the death of 7-year-old Maria Colwell in the early 1970s (Department of Health and Social Security, 1974), there has been an intense focus on the deaths of abused children. Maria Colwell, Jasmine Beckford, Victoria Climbié, Peter Connelly, Daniel Pelka, Arthur Labinjo-Hughes, Star Hobson and Sara Sharif are children to whom the media, policy, practice, academic and public discourse constantly return and cast a dark shadow over the professions which work with children. This is especially so for social workers who have been ritually blamed and shamed in the media for their deaths (Jones, 2014; Warner, 2015; Shoesmith, 2016; Leedham, 2022). In case review reports, typically brief examples are given of how teachers in schools and nurses on hospital wards have been present with abused and neglected children who subsequently died. Or, much more commonly, how social workers were permitted by parents only to see children on doorsteps or glimpse them through windows. Or they got into the home and were even in the same rooms as children who it subsequently emerged had serious injuries, but this wasn't uncovered.

For instance, in the West Midlands of England in 2020, six-year-old Arthur Labinjo-Hughes' grandmother saw bruises on his back and reported it to the police, including sending them photos of the bruises. The police visited him at his grandmother's but did not examine him, or send the photos to the social work department. Three days later Arthur was visited at his home by a social worker and family support worker. The case review into his death states that 'Arthur gave 10/10 when asked to rate how safe and happy he felt' and that he and his brother showed 'all outward signs of being happy, with consistent stories about their injuries, in what looked like a safe and comfortable home' (Child Safeguarding Practice Review Panel, 2022a, p 31). The social worker and family support worker saw a scratch on Arthur's face and faded bruising on his back, believing the parents' account that it was caused by playfighting with his four-year-old step-brother. Yet during the visit Arthur would have had non-accidental injuries and been experiencing the effects of extreme emotional abuse and neglect. We know this because on the day his father and step-mother were convicted of killing him the police released harrowing CCTV recordings from home surveillance footage of Arthur struggling to get up off the living room floor where he was forced to sleep. Arthur could be heard crying 'no one loves me' and 'no one's going to feed me'. The disparity between a child who the police and social care perceived as showing 'all outward signs of being happy' and the appalling abuse he was experiencing could not be starker. A matter of days later news of the murder of 16-month-old Star Hobson by her step-mother and mother hit the headlines and caused further outcry because the health and social care professionals involved failed to protect her.

The joint case review into why these two children were not protected concluded that the professionals needed to provide 'greater challenge to the self-reported explanations' of the parents and there should have been 'greater triangulation of evidence from across agencies' (Child Safeguarding Practice Review Panel, 2022a). This conclusion that the workers did not communicate effectively with one another or demonstrate enough of what similar reports have often referred to as 'professional curiosity' has been a constant in case reviews for several years (Brandon et al, 2010; Burton and Revell, 2018; Dickens et al, 2022a; 2022b; 2023). But *why* the practitioners behaved in this way and what they actually did and did not do is not examined in any detail.

The absence of attention to the detail of practice is in part due to how such reports choose to give prominence to poor multi-agency working. The Arthur and Star review recommends the establishment nationally of 'Multi-Agency Child Protection Units' made up of experienced, skilled social workers, police, psychologists, doctors and other health staff. Getting multi-agency collaboration and communication right is of course vitally important, but no equivalent attempt was made to examine in depth what actually happened in the encounters between professionals and family members. We don't know enough about how close to the children workers got, whether they saw them on their own, examined them, what the atmosphere in the home was like, how the workers felt, and how this may have influenced what they did or did not do. The question remains: even in the event of effective multi-agency coordination taking place, how should professionals interact with parents and relate to children in ways that ensure they are kept safe?

Bringing child protection to life: a forward-facing approach

In seeking to answer such questions in this book, the concept of 'making' is pivotal and involves shifting perspectives from approaches dominated by retrospective thinking to a forward-facing approach. For instance, the report into Arthur and Star's deaths concludes that '[a] multi-agency strategy meeting would have been the place to bring together everything that was known' (Child Safeguarding Practice Review Panel, 2022a). Of course, with the benefit of hindsight, we know this to be true. What we still don't understand is why this and meaningful relating with the children didn't happen *at the time*.

However well meaning, the kind of analysis presented in these reports reads practice 'backwards' from the perspective of the known final outcome, the children's deaths. Reviews identify a sequence of events and then link them to an idea in the mind of a person or system – such as an absence of 'professional curiosity'. Or the popular idea that practitioners were too 'optimistic', that a 'rule of optimism' results in them naively believing what parents tell them and denying the abuse that is in front of them (Dingwall et al, 1983; Coventry LCSB, 2013, p 43). This kind of simplistic analysis and conclusion barely touches the surface of what was going on in the life of the family and caseworkers, their interactions and experiences. Hindsight thinking has a huge deadening effect in how it drains away the relational dynamics, feelings, energy, atmospheres, grit, the very life and soul that is at the heart of child protection work as it is being done.

There is a huge amount of valuable research and writing on child protection. However, when I wrote *Child Protection Practice* (2011), virtually no other research had been done that observed face-to-face practice as it was going on. This has begun to change, with observational studies of mostly one-off encounters between practitioners and service users (Broadhurst and Mason, 2012; Ferguson, 2016a; 2016b; Ruch et al, 2017; Winter et al, 2017; Henderson, 2018; Jeyasingham, 2018; Noyes, 2018; Forrester et al, 2019; Critchley, 2020; O'Connor, 2022; Murphy, 2022; 2023a; 2023b). This book builds on that work and breaks new ground in the way it uses ethnographic methods to get close enough to observe both short- and long-term practice and relationships in a sustained way (Ferguson et al, 2020a).

My aim in this book is to replace explanation that is based on hindsight with an approach that is *forward-facing* and gives primacy to *life*. This involves seeking understanding of how meaning and everyday life are created through practices and relationships *as they are going on and unfolding in real time*. The anthropologist Tim Ingold (2011) has developed the concept of 'making' to capture this way of seeing and studying life as it is lived through forward movement. This turns the focus onto the movement, creativity, improvisation and skills that social workers and other professionals use and the materials they draw on (computers, cars, toys and so on) to make their practice (cf Ingold, 2011, p 210; Ingold and Hallam, 2007; Page, 2021). This approach also brings attention to the skills and creativity families use in making relationships with professionals.

The overarching theoretical orientation for the book is psycho-social in that it integrates the kinds of social theory from sociology and anthropology that I have mentioned, with thinking from psychology that provides insights into relating and relationships. It draws particularly on psychoanalytic thinking as developed initially by Sigmund Freud, then by Melanie Klein (Salzberger-Wittenberg, 1970), Wilfred Bion (1962), Donald Winnicott (1957; 1971) and Clare Winnicott (1963). For the Winnicotts, the mother–infant relationship was the basis for understanding practitioner–service user dynamics. A parent's unconditional love and deep empathy establish a 'facilitating environment' that is vital to the infant's emotional health and development. Winnicott (1957) extended this concept to psychotherapy, describing the therapist's role as creating a 'holding environment' for clients. As I am developing it for social work and child protection, safe and therapeutic practice involves practitioners and service users having 'holding' encounters and relationships.

This theory helps us to consider how difficult it can be to think clearly about service users, to 'hold them in mind'. This is especially the case in stressful situations, when anxiety is high (Bower, 2005). To help someone requires a capacity to think about them and become emotionally attuned to their experience. Invisible and unheld children in child protection work are those who become 'unthought' about and are not held in mind – or, indeed, physically – by workers and systems. This perspective is complemented by sociological thinking about relationships and modern life, particularly the work of Hartmut Rosa (2015; 2019; 2023). As I explained earlier, this helps to bring to life the energetic quality of relationships and how people connect and 'resonate' with one another, or this does not happen and what I call 'automated' or 'disorganised' patterns of relating occur.

None of these forms of relating and relationships happen in a vacuum. They are embedded in networks of power and institutions that have to be taken fully into account. Child protection work is a product of the interplay between practitioners' lived experience, emotional lives and the organisations, systems and structures of power they work in and service users live within (Reder et al, 1993; Munro, 2011; Trevithick, 2012; Featherstone et al, 2018; 2019; Ruch et al, 2018; Coulter et al, 2020). It is a complex system (Munro, 2005; Hood, 2018). This includes the influence of the powerful state institutions that govern everyday policy and practice and set the parameters within which 'child abuse' is defined, what 'child protection' means, and the services and resources that can be provided. Families experiencing multiple and enduring difficulties who come from lower socio-economic areas are much more likely to be involved with child protection services and have their children taken into care (Morris, 2013; Yang, 2015; Featherstone et al, 2018; 2019; Keddell, 2020; 2022; Keddell et al, 2023) and to experience multiple removals of babies (Broadhurst et al, 2015). This has led to critiques that argue the child protection system is broken and punitive because it individualises family problems rather than providing families with resources and adequate social support (Bywaters et al, 2016; 2022; Gupta, 2017; Keddell, 2020; Keddell et al, 2022). Attention to inequalities, power and human rights within the context of capitalism and austerity politics, and patriarchal structures where the focus is so much on regulating mothers, is essential to understanding family experiences, decision-making and the making of child protection work.

The core argument of this book, then, is that making child protection work is – or should be – fundamentally about entering children's worlds in ways that are intimate, 'alive' and 'resonant'. It involves having relationships with parents and families that are reliable, humane, authoritative and therapeutic, where their adversities are fully considered and they feel 'held'. This is only possible if practitioners themselves feel held within organisations that support them to deal with the emotional impact of the work and that provide them and families with the time and resources to form meaningful relationships that can make child protection work.

Structure of the book

Chapter 1 sets out the broad parameters of the child protection system and how practice is made through creativity and improvisation. It outlines the Practice

Cycle, which is a way of mapping what occurs from the moment information about a child comes into social workers and checks are made with other agencies, managers consulted and the worker travels to and sees the family. Chapter 2 discusses the nature and experience of short-term investigative work and how it fundamentally relies on movement and contending with the uncertainty of going into the unknown. By contrast, Chapter 3 considers the overarching character of long-term relational practice with families. It expands upon the theoretical framework for the book by discussing key concepts such as 'holding', reliability, and relational rupture and repair. It also sets the scene for Chapters 4, 5 and 6, which provide in-depth analysis of patterns and forms of relationship-based practice that emerge from the Practice Cycle. Patterns of avoidant practice will be identified where workers are either robotic and automated in how they relate (Chapter 4), or disorganised (Chapter 5), resulting in invisible and unheld children. Or the relating is close and intimate, the energy of encounters full of resonance and children are seen, heard and held (Chapter 6).

Chapter 7 takes the exploration of intimate practice further by giving detailed consideration to making relationships with babies and younger children. Chapter 8 considers the key components in making co-operative and therapeutic 'holding relationships' that help parents to change and develop their relationships and capacities to care. Chapter 9 deals with the different challenge of working with involuntary service users and argues that the best chance of establishing a working relationship is through the use of 'good authority' and engaging in 'Practice by Negotiation'.

Detailed attention is then given to more general themes and key issues that affect relationships and child protection work. In Chapter 10, the different 'relational styles' of practitioners are identified and placed on a relational continuum between avoidant and intimate. A concept of the 'professional self' is posited as a way of trying to ensure that practice has resonance and is relational and intimate. The effects of domestic, public and digital spaces on practice and relationships are considered in Chapter 11. In Chapter 12, the influential concept of 'reflective practice' is analysed and shown to have limitations. Practitioners being supported to think clearly and manage anxiety is crucial and it is argued that this can be advanced through the development of an 'internal supervisor'. Chapter 13 deepens the analysis of these issues by examining the organisational setting and the formal and 'live' supervision needed to support staff well-being and retention. It highlights the importance of sustaining professionals in ways that enable them to possess the aliveness, energy, desire, courage and skills to engage in resonant relationship-based practice with children and families. Chapter 14 concludes the book by drawing together the arguments and key learning about the nature of practice and relationships and what needs to be maintained and changed to make child protection work well.

Finally, it is important to also stress what this book does not attempt to do. While the practice issues it addresses have relevance to all professions who are involved in child protection work, it is heavily focused on social work. The involvement of some other professionals is considered in the context of some case studies, but I haven't provided a detailed analysis of multi-agency working. This is not because it is not important, but due to the decision to focus intensely on the dynamics of interactions and relationships with children and families. Nor does the book seek to provide a rigorous analysis of the effectiveness of key policies, legislation and procedures in the UK or elsewhere, although some hopefully helpful insights in this regard are provided. It is rather a sociologically and psycho-dynamically informed study of practice that seeks to provide new insights into relationship-based practice and the variety of forms it takes, the experience of doing, receiving and making child protection work, and how it can best keep children safe, help parents and support families.

1
The child protection system and the making of practice

The central aim of this book is to show how everyday child protection work is done, to learn from practice that is good enough, analyse why sometimes it isn't and explore how it can be made better. This 'making' of practice occurs through a variety of actions carried out by practitioners and families within the context of organisational and wider systemic influences. It is vital to examine how systems enable, block and frustrate good practice and to identify the creative ways in which social workers and other professionals improvise and adapt their practice to keep children safe and help parents. As I argued in the Introduction, this requires us to explore practice in a forward-facing way as it unfolds in real time. The aim is to capture what Stern (2004, p 14) calls 'lived present moments as they are unfolding, not as they are remembered or narrated'. This chapter begins to show how this *making process* occurs by providing an outline of the child protection system, the organisational context, what I call the 'Practice Cycle' and some key aspects of how the work is creatively done and experienced by practitioners and families.

In the office and beyond

Not long after beginning to observe what goes on in social work offices, two things in particular stood out for me. The first of these was the range of concerns social workers have to respond to and the knowledge, sensitivity and skills required to do so effectively and humanely. For example, in the first couple of weeks alone, the visits I accompanied social workers on included going to see a four-year-old girl with a black eye who said her mother had caused it. Then there was a case of 'neglect' of two children aged two and four where the home conditions were described as 'very poor, chaotic, dirty' and the social worker had previously written to the parents telling them that they would have to clean up. There was a 14-year-old girl who told her school that a man her mother was in a relationship with tried to get into bed with her. And there was a visit to a school to see a 12-year-old boy who had recently been moved to live with his grandparents due to his mother's drinking and father's absence, which involved the social worker seeing him on his own as well as discussing matters with his carers.

Although I had done this work myself many years before, I'd lost touch with just how complex, sensitive and intellectually, emotionally and viscerally demanding it is. This is true not just for practitioners but for families too. The parents of the four-year-old with the black eye were visibly shocked and annoyed at the suggestion it was inflicted by her mother and insisted that it was caused by the child falling over and they showed the worker the exact spot outside where they said it happened. They also had to endure the social worker asking for the child's clothing to be removed and watching her check her body for bruises. This the social worker did with great sensitivity, having first spent time building rapport through getting down onto the floor to play and talk with her.

During the visit to the 'neglect' case the children's mother spoke of her depression and cried, sobbing throughout, expressing what she saw as the unfairness of social work needing to be involved and the confrontational way they had written her a threatening letter. She felt that what she needed was compassion and practical help with cleaning the home and therapeutic help for her mental health, none of which the social worker showed signs of offering. During the encounters with the 12- and 14-year-olds, care was taken not only to tailor interactions to the children's ages and ensure their voices were heard, but also to choose settings that respected their privacy. The 12-year-old preferred to be seen in school so that no one at home could overhear him expressing his feelings and views about his family and where he'd prefer to live. As well as talking to the 14-year-old girl on the home visit and establishing that the man did not succeed in getting into her bed, the social worker pressed the child's mother about the events, probing how safe the man was and what could be done to protect her daughter. These observations of their practice generated discussions with social workers in their cars and offices about many philosophical, ethical and practice dilemmas that will be considered at length in the book.

The second standout feature of this world of work that it doesn't take long in a social work office to notice is that those same social workers spend a great deal of their time sitting at computers, typing. The ever-present sound of keyboards is punctuated by the chatter of voices as practitioners talk to one another about their cases, or themselves, or to other professionals, or service users on the phone. On rare occasions children's voices can be heard, such as when they accompany their parents to the office for a case conference or, having been taken into care, are there on a 'contact' visit for 'family time' with their parents. Virtually all of this typing and administrative effort is put into electronic record-keeping and report-writing about families. After a while in this environment it is possible to believe that being a computer operative and typist is what social work has become. Before computers, when I was in practice, there were 'secretaries' who typed up case notes from our tape recordings. Today bureaucracy is such a major concern of managers and therefore social workers that it creates what I call in this book 'bureaucratic preoccupation' that has significant effects on work with children and families.

At the same time, however, the work is much more complex and nuanced than that because so much of what is important about child protection (*what they are typing about*) doesn't happen in the office at all, but beyond it in a whole range of different sites and settings, most commonly on home visits to families. This means that to be effective practitioners are compelled to travel, to *move and to improvise*. A core challenge social workers face is how to shift their attention away from bureaucracy so that what they are primarily preoccupied with is *practice* and relational work with children and families. It is through the tense relationship between top-down policy, law, regulation, bureaucracy and organisational routines and culture on the one hand, and on the other the movement, improvisation and creativity of workers and families evident in the case examples mentioned earlier that child protection work is *made*.

The child protection system

These tensions, possibilities and barriers can be further illuminated by setting out how the child protection system is organised and meant to work. Becoming a child protection 'case' begins with social work receiving a referral from the general public or other professionals expressing concern. Referrals then need to reach the threshold for intervention and a decision on a course of action must be made within one working day (DfE, 2018; 2023). Government guidance sets timescales within which investigations and assessments are meant to be completed. In the 2010s in England ten days were allowed for an 'initial assessment' and a more comprehensive 'core assessment' had to be completed within 35 days (DCSF, 2010). This was subsequently changed to a full assessment needing to be completed within 45 days (DfE, 2018, p 38). Concerns about children are put to the parents, most often in their homes, and information gathered about children's health and development, parents' histories and sources of family support, housing and the involvement of other professionals (Department of Health, 2000).

Those families regarded as having complex needs rather than representing serious risks to children are formally classified as 'Children in Need'. They become the subjects of 'Children in Need plans' that are drawn up by the multi-agency professionals involved, along with the parents. Children in Need involvement is voluntary and parents are free to decide whether or not to receive a service. Where children are assessed to be at a higher level of risk the case is classified as 'child protection' and in England dealt with under Section 47 of the Children Act 1989. What are colloquially referred to as 'Section 47 inquiries' often involve social work managers engaging the police and doctors in initial 'strategy' discussions about what is known about the family and how to proceed. This happened in the case of the four-year-old with the black eye discussed earlier and neither police or medical involvement were deemed necessary. Where what constitutes 'significant harm' is substantiated children are placed on a 'Child Protection Plan' through a multi-agency case conference which categorises the nature of the harm involved as being either neglect, physical, emotional or sexual abuse. The latter now includes the more recent classifications of child sexual exploitation and online abuse (DfE, 2018; 2023). Children on Child Protection Plans have to receive 'statutory visits' at least once a month, although some local authorities set the time limit as at least every ten days. Oddly, such local differences are permitted in this highly regulated area. When risks to children are considered high it is common for families to be visited more regularly anyway, but sometimes I have seen the once a month yardstick used to justify a low level of contact. Children on Child Protection Plans must be reviewed by the multi-agency network at case conferences every three or six months, depending on how long they have been on a plan.

In recent years, policies and procedures have made explicit an expectation that where there are child protection concerns, children should be seen on their own by social workers to establish their 'wishes and feelings', 'lived experiences' and level of safety (DCSF, 2010; DfE, 2013; 2018; 2023). It is a key target, and on the standardised case recording forms there is a box to tick to signal if it has been done. To be regarded as a legitimate statutory visit it is common policy for it to have to be done in the child's home and include seeing their bedroom.

At a local level there is variety in how services are organised, with them often being split into separate teams doing short-term and long-term work. Short-term teams deal with new referrals and are variously known as 'intake', 'reception', 'duty', 'referral and assessment' or 'duty and assessment'. In some areas there are also 'MASH' (Multi-Agency Safeguarding Hubs) teams, made up of social workers, police and health professionals, who assess new referrals and decide whether they reach a threshold where the concerns need to be passed onto the 'duty' social work team to 'go out on it'. Cases assessed as substantiated Children in Need and Child Protection are usually passed on to long-term teams at the point of the completion of a comprehensive assessment and/or at the first case conference. Or in some localities case transfer happens at the point when families enter legal proceedings.

Time management and organisational practices

Extensive data capture and auditing processes are in place to monitor the completion of core social work tasks. Typically, a traffic light system flashes up information on the computer screen informing managers and workers whether the children in their cases have been seen within the prescribed timescales for statutory visits, or whether they are 'out of time'. These data are examined at least weekly by team managers and incorporated into supervision and workers' performance assessments. In England they are also central to the evidence used by the regulator Ofsted in their inspections and ratings of children's services.

Office conversations I have observed often refer to these timescales, of which this is a typical example:

> Zara is going through her caseload on her computer screen and then produces a large paper folder which contains a printed version because it's easier to look at. 'It drives me mad' looking at it on screen, she says. Going through each family on her list her narrative is heavily structured around time and deadlines: 'in timescales' … 'I'm not out of date yet' – referring to a young person in care who she says she may have time to see next week. She makes a list of everything she needs to do, that includes some things from last week's

to-do list and talks about all the forms she has to complete for a private fostering assessment, which she says involve so much repetition that it feels like 'an assessment of the assessment of the assessment!'. She mentions that this information on how well they each meet timescales is used to assess performance, or at least it can be.

Challenges in managing busy caseloads and keeping case records up to date are as old as social work itself and at first sight these seem like sensible systems and good uses of technology to track some basic aspects of safe practice and recording. However, they are often experienced as unhelpful. I have observed practitioners and managers hanging onto paper and pen methods by listing the family names and dates by when the statutory visit had to be done on sheets of paper or a whiteboard and ticking them off when completed. They felt this was as effective as any computerised prompt in keeping up with what had to be done, by when. But what computerised data collection makes possible that manual pen and paper usage can't is for managers to have access to the data and easy oversight of the performance of the workforce. For similar monitoring purposes, the data is also supplied to the government. I have heard a great many social workers express unhappiness about this surveillance. It can mean supervision becoming merely an exercise in accountability as managers monotonously check on what has been done in every case, squeezing out attention to relationships with service users and workers' emotional experience and opportunities for reflective thinking and learning (Wilkins et al, 2017; Beddoe et al, 2022).

Some social workers have told me, and shown me on their screens, how they gain satisfaction from crafting their case records and pleasure from knowing they are done and the predictability and order these electronic recording systems provide. But many more have shared dissatisfaction and some regard the system completely negatively. As this social worker from a long-term team put it: 'The key problem is that limited time, procedures, deadlines and bureaucracy is killing our practice. Risk aversion, management, blame culture, overwhelms our individual initiative.'

Some social workers are more conciliatory and, while disliking and feeling frustrated by this bureaucratic preoccupation, pragmatically get on with trying to improvise and develop quality relationships. Perverse consequences undoubtedly flow from this kind of data-driven performance management. A huge issue for staff is the problem of *time* and the ways in which bureaucratic tasks and managerial diktat take practitioners away from being able to do more with and for children and families. This adds to anxieties about whether they are doing enough to keep children safe and fear of blame (Whittaker and Havard, 2016). The point is not that high quality work with children and families is never done – I shall show that it is – but that finding the time and thinking space to do it is often a struggle.

It is vital to understand the fast-paced momentum of the system, and the energy and culture that drives it. Social workers and their managers are not just preoccupied with complying with timescales and procedures but with not *failing*, with *improvement*. A concept that captures these dynamics and changes in experience is what Rosa (2015) calls 'social acceleration'. Acceleration refers to the ways in which modern societies have speeded up and changes in how time is organised and experienced. Put simply, with respect to child protection, social workers have to do more in the same time than previously, or something has to give. And what they do is increasingly optimised in the sense of being measured, audited.

Government inspection of social work organisations is central to this acceleration. In England, inspections by Ofsted follow the four-point scale: *outstanding*; *good*; *requires improvement to be good*; and *inadequate*. Those judged to have failed, who are 'inadequate' or 'require improvement to be good', must go on 'improvement journeys' and evidence to the inspectorate that they have done so. These judgements are available to the public and it is typical for children's services departments who are 'good' or 'outstanding' to use this in their branding and to openly celebrate their achievements on social media. The consequences of failure are usually devastating for senior managers as they lose their jobs, causing shame across the service and destroying staff morale (Gibson, 2019). In social work, like most other human service organisations, the fear is of slipping back. Once 'outstanding' or 'good' are reached, the imperative becomes to improve further and, whatever happens, to never ever go backwards and, nightmare of all nightmares, to be judged 'inadequate'. This involves doing more and accelerating the work simply to stand still, to not slip back (a process Rosa [2019] calls 'dynamic stabilization').

This culture is also fuelled by the haunting risk of failing to protect children who are known to be at high risk but who die. As discussed in the Introduction, on top of the grief arising from such tragic loss, workers and managers are publicly blamed and shamed. While only a tiny minority of the workforce ever have direct experience of such tragedies, there is a generalised anxiety and fear of it and the fallout. Sharon Shoesmith, who was the head of the children's services department involved with Peter Connelly at the time of his death in 2007, aged 17 months, has analysed her horrendous experience of being made a hate object and publicly persecuted in the media and parliament. This shows the devastating personal as well as professional impact of such hate and blame (Shoesmith, 2016; see also, Jones, 2014).

There is nothing wrong with, and much to be said for, the organisational and personal desire for improvement. The problems arise when this is driven by what Rosa (2023, p 149) calls the 'motivational energy' of fear and anxiety, resulting in managerial regimes of command and control, rather than trust and creativity. This accelerates processes that bureaucratise the work by making data and what is *written about practice* the key way of demonstrating and measuring the quality and impact of the service (Murphy, 2022). Time and energy are diverted away from a primary focus on *actual practice* and the relational components of the work (Munro, 2011; Yuill, 2018). For instance, Ofsted inspections rely heavily on data and contain no direct observations of practice and little or no feedback from children and families (Ferguson et al, 2019; Hood and Goldacre, 2021).

Little wonder then that practitioners often express concerns about the impact of the lack of time and the data-centred priorities on their relating to children. A typical example was a social worker who, after I observed her interviewing Grace, a ten-year-old girl in school about her experience of physical abuse and neglect, said:

> In an ideal world I would have liked to have sat with Grace and done some art or stuff like that, because she really enjoys art, and sat and done that for a while before even thinking about asking her all the horrible stuff, you know. But you're on duty, doing an IA [Initial Assessment], which you know people expect you to be out of the office for an hour, hour and a half, generally, and you've got to go round and see mum afterwards, and there's always more stuff on duty, you know. But I think we also get used to just going in and expecting to get information, information, information, and not you know … and I think, you know, the cultures develop because of the time pressures really, and the time pressures that we're under you know, what you're expected to get out of an initial visit and it's very much information, information, information rather than relationship building and stuff. And on the other hand it's like how much do you want to build a relationship with this child when you don't know if they're ever going to see you again, when you're starting off like that.

The worker articulates a state of mind that is preoccupied with bureaucratic tasks and accountability, that makes it difficult to leave the office and having done so feeling under pressure to return to it. She feels unable to do the extended playful therapeutic work with children she would like to, and which the child needs, and to trust that she will have time and institutional backing to return to see them again. As Duschinsky, Lampitt and Bell (2016, p 147) observe, when such a lack of alignment occurs between what workers experience and what they still hope for it results in what Berlant (2011) calls 'cruel optimism'. Workers badly want to be creative and relational and hoping for it helps get them through the day, but not being able to achieve it often enough depletes or harms them and service users.

As the social worker quoted here exemplifies, instead of being just collectors of 'information, information, information', practitioners need to be able to have meaningful relationships with service users that enable them to be helpful. The challenge is to replace the restrictions of bureaucratic preoccupation with a primary focus on *practice*. A far more productive balance needs to be found between risk management, accountability and record-keeping on the one hand, and staff support and time and space for relationship-based practice on the other. The aim should be to enable practitioners to *be as skilful, improvisational and fully emotionally and intuitively present with children and families in the time that is available and needed to be able to help them.*

The Practice Cycle and spaces for creativity

While that is the overarching social system and context for child protection, how do these regulatory, organisational and cultural issues play out in practice from place to place and from worker to worker? Every organisational leader, team, manager and practitioner has to reckon with these systems, but I have found some teams to be more bureaucratically preoccupied than others. On a case-by-case basis, the form that relationships with families take, the kind of practice and relationships that are made, will vary depending on how the work progresses through different stages in what I call the Practice Cycle (see Figure 1.1).

Stage 1 is *preparation and readiness* and begins when information about a child comes into the office. Achieving a state of *readiness* to see the child and family involves gathering information from other professionals and practitioners being helped by managers to have clear goals for their meetings with families. This needs to include being supported to deal with feelings of anxiety and any fears about the impending encounter with the child and family. In her study of practice O'Connor (2022) refers to this as social workers engaging in 'anticipatory emotion practices' when preparing for the encounter.

Another vital component of practitioners getting prepared and ready is for them to be helped to set off in the right state of mind and to be what I call 'energised'. The office is potentially a place of safety and emotional renewal, a 'secure base' (Biggart et al, 2017; Cook et al, 2020) where workers can let off steam, be irreverent, share light-hearted moments, eat (especially cake) and drink together, express fears, anxiety and joy. Yet the office may also be stultifying due to the sedentary, computer-dominated work environment, where the mind is

Figure 1.1: The Practice Cycle

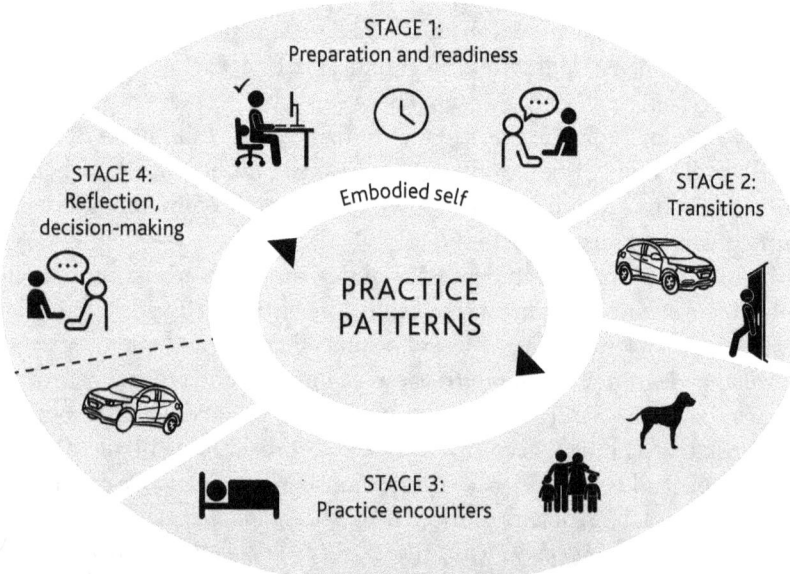

largely used in selective ways to process information. The body becomes stiff and desensitised and, apart from the use of sight to view the screen, the other senses are numbed (Bissell et al, 2020). As one worker noted, 'When you are on duty in the morning, you have a sort of duty head on.' To engage relationally with children and families – and to bring the necessary energy, agility and presence to their practice – the practitioner must move beyond this 'duty head' and awaken both body and mind. They need to come fully *alive*. Managers have a crucial responsibility in enabling this to happen.

Stage 2 is the *transitional* phase where the worker leaves their desk and the office and sets out on a journey to see the child and family. The car journey is the classic transitional space where workers can build on any support they have had in the office to be physically and emotionally attuned to the challenges ahead and the needs of the child (Ferguson, 2010). Becoming fully alive requires letting go of their preoccupation with bureaucracy and rehearsing a plan for what they want to say and do when with service users. The aim should be to achieve a state of kinaesthetic awareness, freedom of movement and emotional attunement that will aid effective practice. This social worker articulates how the emotions involved are felt in the body as well as the mind: 'Well, [with] cases I don't know I am anxious and I have little butterflies in my tummy, so hence the prepping in the car or talking to a colleague in the car about what we're going to do and how we are going to do it.' The 'prepping in the car', what I call 'car therapy', is a vital part of having strategies for the encounter, managing emotions and becoming energised and alive. It should build on the mindfulness and preparatory work the practitioner needs to have received support with before leaving the office (Kinman et al, 2020). The aim is to ensure a thoughtful and attuned presence upon arrival at the encounter.

Stage 3 concerns the *practice encounter* that occurs when the worker arrives at the place of meeting the child and/or family. On home visits it involves walking from the car (or much less often, public transport), negotiating the neighbourhood and gaining access to the house, and interacting with the child, parents and other family or friends and pets in various rooms. All the preparation to be fully present for the children and family and engage in what I call intimate child protection practice needs to come to life. It concerns how to provide what Bülow and Simpson call the best 'practice of attention' to children and families that it is possible to offer, especially in conditions of uncertainty (Bülow and Simpson, 2022). This involves a complex set of skills, awareness, attention, movements and a capacity to attune, relate and respond in the moment. A deep visceral experience of the body, emotions and all the senses occurs, that will be explored at length in this book.

Stage 4 involves the worker journeying back to the office, or on to another visit, or to their own home. Being back in the transitional space of walking and travelling provides them the opportunity to begin to process the encounter they've just had. This continues on arrival back in the office when debriefs with their manager and peers should help them to further process what has just happened and to be able to think clearly and make decisions. As was shown earlier, there are systemic pressures that shape what managers and practitioners are expected and able to do, but how these are managed and moderated in offices and teams and translated into practice by individual social workers matters greatly. This is why in Figure 1.1 the practitioner's 'embodied self' is at the heart of the cycle, because from a relational perspective everything is mediated through their mind and body. This does not mean to say that individual practitioners are solely responsible for the quality of practice, nor does it assume they should ultimately possess the creativity and skill to overcome the influence of all other stages in the cycle. As well as taking individual relational styles seriously, it is vital to ground them in the context of the power relations, systemic processes and resources available that also shape how practice is performed, made and what relationships become.

Recognising the different stages involved in the Practice Cycle when undertaking work with children and families helps to reveal its complexity, organisational supports and constraints and the spaces for creativity and improvisation that exist beyond the computer. As Figure 1.1 depicts it, it is through the interactions between the four stages in the cycle and the embodied selves and experiences of participants that patterns of practice and relationships are made. A wide range of human and non-human systems, actors and materials – laws, procedures, managers, computers, service users, strangers, streets, homes, cars, toys, pets and more – are involved and must be considered (Deleuze and Guattari, 1987; Hood, 2018). Rather than always being a smooth, circular process, activity within the stages and movement between them and around the cycle can happen in disjointed, uneven ways that reflect the messiness of social work (Devine, 2025). The book will provide an in-depth analysis of this dynamic process of making and the energies and patterns of practice and relationships that emerge from them.

Improvising and making practice

Lynne was typical of the social workers who taught me a lot about the Practice Cycle and this dynamic unfolding process of making practice and relationships. This is exemplified by her work with a family of three children, here called Justin (six), Florence (five) and Liam (three). The referral that led to this phase of social work involvement concerned bruising on Justin, allegedly by his stepfather Neil who had been living with Emma, the children's mother. Neil had moved out and a new boyfriend, Gareth, had moved in. Gareth had a history of domestic violence offences for which he had recently served a prison sentence. The social worker had been involved with the family for a couple of months and was meeting Gareth for the first time on this home visit.

In the office before the visit Lynne discussed her aims with her manager who helped her to have a clear plan to see Gareth and check on the children and their mother, Emma. On the way there Lynne told me about the importance of the journey for helping her prepare emotionally for the visit and feel energised, and how she planned to see Gareth on his own, Emma alone and the children on their own.

On arrival, Lynne went into the sitting room where she excitedly spoke to Florence and sat on the sofa beside her and Justin. Lynne held Florence and nestled her into her while she related to Justin who gathered himself up in the other corner of the sofa. Emma was standing close by and Gareth then entered the living room and Lynne got up, walked towards him and introduced herself, initiating a handshake. Lynne said she wanted to see Emma in the kitchen alone and negotiated with the children that she'd spend time with them later. She gave them some pens and paper she had brought along to play with.

The visit lasted 46 minutes, four of which were at the start with the children in the sitting room and five in the kitchen with Emma alone catching up on issues to do with Neil. Lynne then requested to see Gareth on his own and decided that the garden was the best place to do that and spent six minutes there alone with him. She told me afterwards that she chose to do this early on in the visit to check with him what Emma knew about his violent past (he said she knew everything), to ask him if he was still using drugs (he said he wasn't) and also so that she could check out information that he keeps a dangerous dog hidden there. She cleverly chose the garden not just to create confidential space away from Emma and the children but so that she could see whether he was keeping the dog there (he wasn't). Lynne then asked to see Emma and Gareth together in the kitchen where she spent six minutes authoritatively discussing her concerns about the risk of domestic abuse. Lynne followed this by spending 13 minutes in the bedroom with the children, alone, exploring among other things their feelings towards Gareth. This was followed by another six minutes with the adults together in the kitchen reiterating her concerns about the risks of violence and the harm and consequences that can occur should it happen. She then spent four minutes with Emma alone in the kitchen, which included checking out her vulnerability and whether she was experiencing any domestic abuse and, finally, two minutes saying goodbye to the children.

This example typifies the commonplace ways in which some practitioners crafted home visits: by moving through the home, standing, sitting and playing for periods, the clever use of space to see individuals alone and in various combinations in different rooms and the garden and the energy, improvisation and agility this required. Even the 13 minutes this worker spent with the children in the bedroom involved a mixture of being seated and still and moving around as the children got up onto the window sill where the window was open and a danger to them. The worker was twice sat on the bed, twice at the window sill, and once sat on the floor, all the while communicating with the children and using objects like toys, pens and paper, as well as talk in the process. The craft and intimacy involved in such skilful communication was also enacted through embodied practices of touch – like when the worker nestled the children close to her when sat on the sofa and initiated the handshake with Gareth.

My first words to Lynne in the car on the way back to the office were: 'Well you got through a lot there didn't you?', to which she replied:

> Yes. Well that was my, well you have to don't you. I mean if you think about the reality of the job, timescales, caseloads, you have to. It's quite task-centred at times and lots of people argue that it shouldn't be that way, but in the reality of the job, I mean, Jesus.

She then spoke of how she would like more time and how she would use it:

> I would rather have half a day where I could talk to mum and dad separately, then talk to them together, then take the kids out to the park, have a nice hour chat with them, play with them, get to know them, bring them back home. But that's not real is it? We don't get to do that, you have to work with what you've got and because it's short you have to, you have to have a plan.

While apt, this depiction of the work as 'task-centred' should not be interpreted to mean that all such practice is simply functional and devoid of meaning, depth and impact. It means rather that to have any chance of forging meaningful connections and for the encounter to have what I am calling resonance, the work has to be planned and implemented with great skill, resourcefulness and *presence*. The worker wishes they had the opportunity to relate to the family in a longer timeframe, which shows how the first stage of the Practice Cycle – the wider system and organisation – placed limits on what she could do. However, within those limitations her manager helped her focus and get energised and as she moved through the cycle, her 'prepping' and planning on the journey to the family ensured she achieved the state of 'aliveness' and agility that is necessary in child protection to be relational. There was a depth and energy to the encounter, a vibrating quality of positive connection between the worker and family members, that I call resonance. The social worker's skill, confidence and dynamic energy enabled her to make the best practice possible within the parameters of the system she had to work in. This can be defined as *squeezing every piece of value and possibility for relatedness into the time available*.

Afterwards, I asked Lynne about what I spontaneously referred to as her 'choreographed' approach and what lay behind how she moved around and saw different family members in different combinations and rooms: 'Yeah, but I didn't have that planned in my head, though, because you don't know what you are walking into, so you have to be able to, it is just all very spontaneous.' She said it was about knowing 'how to work a house, how to work a family'. What this social worker describes as 'just all very spontaneous' is another way of articulating what I call *improvisation*. As she also notes, it is the conditions of uncertainty that home visiting and encounters in other spaces routinely involve that demand it (see also Pink et al, 2015). 'Working the house' gives expression to social workers' and family members' craft and improvisation in using the home, including gardens, and other materials like pens and papers, toys, the car, to make their practice, relationships and achieve their aims.

Conclusion

This chapter has begun to show the intricate, dynamic nature of child protection work as it unfolds in real time.

Key learning points

- Social structures, power relations and systemic processes, ranging from legislation and bureaucratic procedures to performance metrics and managerial oversight, are highly influential in shaping practice.

- Yet, despite these top-down influences, the chapter has shown that making child protection work is a process of professionals and service users creating lived experiences and meaningful protection of children that depends heavily on the humanity, energy, skill, creativity, intuition and perseverance of practitioners and families on the ground.

- Central to this work is the 'Practice Cycle', which I have introduced to provide a framework that captures how practitioners prepare for, transition into, engage with and reflect on their interactions with children and families. From the careful gathering of information in the office and preparation for emotional readiness, through using the journey to see the family as a thinking space, to the intimate and improvisational nature of seeing families on home visits or elsewhere and finally the post-encounter reflective debriefing, each stage is vital. The worker's aliveness, skill and ability to improvise can make practice as safe, intimate and resonant as it is possible to be within the systemic constraints under which it is carried out.

- The chapter has illustrated the tension between bureaucratic preoccupation and the need for relational engagement. While managers and regulators emphasise time-consuming data recording and fixed timescales, practitioners must continually strive to squeeze every piece of value out of the time available to truly connect with service users. This constant struggle to balance accountability with flexibility, risk management with compassion, reveals that effective child protection is not solely the product of following procedures, but of innovative, adaptive and deeply relational practice.

These insights have set the context for the next chapter, where the practices, rhythms and challenges of starting relationships and conducting short-term work will be further illuminated. This will show further how making child protection work is a process of constant negotiation between systemic pressures and the transformative potential of human creativity and relationships. In that delicate balance lies the promise of good enough practice that is realistic, resourceful and fundamentally about nurturing secure, intimate and trusting connections with children and families.

2

Starting relationships: investigating and assessing child protection concerns

This chapter continues our exploration of how child protection work is made, through an examination of how children and families come to be known, how concerns are investigated and assessed, and what short-term work looks like. It highlights the range of skills, actions and virtues needed to start relationships during initial investigations and assessments (Kohli and Dutton, 2018). But what does is it really feel like to do this work? As I have already argued, it is vital to explore not just the tasks and 'doing' of practice but the *experience* of it, the places, challenges, feelings, energies and atmospheres involved (Jeyashingham, 2018). It will be shown how the work involves calm, broadly co-operative encounters with some families, and dread, excitement and high drama with others.

By looking at child protection work as it unfolds in real time, we see that both managers and practitioners face the challenge of stepping into the unknown. They never know exactly what to expect when engaging with a child or family. So, how can we better understand these unpredictable encounters? This chapter takes forward the book's argument that child protection must be understood as a truly mobile practice, moving between the office and homes or other settings where families are seen – the process I call the Practice Cycle. Why is it important to capture this movement? Because it is in these dynamic transitions that the full complexity of an encounter is revealed, the atmospheres, smells, sounds, textures and emotions that bring a practice to life (Ingold, 2011; Hollway, 2015, p 123). It will be shown that although practitioners leave the office and navigate the Practice Cycle, often they bring the organisation with them by staying connected with managers and receiving real-time support, which becomes vital for managing both the complexity and the anxiety that come with the work. It is important to consider then not just the work itself, but what new strategies might ensure that effective, 'live' support sustains these practices in the face of uncertainty?

Routine everyday practices in duty and assessment work

The work involved in child protection begins well before the practitioner enters the actual encounter with service users, as prior to setting off from the office they imagine and anticipate what might happen. Risk assessing and planning the encounter with the children and family goes on with team managers and by making inquiries with other agencies to find out what is known about them. The following extract from my field notes illustrates this:

> A dull rainy day. There is a sense of quiet busy-ness on the duty desks. Discussions take place at various times between the two social workers about referral information that is coming in. They are pretty constantly processing information, making telephone inquiries with other agencies, typing up records. Lynne is speaking to a woman caller in a reassuring tone which she finishes with 'you're worth it'. The duty system works in such a way that duty workers make lots of inquiries and where a visit is needed they either go out on it straightaway or make appointments in the diary for the person on duty that day to visit.

Children are seen in a variety of places depending on the needs of the situation: in social work offices, cars, schools, police stations, hospitals or clinics, parks, in children's or family centres, nurseries, and most commonly in their homes. Social workers do two kinds of home visits: announced, where they are expected, and unannounced, where they visit without prior warning so that they can find the family as they normally are and not after they have prepared for it. Child protection is complex work, not least because home visiting is very different to work that goes on in the office, the clinic or the psychotherapy consulting room. Even when they are expected it is rare for workers to find families all set up and waiting for them in an orderly fashion to go through what needs to be done. The daily experience of family life is fluid and lively as adults and children interact, play, eat, cry, fight, the TV is on, phones ping or ring, dog(s) bark, growl, demand attention, or other adults whose identities are often unknown to social workers are present. Then there is the impact of the home itself, such as smells and atmospheres (welcome, hostile) to contend with. As Hicks (2020) puts it, the 'feel of the place' matters, a lot. This flow and flux of family life provides crucial observational information that helps social workers to reach an assessment of child welfare (Trevithick, 2012; Page, 2021). But it also threatens to be disruptive of the orderly conditions required to communicate and gather the range of information needed.

The key implication of this is that the conditions that enable meaningful work to be done have to be *made* and the following field notes provide a typical example of the craft involved:

> Mother ('Lisa') answered the door. As soon as the social worker stepped into the home the dog was jumping up to try and escape outside and Lisa was roaring at and hitting it to try and stop it. The social worker walked into the dining area and was met by five-year-old Leon doing dangerous swings from the bannisters of the stairs and his seven-year-old sister soon joined in. The dog came into the room and was tearing round and chewed up an entire cushion. The social worker had negotiated with Lisa prior to the visit to spend some time alone with the children but on arrival there was nowhere suitable where

she could do so. The small bedrooms were too cluttered and there were no armchairs or sofa, so at the social worker's request the dining room table and chairs were set up.

Lisa left and the worker then did 20 minutes work with the children. She worked hard to hold their attention and used a drawing exercise through which both children spoke about family relationships and their feelings.

The social worker commented afterwards on how much calmer it was today and how delighted she was to have get 15 minutes of good work done with the children that contributed to her assessment. Through improvisation, movement, adept use of the space and the family's co-operation and help, the worker managed to create enough order to enable some meaningful work to be done with the children and parent. This 'order-making' and creating of the conditions that enable meaningful work is a key skill that deserves much greater recognition in training and how the challenges of everyday practice are understood.

Often when they aren't expected, despite the surprise visit social workers are greeted calmly by parents and allowed in. However, unannounced visits can be very awkward, like the time the social worker I was shadowing turned up shortly before the child's birthday party was about to start. Sometimes social workers aren't welcomed in and are greeted by a range of responses, such as shouting, crying, anger, fear, threats and outright rejection and assaults. On one visit the social worker spent 14 minutes trying to persuade a distressed, crying mother to allow her in but she wouldn't. Having already had five of her children taken into care she virtually begged the social worker to reassure her that her one remaining child would not be removed. She had had serious addiction problems and her cries, fears and desperation to hang on to her child were deeply upsetting and moving. But the social worker held her ground and maintained her composure, showing compassion and empathising with her, while not making any promises or giving false reassurance about the outcome, which was at this point unknown. She had to leave without getting in, but was allowed in at a later date.

In situations where there is no perceived value in trying to see the family 'cold' and unprepared for a visit, social workers often try to make a prior appointment with the parents. A common approach is to time the visit for around 4pm when children are home from school, enabling them, the parent(s) and the home to be seen. Chapter 1 outlined how social workers are required to see children for some of the time on a visit to the home, or elsewhere, on their own to find out about their experience and it is important to pay close attention to where this happens and the amount of time devoted to it (Ferguson, 2016b). Bedrooms are a popular place where social workers see children alone, in part because they are a convenient space to go to be separate from other family members and also because they contain a lot of children's personal things that can potentially be used to play and communicate through. In addition, being in their bedroom is regarded as a valuable way to experience the child's inner world and lived experience and for some workers is preferable to the formality of, say, sitting with a child at a dining room table, face to face. Some – a minority in my experience and most often male workers – avoid bedrooms for fear of allegations of inappropriate behaviour. Conversely, bedrooms can be perceived as unreliable and unsafe spaces because of the lack of privacy as parents are in the house and can eavesdrop. If this is suspected the preference should be to see children outside the home, such as at school, in parks, cars, on walks or other public places (see Chapter 11). The choice of location and timing of seeing the child is most problematic when managers prefer it that children are seen at home after school for the pragmatic reason that it is less time-consuming than visiting them in the home and school separately.

In my experience of observing duty and assessment work on first and early visits, children are typically seen alone for between five and 20 minutes. This is evident in the 20 minutes the social worker in the previous example spent with Lisa's children, while another typical example is the Nolan family I opened the book with, where the six-year-old was seen in their bedroom for 12 minutes and her 10-year-old brother for 11 minutes. Overall, three times longer is spent engaging with parents and seeing them and their children *together*. Children below the age of four and sometimes five are generally not seen on their own because they are less able to communicate their experience (see also, Ferguson, 2016b). A key issue, then, is how practitioners relate with infants and pre-school children. This book will show that some do so by getting close to them, interacting through eye contact, facial expressions, sounds, play and sometimes touch and actual holding, while some workers remain at a distance.

Effective interviews with children require more than just a simple conversation. To help children open up about their lives, it is necessary to guide them through several stages – both during a single encounter and over time as trust builds (Jones, 2003; Winter, 2011; Horwath and Platt, 2018; Lefevre, 2018). The process should start with introductions, building rapport and the worker explaining their role and setting boundaries. The goal is to create a safe space by using empathy, offering reassurance, clarifying what the child shares and gently moving forward. This approach helps to contain the child's fears, past traumas and worries in a therapeutic way. The final stage focuses on wrapping up the encounter, ensuring that any implications of what the child has said are properly addressed. As Ruch, Winter and colleagues put it, based on their observations of social workers communicating with children in a range of settings, done well the process has four key dimensions: getting the mindset right; creating the space; communicating with a purpose; and making good endings (Ruch et al, 2017; Winter et al, 2017).

In some cases, especially when gathering 'best evidence' for victims of criminal offences, the interview process is very formalised and takes place in designated rooms at police stations or social work offices (Bull, 2018). Yet in everyday practice – whether in family homes or other settings – these conversations tend to be messier and follow a non-linear path. The simple notion of an 'interview' as just a static face-to-face conversation fails to capture the dynamic, mobile and creative nature of interactions between social workers and children – as the examples in this book of social workers combining time sat on the bed talking, on the floor, doing art, moving around and playing illustrate. This is why it is far more accurate to call them 'encounters' than interviews.

There are essential components to working with children that constitute good practice. I have observed encounters where rapport-building with children on their own and even introductions didn't happen and workers went straight into asking direct questions about specific incidents and concerns. This leaves children with limited or no understanding of who is asking them questions and what the possible implications of their answers could be. Their perception of the social worker will be based in part on anything they have been told by their parents or others prior to the encounter, which may be a negative and fearful portrayal of what will happen. Ethical, rights-based practice needs to be based on an appreciation of the 'competencies and capacities of young children to engage in relationships with adults' (Winter, 2011, p 3).

The nature and duration of social worker–children encounters are shaped by workloads, the timescales that practitioners have to adhere to and their skills, playfulness and comfort with getting close to children. The degree of parental co-operation or reluctance is also a crucial factor. Not surprisingly, parents often find their children being seen on their own by social workers difficult. Some don't agree to it and even some others who initially give their permission for it then walk into the room to interrupt or make noise nearby to signal that enough is enough. This shows how problematic talking alone with children in the home when parents are in the vicinity can be and how children can, with justification, fear being overheard and not speak their truth. When this is suspected, seeing them in other safer confidential spaces is very important.

Whether the time spent with children is long enough is situation specific. In some cases, when spread across two or three encounters, practitioners and their managers feel that sufficient time has been given to reach a confident assessment of the children's well-being and level of safety. Relatively short sessions with children can be productive, but a significant issue concerns their frequency. When workers do not have enough time to keep going back for as long as it might take to gain as deep as possible an understanding of the child's life, the work has to be crammed into brief encounters and fewer of them. A very troubling illustration of this problem occurred on a visit I shadowed where, ironically, the social worker spent what, within the parameters of the norms for her social work team and agency, was a relatively long period of 27 minutes alone in the sitting room with an 11-year-old boy and another 16 minutes talking separately to his nine-year-old brother, discussing concerns about their care and emotional needs. The worker introduced herself and explained her role in a clear, accessible way. She saw the boys separately in the sitting room, the door of which was off its hinges. Their mother was in the kitchen and could be heard shouting things into the room, which culminated in the 11-year-old getting up from the sofa and lifting the door up and placing it over the empty doorway. The social worker did not budge and ploughed on, which included pushing the boy to talk about highly sensitive issues, such as the fact that, according to his mother, he soils himself. Clearly embarrassed and agitated, he closed down and simply refused to discuss the matter.

Interviewed in the car straight afterwards, the worker said she felt she had to force discussion of this highly personal issue and gather as much information as possible due to the agency requirement to have the initial assessment completed and written up within the timescale, which was by the following day. She knew that due to that deadline and workload pressures she would not be able to go back and it was imperative to make an assessment of whether long-term intervention was needed, which she felt it was. Framed within the concept of the Practice Cycle that I introduced in the last chapter, the worker received no support at stage 1 in the office to move beyond a preoccupation with timescales and other bureaucratic requirements and did not achieve a state of relational attunement and aliveness as she travelled through the stages of the cycle. This shows the harm that limiting practitioners' discretion can have, in how system needs and relating that are rushed block work with children that is paced compassionately, skilfully and therapeutically to meet their needs (Murphy, 2023b). Some children end up distressed and probably harmed by the experience.

Yet the length and quality of practice encounters is not simply determined by organisations, time limits, parental attitudes, and children's willingness and capacity to engage. Workers' skills, playfulness and relational styles also matter. In the last mentioned practice scenario, for instance, at the outset of their time together the 11-year-old was playing with a handheld electronic game device, but instead of taking the opportunity to connect with him by getting alongside and involved in the game the worker instead sat opposite him and tried to stop him using it so that she could get on with the talk-based interview. The worker was impatient and seemed to lack skills of playfulness to build rapport and communication. She had been qualified for two years and may never have had the skills and qualities and energetic presence needed. It is also possible that she once had some of these skills and desire for relational closeness and that these were diminished by the demoralising organisational context she had to work in. What was clear was that the agency was doing little or nothing to enable this worker to use and develop her relational skills and confidence, or to help her turn up to families feeling energised and alive with the possibilities of connecting in meaningful, resonant ways.

In marked contrast there were other workers who creatively used talk, play, toys, pens and paper, phones, other electronic devices and positive motivational energy to communicate with children skilfully and productively in the time available. Very detailed illustrations of this will be given in later chapters and a striking example that brings the issues to life at this point occurred on a home visit when a social worker entered the bedroom of an eight-year-old boy she was meeting for the first time to speak to him away from his parents. The boy immediately produced a hand puppet through which he spoke and the social worker responded not by getting him to put it away, but creatively by welcoming it and communicating with him through the puppet for the entire discussion. The child responded enthusiastically, clearly feeling heard, benefiting from the relational connection that he and the worker ensured infused the encounter.

Into the unknown: drama, risk and inquisitiveness

Having set out some key dimensions of how short-term practice is done, the focus will now be on the experience of doing it. How does it feel to step into the unknown, as a social worker arriving unannounced at a family's door, where you're neither expected nor familiar, and anxiety and dread, mixed with excitement, can be intense? As this social worker put it when on their way to an unannounced first visit:

> You're going into an unknown situation and you don't know what's going to happen and you don't know how people are going to react to you. I mean I've never met these parents before, I can see on [the case record system] that Dad has got previous sort of behaviour issues, so it makes me think, oh, is he going to sort of take that out on me?

A common way in which those who do this work talk about and make sense of it is through stories of uncertainty, risk and drama. Families' experiences of the child protection system may also be uncertain, risky, fearful and dramatic, but for reasons that are different to social workers. In social work education, literature and in practice the value base rightly emphasises the need to aim for respectful, 'partnership' working with families (Featherstone et al, 2018). This is difficult to reconcile with the investigative dimension at the heart of statutory work, which one social worker summed up as the need to be 'inquisitive and assertive'. Parents have a vested interest in presenting as positive a picture of their care and family as possible, while social workers try to delve into whether it is true or not. The complexity can seem akin to entering what Critchley (2020) calls a 'lion's den'.

Sometimes the expectation of drama and danger is fuelled by stories from and about service users, as illustrated by this extract from my field notes:

> I get into the office at 9.15 and go straight to the duty desk. A referral has come in that Jackie is going out on which has a history of social work involvement in which the mother has told the health visitor that her and her partner have a baseball bat and iron bar in the house to use against social workers.

Such fearful stories may turn out to be mythical and discriminatory towards certain families or individuals, based on social class, gender or racial stereotypes. Or they may be true and the workers are actually in danger. Assessing the risks to workers is vital and one expression of this is lone-worker safety policies and whiteboards in offices which record where the worker is and their expected time of return. The intensity of encounters and what is at stake in them is ramped up by sensationalist media reporting of child deaths that blames social workers and feeds parents' fears that they have come to remove their children. Jeyasingham (2018) cautions against over-dramatising and sensationalising everyday practice that he suggests is in reality mostly 'mundane and quotidian', that is, unremarkable. This is because it most often involves families struggling to parent well in conditions of disadvantage who need compassionate support and not to be portrayed in dramatic, stigmatising ways as 'dangerous' (Featherstone et al, 2019). However, often the underlying existential experience of doing social work doesn't feel so mundane. A lot of the time it may indeed turn out to feel routine but it is vitally important to understand how even then practice remains alive with the possibilities of the unknown, full of complex challenges and emotions and sometimes actual drama. As one social worker, Leroy, expressed it: '[T]here's a routine element and even the mundane and boring element, but there's absolutely always that potential for things to spike up into, you know, unknown and potentially dramatic situations.'

For some it is the excitement of the unknown that attracts them to the job, especially short-term 'duty' work and responding to new referrals. Maria goes so far as to say 'I don't think I could do any other job than social work, apart [*thinks for a few seconds*] from maybe the police … or being a movie star. I need the excitement.' It is rare in my experience for social workers to liken the job to anything as glamorous as being a movie star! But Maria's point about excitement makes sense with respect to the police comparison. Many social workers have told me how much they enjoy the 'buzz' of duty work and going into the unknown. Others prefer the somewhat more predictable and controllable experience of long-term work, even though it too can often involve some crises and uncertainty.

Jim, a very experienced social worker, talks about the 'jumpiness' of duty work, which he explains is about excitement but can also include a more troubling anxiety and edginess about what might come in and have to be faced. He summed up how the work is made up of 'the dramatic, the mundane and the boring'. A new referral I shadowed him on typified the 'dramatic'. The referral comes in early on a Friday morning from a school about a Black British mother, Shanice, who has just turned up appearing to be under the influence of drugs or alcohol, staggering and falling over. Her five-year-old son, Jermaine, is hungry and school have given him two slices of toast. Pre-schoolers Ebony (four) and Kai (two) are with their mother at the school. Jim is on duty, and the imperative for him and his team manager, Raymond, is to find Shanice and assess her capacity to care for her children. I go along with him as he heads to the family home, but on arrival there is no reply. He then drives to the addresses of two people thought to be friends of Shanice. At the first address, one of Shanice's friends shouts loudly at Jim as he walks up the path, declaring, 'I don't want you coming into my house!' She appears either drunk or heavily under the influence of drugs. A man, who is big and probably mid-50s, soon arrives, and she tells him, 'They're social workers!' Jim responds respectfully, apologising for the intrusion while firing questions at her about whether she has seen Shanice. She continues to hurl abuse, and Jim eventually leaves.

Starting relationships

At the next house, two women and three teenagers come to the door. One of them says she saw Shanice last night when she appeared upset. They are anxious to help, and the youngest teenager sets off up the street in her pyjamas to see if she can rouse Shanice – even though Jim tells her it isn't her responsibility. As he drives, Jim describes the area as having notorious streets, inhabited by many transient individuals and families, many of whom are 'chaotic'. On the drive back to the family home, Jim explains that he knows Shanice's phone number but doesn't want to call her because he wants to visit unannounced so he can see her as she naturally is – to catch her 'cold'.

On arrival at the family home, he knocks hard on the door and calls through the letterbox, but there is no reply. He returns to the car and phones the duty team manager, Raymond, who advises him to ring Shanice. Shanice answers, talks a lot, and Jim struggles to get a word in. He is very polite but firm, saying that he needs to see her at home at 12.30. He rings Raymond to update him, and Raymond suggests that he go to the school to view the CCTV footage. At the school, Jim feels that in the footage, Shanice definitely looks unsteady, as she can't get the buggy through the door.

We drive to a shop and buy lunch, and Jim rings Raymond again to talk it through. Jim tells me about the value of having a team manager who listens and advises, and he explains how much important work can be done from the office while the worker is in the field. For instance, Raymond arranges a telephone strategy meeting with the police.

As we arrive back at the home at 12.30, Shanice is there. Four-year-old Ebony is standing in the garden in a pyjama jumpsuit, and Jim greets her warmly. Then the woman who earlier screamed her hatred of social workers at Jim appears from inside the house and, even before we enter, immediately apologises for her outburst. A man – probably in his mid-60s – is also present, drinking a can of beer and looking noticeably drunk; he steps forward and initiates a handshake with Jim (and me). Shanice lets Jim in, and he sits at the end of the dining table near the sofa where Shanice sits. The intoxicated female friend never sits down; instead, she parades around, forcefully declaring that things aren't as they seem and that Shanice is a good mother. Shanice, however, looks unwell and uncared for. She is clearly under the influence of something, speaking with a slurred voice, and has a vacant expression. During the hour he spends there, Jim heads into the kitchen, searches the fridge and freezer, and finds food. He inspects all the bedrooms, tenderly taking two-year-old Kai by the hand as they walk up the stairs. Jim finally learns from Shanice that she took heroin in the early hours that morning, along with anti-depressants and painkillers.

Afterwards, in the car, Jim's assessment reveals some positives – Shanice has food and 'she has a plan for tea'. He notes that the children aren't distressed and emphasises how emotionally traumatic it usually is for young children to be removed from home. Back at the office, Jim, Raymond and another senior practitioner discuss the situation. Their consensus emerges: 'So it's just about good enough.' They decide it isn't appropriate to remove the children immediately and agree to rely on the Emergency Duty Team and the police to keep an eye on things over the weekend.

Back in the office on Monday morning, Jim and Raymond learned that at 2am on Friday night Shanice went around the neighbours 'dumping the children', one of who informed the Emergency Duty Team. The emergency social worker visited on the Saturday and Shanice consented to the children staying temporarily with their aunt, who was regarded as an imperfect solution as her own son was in care. The police visited the children there on Sunday to do a welfare check. This morning duty social workers had just visited and found Shanice had taken drugs again and 'has crashed'. Raymond said he now felt he was wrong not to take decisive action to remove the children on Friday and decides now that 'enough is enough' and that the children need to go into care. Huge efforts were made to try to find appropriate family members who could have the children, but none were regarded as safe enough and they were placed in foster care.

This is child protection work at its most investigative, dramatic and adrenaline-pumping in terms of urgency, uncertainty and high energy momentum. It was all done at pace and in the midst of it Jim said he likes the challenge of having to deal with the aggression and flux he faced on the streets and in the family home and unknown, unpredictable people: 'You've got to immediately take control', he said, which he regarded as 'one of those experience things'. It is vital to consider the critical question of whether there were other possibly 'calmer' and more empowering ways of responding to the children and their mother than the dramatic, investigative approach the social worker was expected to take. This could perhaps have been through the school taking their initial concerns up with Shanice and the social worker at first meeting up with her there. And by also involving extended family as quickly as possible, who can provide support and advocacy for vulnerable lone-parent women (Ferguson, Featherstone and Morris, 2020). In this instance, neither option worked out because Shanice would not remain at the school and no wider family were known who were viewed as suitable to have the children.

This kind of highly charged investigative approach seems destined to always be needed in some situations and how to do it well and humanely must be part of the repertoire of skills and virtues child protection workers need to have. In that event such work should not be done alone – even though often it is – and we have seen the vital importance of live, mobile supervisory support through a close connection between managers in the office and practitioners when they are out there doing the work. This enables practitioners to feel held and guided in the face of such anxiety, risk and uncertainty. It means that while thus far I have depicted the Practice Cycle as involving a clean break with the organisational setting in order to see the child and family, when live, mobile supervisory support occurs practitioners never fully leave the office behind and nor should they.

Courage and composure under pressure

It should be clear that there are significant risks involved in doing child protection work. Yet the courage and composure it takes to do the work is rarely given the recognition it deserves (Dickens et al, 2023). Understanding the courage and resilience that families need in the face of child protection investigations is no less important. Another significant aspect of this is that social workers' caseloads typically involve violent and abusive individuals. Most often this involves men who social workers engage with either directly when they are still living in or involved with the family, or indirectly when they are no longer around but have left a legacy of trauma for women and children.

Jennifer was making her first home visit as part of her assessment of Natalie, a very vulnerable 21-year-old mother of four-year-old Maisie. Natalie had been assaulted by her partner and during the first section of the visit Jennifer addressed a range of questions to her about him, the assault and how the child was caught up in it. Then 17 minutes into the visit Jennifer received a phone call from the social work office saying that Natalie's mother and Maisie were at the office because Natalie's partner had assaulted a man in a shop and was supposedly on his way to the flat. Natalie immediately got extremely anxious and became distressed, crying, sobbing, remarking on how difficult her life is: 'All I have had in my life is people that treat me like shit, and passing me backwards and forwards, because they don't know what they want to do.' The atmosphere changed completely to one of tension and panic.

Jennifer responded in two key ways. She maintained her composure, taking up a caring and compassionate body position, sitting forward facing, making eye to eye contact with Natalie. She focused firmly and very determinedly on what needed to happen *right now* to ensure that Natalie and her child are safe. In case the boyfriend carried through on the threat to visit she advised Natalie to give the impression she was not in by closing the windows. Second, Jennifer offered this vulnerable woman hope and reassured her that social work will support and help her: 'We can change this ...'; 'It does sound like at the moment you have some very controlling men in your life'; 'Social work can help ...'. Twenty minutes after the first phone call the team manager rang again to say that the police had put a 'Treat as Urgent' on Natalie's address, meaning they have to respond immediately if they get a call.

The social worker then drove Natalie to the social work office to meet her daughter and mother, whose home she would stay at that night. Jennifer spent a long period with her in an interview room calming her and putting a safety plan in place. After this Jennifer went straight to her desk, took a mirror out of her bag, looked at herself and said 'Oh my face is all dried up', referring to the blotchy marks that were plainly visible. She implied that this was connected to the stress of the experience she'd just been through, which when I asked her about it she seemed to play down. My sense was that Jennifer wasn't ready yet to express in words the risks and range of feelings she had just been through, but her body spoke volumes for the stress, anxiety and other feelings she was carrying that burst out on her face.

Another typical example of danger, risk-taking, courage and composure involved a father who was not supposed to have any contact with his children due to his violence but his ex-partner was suspected of visiting his home with the children. The man became very aggressive towards Priya, the social worker, after she raised suspicions that the children's mother had been present when she arrived at the home and had escaped out the back door and through the garden. The social worker even ran around the back of the house in the dark to try and catch her in the act of escaping, but there was no sign of her. The worker authoritatively reminded him that at present he must not have contact with his daughter. Afterwards Priya reflected:

> I think you've got to have some balls about you. … I think if you are really really placid, you really, I think you would fail. What we face, especially in child protection, is a lot of anger, a lot of people not wanting us around. You've got to have the courage to fight against that, to get in and do what you need to do.

Although symbols of masculine strength are often evoked to suggest authority, both male and especially social work's predominantly female workforce routinely take significant personal risks and display courage to protect children and vulnerable women.

Conclusion

This chapter has illuminated the mobile, complex, dynamic nature of child protection work and how relationships are initiated and concerns assessed, often under unpredictable conditions.

Key learning points

- It has shown that short-term practice requires practitioners to venture into people's lives, frequently unannounced, and navigate various environments, people, pets, family routines and emotional atmospheres. These experiences offer valuable perspectives on children's and families' lives.

- Good practice skills in starting relationships with children include clear introductions, rapport-building, containment of the child's worries and trauma and clarity about what happens next. The process of investigating and assessing concerns is far more fluid than the literature on conducting traditional 'interviews' suggests. Rather than adhering to a static scripted question-and-answer format, encounters regularly unfold through agile movement, improvisation, playfulness and creative use of space, be it in the family home or elsewhere.

- Creating an environment in family homes that is orderly enough to allow meaningful interactions – with children and parents, both together and individually – is a vital skill.

- Practitioners must not only gather information but also manage their own emotions and those of service users. The capacity to work calmly under pressure and maintain one's composure is as crucial as practice skills and enables social workers to cope with the inherent risks, crises and sometimes dramatic situations they encounter. Ways of handling such situations calmly, that defuse drama and empower families, should always be sought.

- The concept of the Practice Cycle has been further developed to account for the importance of a mobile, adaptive process that extends beyond the office. This has highlighted the vital role of real-time, live supervisory support from office-based managers, to help practitioners navigate the unpredictable rhythms of family life and community relations and manage complex, sometimes high-energy, risky situations.

- Child protection encounters and relationships demand courage from both practitioners and families. Social workers may risk their own safety and emotional well-being in volatile encounters, while families must display remarkable resilience in the face of intense scrutiny and potentially life-changing interventions.

Together, these insights lay a solid foundation for the next chapter, which explores the nature of long-term relationships, and later chapters that will consider the dynamics of beginning relationships and making child protection work in great depth.

3

Relationships over time: care, holding and reliability

Having provided an initial overview of the ways short-term investigatory and assessment work is done and the skills, emotions, lived experiences and challenges involved, I will now consider the broad outlines of the nature and experience of work with children and families that goes on over the longer term. Some similar skills, knowledge and virtues are needed, but developing and sustaining relationships over longer periods involves particular kinds of relational work and presents some unique challenges. Crucial among these are honesty, openness, trustworthiness, endurance and reliability. A deep understanding is required of the complex dynamics of human relationships, how they ebb and flow over time, go through cycles of rupture and repair, love and hate and are deeply affected by unconscious as well as conscious processes. This is especially the case in statutory work like child protection because these relationships always involve power and authority.

At the heart of this relational work is using what I call 'good authority' (Ferguson, 2011), which means finding a careful balance between empathy and directiveness, care and control. This includes providing service users with reliable encounters and relationships where they feel emotionally 'held'. The chapter further develops this theory of 'holding' and applies it to practice, beginning to show its relevance to working with children and families, not least those who are angry and dismissive of child protection interventions. The chapter also highlights another aspect of the work, where children and families feel positively about the help they receive. These varied experiences show how understanding long-term work requires becoming immersed in the complexities of love and hate in relationship dynamics (Froggett, 2002). Love, care and making a positive difference are obviously crucially important to children and families. But they are also vital for sustaining and nourishing practitioners and teams, inspiring them to persevere and find ways to overcome or cope with the many challenges they face.

Holding practices

It is important to begin by setting the context for the analysis that follows by elaborating on the theory of 'holding' that is central to this chapter and the book. As mentioned in the Introduction, the concept of 'holding' was developed in the influential work of Donald Winnicott (1965; 1971) and Clare Winnicott (1963). Donald's idea of the 'good enough parent' refers to those who create a 'setting' for the baby, a holding, 'facilitating environment' in which the infant becomes able to have a self (Abram, 1996, p 166). This theory of 'holding' is similar to Bion's (1962) concept of 'containment', where a parent accepts and processes their infant's anxious feelings – such as helplessness, frustration and rage when not immediately fed – and returns them in a tolerable, digestible form. This provides the baby with the emotional reassurance, comfort and security that form the foundation for healthy development.

The Winnicotts applied these ideas to the therapeutic settings created for clients, and I suggest that a similar argument can be made for social workers. They can 'hold' service users in reliable, caring ways, enabling those who have experienced harm and trauma as children and/or adults to develop their capacities to love and care and be 'good enough parents' (Abram, 1996, p 166). This is achieved through the therapeutic effects of the relationship, which is an idea that is fundamental to relationship-based practice (Ruch et al, 2018). Similarly, John Forrester (2017) notes that 'holding' for Winnicott is about 'care-cure'. By being held, 'the patient can (re)experience and repair the past, allowing a maturational process to occur'. Similar forms of holding work are practised and theorised by leading child psychotherapists (Music, 2019).

Clare Winnicott summarises what is involved in social work when holding occurs and reliable helping relationships are made:

> I think it ['the caseworker's basic technique'] lies in the provision of a reliable medium within which people can find themselves or that bit of themselves which they are uncertain about. We *become*, so to speak, a reliable environment, which is what they so much need: reliable in time and place – and we take great trouble to be where we said we would be, at the right time. ... We are not only reliable in time and place but in the consistent attitudes which we maintain towards people. They know how they will find us. ... And not only do we hold a consistent idea of people, but we hold the difficult situation which brought the client to us by tolerating it until he either finds a way through it or tolerates it himself [*sic*]. If we can hold the painful experience, recognizing its importance and not turning aside from it as the client re-lives it with us in talking about it, we can help him [*sic*] to have the courage to feel its full impact ... I have deliberately used the word 'hold' in what I have been saying, because while it obviously includes 'acceptance' of the client and what he gives us, it also includes *what we do with what we accept*. To sum up, the professional relationship is the technique whereby we provide a limited and enclosed environmental setting which is personal because it contains all that the client has put into it himself, and which is reliable because it is accepting and holding. (C. Winnicott, in Kanter, 2004, p 152; original emphasis)

The question arises: do social workers in child protection today engage in these kinds of holding practices and relationships? I will argue that they do and that we can go further. 'Holding' is also relevant when professionals are 'held in mind' by peers and supervisors, helping them process their emotions and gain clarity in their thinking (Ruch, 2007). As shown in Chapter 2, practitioners staying connected to the team manager and office, even when out in the community doing casework, is a crucial dimension of feeling cared about and 'held in mind'.

This means that the concept of 'holding', as developed here, is more expansive than containment. It encompasses both individual acts of care and a network of care and control by various agencies and professionals that envelop the service user. John Forrester illustrates how, for Winnicott, case managing was an extension of holding: 'Psychotherapy, medicine, and social work were like concentric circles of holding, centred on the fundamental metaphor of a child being held by its mother' (Forrester, 2017, p 101). Bloom (2006) suggests there is often vagueness and uncertainty in the psychotherapy literature about whether 'holding' and being 'held' are used as metaphors or to refer to actual tactile contact. In this book, it will be made clear when 'holding' and being 'held' refer to actual tactile contact and when they are used metaphorically to symbolise being 'held in mind'.

The contexts for long-term work

We can now consider how these ideas and concepts apply to practice. Social workers in long-term teams generally do not have to work to such strict timescales as the book has shown their colleagues doing initial investigations and assessments do. In theory, the relationship has time to develop over the weeks and months that lie ahead. However, paperwork, deadlines for extensive court reports and workloads make it a struggle to find the time to be as intensively involved with *all* the children and families on their caseloads as they would like. Spending a lot of time on some families, or even one, can mean not being able to give others the attention they need. This is exemplified by a social worker explaining: 'It's been a bit of a crazy, crazy, crazy, crazy week – I've just been doing this, I've written a 19-page chronology going back from when the first child was born.' The children had been taken into care and the chronology was only one aspect of the considerable extra paperwork required. It is the complexity of the cases and not just the number of them on caseloads that matters. For instance, working on several court cases at once is extremely demanding on time due to the administrative burden and practical and emotional labour involved.

Research (Ferguson et al, 2020b) suggests that in long-term casework social workers usually see children and families at least once every two weeks, sometimes more, and the home is the key location where it happens. The length of individual home visits varies from case to case and often differs from week to week, month to month, depending on the purpose of the encounter, and typical visits last around 45 minutes. Families and children are also sometimes seen in the office, on visits to schools, nurseries, foster carers, kinship carers and so on. In addition, parents and sometimes other family members are also seen at meetings involving the whole family, case conferences and other multi-agency meetings. Organisational culture, the way social work teams are staffed and the physical design of offices are crucial to the nature and quality of the service families receive and the holding and support provided for practitioners. I shall examine these crucial organisational issues in detail later in the book.

Honesty, openness and building trust

While Chapter 2 showed that duty and assessment teams usually go into families without an existing relationship, long-term caseworkers start from a point where the family have usually already had involvement. Depending on how the service is organised, transfer to long-term workers can occur after a brief initial assessment, after significant work has been completed and a case conference has taken place with the children already on a Child Protection or Children in Need Plan, or after the children have been removed and legal proceedings have commenced. Due to already having had at the very least short-term social work involvement, the family should know what the assessment of them is and should have input into shaping it. There should also be a plan, including clear objectives for work with the family that have been agreed with them. Despite there having been past involvement, due to the necessity of case transfers between teams, long-term workers and families have to start their particular relationship from scratch. Trust still has to be *earned*; relationships have to be *made*.

Many of the issues involved in making long-term relationships can be illustrated through the experience of 28-year-old Maria Nicholls who had been involved with social work on and off since a child. Some years ago she had her children taken into care due to drug addiction and a very abusive partner. During this most recent phase of involvement she had a new partner, Patrick, and became pregnant. Because Maria's children had been removed, social work did a pre-birth assessment which resulted in a decision that she now had the capacity and circumstances to provide good enough care and she and Patrick kept their baby girl, Isabelle. The network of agencies involved included a drugs counsellor, health visitor and a doctor. Both Maria and the social worker Shelly explained in research interviews how, due to very negative past experiences with some workers, Maria mistrusted Shelly when they first met. Nor does she like or trust the social worker and managers who are currently involved with her children in care and who work in a different office to Shelly.

On the first home visit I shadowed with Shelly, after we were introduced, Maria immediately explained to me how 'Shelly and I got off to a rocky start, but we worked it out'. She felt that some previous social workers had deceived her by saying one thing but doing another, so she insisted that Shelly must show everything that she wrote down to her, and the worker always did this, which helped trust to develop. This typifies how the making of relationships often has to be fashioned out of an initial deep suspicion and mistrust of social work. Family members consistently regard honesty and openness as crucial to the development of trust (see also Bostock and Koprowska, 2022; Baginsky, 2023).

It is one thing to start a relationship and quite another to sustain it. On most of the (seven) encounters between the family and professionals that I observed the social worker gave quality attention to both parents and to the baby, which included physically holding her. The energy generated between them had vibrations of resonance, signalling closeness and connection. It is well known that fathers are often ignored by social care and health services while mothers are invariably seen and held responsible for child safety and well-being (Ferguson, 2016d; Mandel, 2024). On the occasions Patrick was not at work and in the home Shelly made sure she engaged with him most but not all of the time. On one home visit Maria was the only family member who was seen – in the living room – and she explained that Patrick was upstairs with Isabelle. The social worker never asked to see him or the child and explained to me in the car afterwards that she knew that she should have but for some reason that she couldn't explain even to herself, she didn't.

It is sobering to think that if something very serious had happened, resulting in serious harm to this baby, the official case review could easily conclude, with the benefit of hindsight, that the social worker lacked professional curiosity, as many inquiries and case reviews have concluded (Burton and Revell, 2018). The reasons why in the moments of encounters practitioners do not carry out actions that they know they should, why they do not 'reflect in action' (Schon, 1983; Ferguson, 2018a) in textbook ways and realise they need to do the 'right' thing, is a major theme of this book. Relevant here is how at this stage, after five months of seeing how well the parents were coping and caring for their baby, it was regarded as a low-risk situation. In the social worker's mind the father was caring for the baby upstairs, who may have fallen asleep, and the social worker did not want to invade their privacy and possibly wake the child. This is illustrative of the deep dilemma practitioners so often face about how far to go in insisting on seeing children on *every* visit while trying to maintain trust. There is a high risk of rupturing the relationship if what parents say is not accepted by the worker who still insists on seeing the child.

Being able to manage these care/control challenges and tensions by using 'good authority' is a core skill in child protection work. There were occasions when Shelly needed such skill and the courage to use it. While her relationship with the parents was generally positive it was not always harmonious. Some tense, difficult moments were observed, especially in the phase when there was concern about whether Maria was breaking the terms of her authorised use of methadone to come off heroin by stockpiling it. Shelly challenged her about this and it was also explored by the drugs worker at case conference reviews that the parents attended. Maria also consistently expressed anger about her older children still being in care and how badly, as she saw it, the other social work office was dealing with it. Again, Shelly listened attentively, holding and accepting Maria's anger and other intense feelings, letting her know she was willing to learn from this, while at the same time being clear that there were expectations regarding avoiding risky behaviours that were non-negotiable. This shows how resonance in relationships is not just about feeling moved, heard and connected to others in positive ways and with happy outcomes. Painful feelings such as anger and sadness can be at the heart of resonant experiences, such as those cathartic moments that involve re-visiting the pain of trauma and loss. The distress and hurt that are offloaded by the service user and held by the professional creates a supportive, therapeutic experience (Herman, 1992). It is the mutuality and responsiveness of the relationship between worker and service user that produces such important moments of connection, such resonance (Rosa, 2019).

Isabelle was always found to be very well cared for and when she was nine months old she came off the Child Protection Plan and the case was closed. When interviewed at the end of the study Maria and Patrick were very positive about how Shelly related to them and Isabelle, saying that by supporting them to keep and care for their child she had helped them to transform their lives, for the better. On the social worker's final home visit Maria showed her thanks by hugging Shelly. Afterwards, Shelly and her manager, who had supported her positive assessments of the parents and decisions all the way, were very happy for the family and pleased that they had helped them to achieve this positive outcome.

Over the months of involvement, Shelly, supported by her manager, navigated the stages of the Practice Cycle repeatedly, carefully and mindfully, building a close, honest and therapeutic relationship with the family. In long-term work, practitioners must complete the office–transition–family encounter–back to the office cycle many times. Therefore, the concept of the Practice Cycle needs to be developed as an analytical tool to understand the long-term relationship cycle and later chapters will do this.

'Good enough' practice

Overall, while Shelly's practice was not perfect, it was 'good enough'. 'Good enough' does not refer to complacent blasé thinking along the lines of 'that will have to do!'. Rather its value as a concept is that it takes into account what it is possible to achieve in particular circumstances, acknowledging that some mistakes happen and that it isn't possible to be perfect. Winnicott (1971) developed the concept of the 'good enough' parent/mother in recognition of the reality that caretakers too have feelings and needs and being the perfect mother is impossible. The baby isn't always fed on demand because the parent is worn out, or asleep, on their phone, the infant's cries are misinterpreted and so on. Such ruptures in the relationship are repaired by the parent recognising them and soothing the child, by 'holding' them physically and emotionally. Being the 'good enough' mother/father is the best that can be hoped for and rather than being condemned they should be praised for navigating all the pressures, contradictions and joys of parenting to raise broadly healthy children.

The 'good enough' concept is currently gaining renewed popularity and being taken up in a number of ways (Alpert, 2022; Miller, 2024). In psychotherapy,

Sachs (2020) and Cozolino (2004) have adapted Winnicott's concept by substituting 'therapist' for the word 'mother'. They argue that being a 'good enough' practitioner is what is realistic and possible and to be that it is necessary to relinquish the belief that it's possible be a *perfect* one. Mistakes, failures and what Sachs (2020, p 25) calls a feeling of 'clinical futility' need to be accepted as unavoidable at times. Such acceptance can enable professionals to acknowledge their own vulnerability and develop the patience and courage to experience a sense of shared humanity with service users. This supports Steggall and Scollen's (2024) argument that social workers need to embrace what they do not know, which with children can take the form of playfully showing 'their naivety and stupidity' (p 2134), as doing so allows the service user to lead and inform the practitioner's understanding. A huge difficulty for social work in child protection is the blame culture that has become deeply embedded due to the vitriolic public criticism that follows news about child deaths. This makes it very difficult to admit mistakes and failures in everyday practice, generating strong pressures to appear perfect – or, as the social work regulator in England, Ofsted, describes it, 'outstanding'. Shelly's practice overall with Isabelle and family was humane and highly effective. Calling it 'good enough practice' does justice to that and how the work and relationships ebb and flow over time, and rupture and repair, ups and downs, are normal.

Empathy, compassion and endurance

The acknowledgement of heartfelt successes should not detract from families who have very different experiences. For some, child protection interventions are harmful when, for instance, all they get is an investigation that disrupts family relationships without providing any help, leaving them traumatised (Bilson and Martin, 2016; Pappas et al, 2024). With some families where there is known need and risk, a low level of involvement occurs that is not well thought out or purposeful, but reactive. This is often a consequence of workers losing sight of families due to pressure of work or because the physical distance of the family from the office causes them to fall off the radar (Disney et al, 2019). It also happens due to sick leave, or the worker leaving and delay in transferring to a new worker, or because the family don't want involvement and practitioners lack the energy, desire, skills and endurance to keep going back.

Even when families and practitioners become familiar to one another, a degree of uncertainty, risk and anxiety from the unknown remains. A home visit I shadowed with a social worker, Leroy, illustrates this and how the unexpected also occurs even on visits to families who social workers know well. 'Rita' was 18, and her 13-month-old son was on a Child Protection Plan due to domestic abuse by the father who was no longer involved with them. They lived with Rita's mother, sister and two brothers. The social worker regarded it as a routine visit to see how Rita was coping and to help her sustain a childcare routine. She had confirmed calmly by text that morning that she would be in, but as recorded in my field notes the plan quickly had to be abandoned.

> Rita was waiting for the social worker at the front door and was shouting at him in an angry upset way as he approached the front gate and walked down the path. She'd had a row with her sister and mother and was shouting about wanting to get them out of the house. The row continued for the first ten minutes of the visit and the social worker put all his energy into calming things down. Rita kept appealing to the social worker to get her out of the house and into a refuge.

The social worker had to completely revise their plans and improvise on the spot as the entire visit consisted of him calming everybody down and skilfully helping Rita and the other family members to resolve their arguments and discuss options.

Long-term work can be hazardous and frightening. Simone, for instance, told me about a threatening message that had very recently been left on her voicemail: 'It just says: you'd better watch your back because I'm fucking watching yours. So, it, you know, clearly it's a family that isn't happy with what I'm doing, that I'm involved with.' She didn't know who the message was from and obviously found it disturbing and distressing, to the extent that she had become hypervigilant and worried about who is behind her when she is out walking and when driving.

In her classic book *Psychoanalytic Insight and Relationships*, Salzberger-Wittenberg (1970, p 145) suggests that 'caring, containment, courage and endurance, are probably the basis of improvement' for service users in long-term relational work. Following the earlier quote from Clare Winnicott, I would add to this *reliability*, at the heart of which is showing 'care' through empathy, compassion and endurance by keeping going back to see families and trying hard to be helpful. The capacity to endure is just as crucial for the family, for whom involvement with the system is often exhausting due to their fear of losing their children or not getting them back, and the shame and anxiety they feel from being under surveillance and having to deal with the potentially overwhelming amount of procedures and processes involved.

Empathy and compassion are also crucial dimensions of making effective relationships because of the anger, rejection, passive aggression and overt hostility workers often face. For Clare Winnicott (in Kanter, 2004, p 175), a key component of empathic relational work is that the social worker 'creates and maintains a professional relationship which, among other things, eliminates fear of retaliation'. This means that good enough longer-term relational work has to involve responding to service users' anger and other emotions in a reliable non-punitive way while maintaining the necessary drive, endurance, compassion, aliveness and hope to be able to keep going back to see families.

An unconscious process that often occurs for workers under high levels of anxiety and for parents dealing with unbearable feelings about having their children removed involves the psychological defence of the mind 'splitting' people and agencies into 'good' and 'bad' (Trevithick, 2011). Some workers are regarded as 'good' and idealised, while others are seen as unacceptable and hateful, as 'bad objects' (Valentine, 1994). This often has a basis in real events and experiences that are painful and shaming for parents and children (Gibson, 2019). However, at an unconscious level, such splitting may also be a way of making painful experiences and relationships bearable. The 'bad worker' has the service user's fear, anger, resentment, trauma, shame, humiliation and hate projected onto them, while the 'good worker' is idealised with qualities like care, compassion, tolerance and love. This manifests in different ways, one powerful pattern being that following the transfer of a case, the family tells the new worker of their dislike for the previous social worker(s). In Maria Nicholls' situation, described earlier in this chapter, it is some past and current social workers and teams from different offices involved with her children in care who are hated.

We can see this in the experience of Sally, whose three-year-old son was on a Child Protection Plan. She had significant mental health and addiction problems and a long history of hating social workers.

> My aftercare worker and one of the foster placements I was in before I left care, she was the one that probably got me on the right track, she was absolutely brilliant. But all my social workers, I've never got on with any of them and that is in my history and I did headbutt one of my social workers when I was younger, so I've never had a good dealing with social services or with the police. Which is why I wanted to move to a new county to have a fresh start. ... I feel quite sorry for her [Rebecca, the newish social worker] because she has been chucked in at the deep end, halfway through all of this. So this is the thing that I get frustrated with them, they never keep the same workers on you, they change them either halfway through or right at the end there's never a consistent worker who is just dealing with your case. Even though I hated the social workers I had before, I think that's why it got to the point where they wanted to change it anyway because there was a complete breakdown between all of us, so I think for me it is in a way better that I do have Rebecca and sort of like a fresh pair of eyes on it really.

For Sally, all her previous social workers and the entire social work department and care system were hateful, 'bad objects', apart from one aftercare worker and foster carer. The time I spent in this social work department over a lengthy period confirmed Sally's experience of it as a disruptive environment. It struggled to recruit and retain permanent staff and had to rely heavily on agency workers who could leave at any moment. The senior management team kept changing – in part because many service redesigns hadn't worked and they were failing inspections by the regulator. This all meant that the organisation was stuck in a state of constant disruption and crisis. My observations of Rebecca interacting with the family supported Sally's view that she was a humane and skilful practitioner. She 'held' Sally in exactly the way Clare Winnicott refers to earlier: by being reliable and unlike previous people in Sally's life, she did not retaliate when Sally was angry or dismiss or abandon her when she was distressed. This experience of feeling held in a long-term relationship was therapeutic for Sally.

The aim of identifying defences like 'splitting' is not to undermine the authenticity of service users' experiences but to highlight the complexity of these relationships and how organisations, workers and service users become entangled in dynamics of love and hate, fantasy, transference and countertransference (Froggett, 2002; Cooper, 2018; Archard, 2020). One destructive consequence can be retaliatory and punitive responses by workers, referred to by Winnicott (1949) as 'hate in the countertransference', which will be discussed further later in the book.

Sustaining care: being a reliable hate object

These complexities can be further analysed by considering the dynamics of work with some families who need ongoing support and seem likely to for as long as their children are living with them. Unlike the Nicholls family, for whom an end to the Child Protection Plan could be envisaged, this hope is not held out for some others due to the extent of their problems and risks. The James family had been known to social workers for some 20 years and their current social worker, Christina, had been involved for six months. There were four children: Lily, aged 16, who lived at home with her parents; and Tia, 13, who had recently gone into respite foster care with her parents' agreement but still spent some time visiting her family. The other two siblings were in their early 20s, a sister who recently served a prison sentence for violence, and another sister whose two children had recently been taken into care and were in contact with a different social work office. Both these adult children had mental health problems and learning difficulties. Tia and Lily also had significant learning difficulties and Christina described the concerns as also being about emotional and physical neglect and the family's 'chaotic' lifestyle. Her view was that for as long as the children remained at home they would always need their involvement if there was any chance of the family staying together.

Christina didn't hold back in describing home conditions as 'disgusting'.

> What else can I say? They've got nits and fleas and anything you can imagine that shouldn't live in a house, rats and mice wouldn't surprise me either. They had, when we first got involved this time, they had 25 cats and everybody was, all of them were pregnant. ... Mum is trying very hard to make sure that they always have food and something in the house but the youngest one Tia she wets the bed and she just lets her sleep in it and it's disgusting. Last time she was sleeping in there before she went into foster care and oh my God I couldn't, and when I walked close to her room it was so disgusting I couldn't even open my mouth because I was just gagging. ... I couldn't open my mouth because I could taste the urine. It was that

disgusting, really strong. But that's the second mattress we've bought them but it was soaking through, mouldy again and she had … they'd had the top off trying to clean it.

At the insistence of the social workers, the cat population was now thought to be down to around six and Tia spends most of her time in foster care, only going home at weekends. The plan is to keep her in voluntary care to prevent her mental health from declining and experiencing the problems her older siblings have. Lily was the main focus of the visit I shadowed with Christina, which aimed to encourage Lily to consider returning to college.

When we arrived at the home Lily was sweeping and mopping the hallway. Mrs James then arrived home, with milk. Mr James was lying down in the sitting room, unwell. Christina and Lily sat at the table and there was a sense of warmth and good connection between the social worker and the family. Christina raised whether the older daughter (whose children are in care) had been to the house and Mrs James laughed about her other 21-year-old daughter being sent to prison for hitting someone. Christina told her it was no laughing matter. Christina moved through her visit plan systematically and authoritatively. When seated she had an A4 writing pad on her lap but didn't write much, which enabled her to maintain good eye contact with the various family members. Christina spoke to Lily in a probing but supportive way about going back to college, stressing the value to her of meeting with other teenagers, and Lily listened and expressed interest. Some 38 minutes into the visit, the social worker asked to see upstairs and Lily led the way, first into her own room, which Christina thought was tidy. Lily showed her recent photos that were on display and Christina admired a drawing she had done. Then, as the social worker entered Tia's bedroom, four largish kittens ran out and Lily shouted: 'MUM! … Found all the cats Mum!' The overpowering acrid smell in the room was just like the social worker had described it. The (adult) cats were there and there was no litter tray. One of them jumped onto Lily's shoulder and scratched her. Lily said the urine smell wasn't the cats but from Tia's bed-wetting. Christina called to Mrs James to come upstairs and told her that she needed to clean Tia's bed and covers before she comes back for a stay. She agreed. Christina told me afterwards that compared to the past the bedroom was quite clean. After spending five minutes upstairs, the visit concluded in the kitchen where Christina agreed to help the family get a new fridge and discussed ways they could dispose of more of their rubbish.

Afterwards in the car, Christina said that Lily 'has grown up in complete chaos and her family life always functions in chaos. But I think I am somebody who gives her some boundaries – no … she doesn't have any routine'. Christina expressed frustration with regards to the family's lack of capacity to change, while emphasising the meaningful relationship she feels she has with Lily and with Tia and the importance of this: 'A lot of social workers came and went. She really needed someone who didn't back off.' In other words, the social worker recognised the value of endurance and reliability. The positive way in which

Lily responded today was in stark contrast to how she was the week before, as the social worker explained:

> I mean, if you could have heard what Lily gave me last week, it was completely different. She goes off ranting. And I've had her kick off in the corridor before; kicking, screaming, shouting, throwing stuff and saying, 'If you come through here I'll kill you' – a completely different Lily. ... At the beginning it was a lot of Lily shouting, screaming, chaos, and she, she wouldn't talk to me at all; she would leave the room, smash stuff. But I think kind of as I persevered and didn't, don't close [the case] and just hang in here and do crisis management, I think she does appreciate that I haven't just gone away. ... I just go back again and again and again. And I think that probably makes her much easier and more appreciative.

Lily and the social worker had what I would suggest was a resonant therapeutic relationship that contained a hateful side in how irritation, anger, disagreement, conflict and even rejection were part of it. This can be healthy and therapeutic as long as the relationship does not involve *constant* hurtful hostility and nothing else (Rosa, 2019, p 191). The therapeutic value of such long-term relational work, according to Salzberger-Wittenberg (1970, p 155), is that 'the client is expressing his [*sic*] need to empty these feelings into someone in the hope that the caseworker be strong and tolerant enough to contain them ... [and] without retaliating'. In persevering and keeping going back, despite – and because of – how Lily rejects her and the visceral impact of the very poor, 'disgusting' home conditions, the social worker proved her reliability and capacity to hold whatever 'chaos' and hate the service user threw at her. To the service user the social worker was a *reliable hate object*. She achieved this by accepting Lily as she was and her acting out and not retaliating, fulfilling the vital holding role of helping her to bear the impact of the harm she had experienced and the anger and hurt she was not yet able to manage in herself.

Conclusion

This chapter has set out the broad outlines of the core relational components and challenges involved in long-term child protection work.

Key learning points

- Long-term relationships are typified by ups and downs, love and hate, rupture and repair. The Winnicotts' concept of 'holding' has been adopted and developed to provide a way of understanding how social workers can support service users in reliable, caring ways to develop their capacities to love, care and become 'good enough parents'.

- A concept of 'good enough practice' is needed to counteract the unrealistic expectation that social workers and other professionals should never make mistakes and the goal is perfection. Mistakes provide learning opportunities and good enough practice can be very good, and effective.

- Empathy, compassion and reliability are crucial elements in building and sustaining relationships with service users. Trust is developed and maintained through practitioners actively listening to service users, recognising and affirming their feelings and needs. This process must involve workers acknowledging families' criticisms of past and current practitioners and systems and, where possible, adjusting their approach to respect their wishes.

- When service users express anger, pain, or distress, practitioners should accept them as they are and avoid retaliating. By doing so, they can act as a reliable container, a 'hate object', fulfilling a vital holding role that helps service users to bear the impact of harm and begin to manage feelings they cannot yet regulate themselves.

- Just as in duty and assessment work, recognising and managing intense feelings is vital for understanding and sustaining long-term relationships. The concept of 'good authority' has been further developed, emphasising the need for a careful balance between care and control. Exercising good authority has a crucial emotional component which requires the ability to self-regulate and avoid retaliating when confronted with hostility.

- Relationships between families and social workers can sometimes be marked by pessimism, hate and despair, requiring endurance from both sides. However, there is also joy and pleasure to be found in meaningful therapeutic relationships that have resonance and achieve desired outcomes.

This chapter, along with the previous one, has set the stage for a deeper examination of the complex nature of relationships and the psycho-social dynamics of relational work. We are now ready to explore in detail how practitioners sometimes avoid engaging with children and fail to be helpful to parents and families. Understanding the reasons behind such avoidance can provide valuable insights into what constitutes good enough practice.

4
Automated practice: the invisible and unheld child

Practitioners achieve different degrees of closeness to children and families. We have glimpsed how in some short- and long-term work relationships and interactions with children are close and intimate. Achieving this is very challenging due to the complexity of the work and means that the risk of superficial practice that avoids relational closeness, asking difficult questions and to see children is ever present. I have sometimes observed social workers in challenging encounters and environments that threatened to overwhelm and distract them from focusing on the children, but many managed to regain their composure and complete purposeful work. Some social workers, however, were unable to overcome these challenges, leading to varying degrees of disengagement from and avoidance of the children. This chapter will show how in such situations, as practitioners make their way around the Practice Cycle, a number of missteps occur that cumulatively result in the making of what I will call avoidant patterns of practice. Two forms of avoidant practice arise from this that I will refer to as 'automated' and 'disorganised'. Chapter 5 will address the disorganised pattern, while this chapter will demonstrate how automated practice leads practitioners to go through the motions in a rushed, robotic manner, resulting in avoidance and causing children to become invisible and unheld.

Thinking about invisible children

As I referred to in the Introduction to the book, there is a vast literature devoted to trying to make sense of how children died in child protection casework despite the extensive involvement of social workers and other agencies who knew they were at risk. For example, the case review into the death of two-year-old Keanu Williams in 2011 from physical abuse and neglect concluded that 'Keanu became invisible' (Lundberg, 2013, p 51). The Serious Case Review into the death of four-year-old Daniel Pelka in Coventry, England who was sadistically abused and neglected by his mother and her partner and starved despite the attentions of teachers and other professionals concluded that '[a]t times, Daniel appeared to have been "invisible" as a needy child' (Coventry LCSB, 2013).

The concept of 'invisibility' captures an element of how children can be overlooked by workers even when they are right in front of them. However, focusing solely on the visual aspect of the 'invisible child' is problematic, as it might suggest that the goal of good practice is simply to make children *visible*. The nature and goals of good enough practice need to be expressed in terms of a language that incorporates all the senses and intimacy. The book will show that where children are not meaningfully engaged with, it is the absence of intimate practice that involves eye-to-eye contact, talk, active listening, play, touch, holding and close observation that results in crucial aspects of their experience remaining unknown. A more suitable term for this phenomenon is the 'unheld child', which speaks to the absence of the physical and emotional closeness required to truly enter the child's world and lived experience. The emphasis on the visual in the commonly used terminology of 'seeing children' is also highly problematic because practitioners can say they saw children and tick that box on the recording system, when in reality they did not 'see' them in any meaningful sense at all (Kennedy, 2020). Incorporating attention to physical closeness and whether children were held or not brings the children and the encounter to life and they can become much more physically and emotionally present in the hands, minds and hearts of practitioners and managers (Ferguson, 2017).

As the Introduction to the book showed, the most cited reason why children who are known to be at risk are not protected is breakdowns in communication between professionals and agencies. Another influential explanation is that the scope for social workers to get to know children sufficiently is constrained by excessive levels of case recording, tight timescales for completing work and high caseloads (Pascoe et al, 2023). This bureaucratic preoccupation leaves practitioners without enough time to develop the depth of relationship necessary to keep children safe (Munro, 2011, p 128). Brandon et al (2008) identify the 'Start Again Syndrome' where social workers pay insufficient attention to the history of the parents and patterns of risk to the children. Other research shows the forms of reasoning that can lead professionals to remain wedded to their initial assessment and not revise the level of concern despite new information (Munro, 1999; Whittaker, 2018). High levels of conflict with families can result in social workers either avoiding or over-identifying with parents and losing focus on the child (Laird, 2013; Tuck, 2013; Ferguson et al, 2020c). An influential argument is that the thinking of child protection professionals is governed by a 'rule of optimism', which 'is where a positive stance is taken of a child's circumstances or level of risk, which is not necessarily supported by the objective evidence or information available' (Coventry LCSB, 2013, p 43). This is said to result in social workers avoiding 'robust challenge' of parents by emphasising their strengths and failing to focus on children.

As I am arguing throughout this book, these understandings of practice are limited by the fact that they are based on retrospective analyses of tragic events that have already occurred, or research into work that has already been done, as opposed to gathering evidence about what happens in practice as it is happening. When a forward-facing approach is taken and the making of practice is examined as it happens in real time this shows that not only were different degrees of closeness with children achieved, but workers had different levels of awareness of how close to children they had managed to get. Some practitioners know when they have not done what they know they should, they acknowledge that it was very difficult and that their practice lacked rigour and is unfinished.

A good example of this involved an initial home visit to inquire into concerns about domestic abuse and alleged poor childcare standards/possible neglect. The social worker spent the duration of the visit interviewing the children's mother in the sitting room, while the three-year-old child spent most of it upstairs, playing with a friend. The social worker did not directly engage with the child on the one occasion he came into the living room. Nor did she seek out the child or inspect the children's bedrooms, which she did where required on the five other visits to different families that I shadowed her on. On those, she addressed concerns openly and honestly with parents, was empathic and strengths-based in her approach, she saw the children on their own and observed them interacting with their parents.

What most seemed to throw the worker off balance on this visit was the presence of a family friend who stayed in the kitchen for all of the visit except for one moment when she entered the sitting room, walked across the room and stuck her head through the hall doorway and shouted upstairs very loudly to the children: 'Fucking behave!' From the outset of the visit, the children's mother seemed to be superficially co-operative, but the atmosphere was awkward and felt slightly menacing. The family friend was not introduced even though the social worker had to walk past her to get to the living room. This friend's intervention had the effect of significantly increasing the tension. It felt like an aggressive act that was directed towards not the children upstairs, but the worker, who was the one who was really being given the message to 'fucking behave'. When interviewed afterwards, the worker had a sense that things were messy, incomplete and that she needed to go further and deeper in engaging with the children. This she did by going back much sooner than she had committed herself to doing at the end of the first visit.

It is when workers fail to engage with children and are unaware of this at the time that the children can be considered *fully* invisible and unheld. I will now show how, in the heat of the moment, workers often struggle to think clearly, leading to a lack of awareness about their avoidance. As a result, the children, despite being right in front of them, become invisible.

A case of fully invisible and unheld children

A case that vividly illustrates the full invisibility and lack of holding of children involved a social worker, Ada, on a visit concerning a two-year-old girl, Amelia, who allegedly was left unsupervised and found a long way from home. The mother, Mrs Brown, was a White British lone parent, who had one other child, five-year-old Jamie. It was an announced visit and the social worker arrived as planned at 3.30pm. Mrs Brown was dressed in pyjamas and dressing gown, and led Ada into the living room, where another adult was sat on the sofa. Mrs Brown sat down beside this other adult and Amelia, while Jamie was sitting on the armchair. Ada sat on the other armchair. I sat on a chair to one side, positioning myself as always as discretely as possible so as to be able to see and hear, while being somewhat detached. The home was a council property and beautifully presented.

Ada began by reading the concerns from the referral sheet. Unlike most such opening moments observed in my research, the worker did not engage in any rapport-building or introduce her purpose as being wider than investigating the specified concerns, such as being a possible source of help. Going straight into the alleged incident seemed to compound an oppositional atmosphere that was evident as soon as the social worker stepped into the home. Mrs Brown flatly denied that Amelia had been left unsupervised and blamed the person who reported it for persecuting her. The worker did not challenge Mrs Brown's account, or try to come at the issues from other directions, but quickly moved on.

From the outset, Ada seemed to be at a loss to achieve any composure. She forgot to introduce herself to Mrs Brown and became aware of this 11 minutes into the visit and apologised. Although the children were present and in the same room as her throughout, she did not directly relate to them at any point. Jamie moved around the room at times, while Amelia was also active or snuggled up to her mother on the sofa. Neither of the children initiated any verbal or play-based contact with the social worker, who in turn, paid no attention to them. This contrasts with practitioners who use children's movement in the room as an opportunity for beginning playful engagement. Nor did the social worker have any direct interaction with the other adult who was present. At one point that person left the house and came back five minutes later but Ada did not even take that opportunity to ask Mrs Brown about who they were or about their relationship with the children.

Ada asked many leading questions, for instance, when asking about the children: 'What about their behaviour, have you got any worries about that? They seem lovely.' Mrs Brown answered in the affirmative ('Yes, they are lovely!') and this seemed to be what the social worker wished for as it enabled minimal engagement rather than longer dialogue. The learning here is how questioning styles can consciously and unconsciously mirror the worker's internal state. The social worker was struggling and wanted to get it over with.

A key source of the worker's discomfort was that Mrs Brown was clearly angry. The atmosphere was tense:

Mrs Brown:	Yeah, do what you want. There's nothing wrong with my kids, I can assure you of that. There's nothing wrong with my kids.
Social worker:	The thing is, when we come out we've got to do these …
Mrs Brown [*interrupting*]:	Yeah, that's what I'm saying, you can do what you want because there's nothing wrong with my kids.

When it came to doing what the social worker wanted, however, Mrs Brown was less than happy to co-operate. She challenged why Ada wished to see upstairs, wanting to know why it was necessary, and very reluctantly led the way. Jamie's bed and the state of the bedroom looked comfortable and had toys and photos. In passing, Mrs Brown's bedroom could be seen and looked very well equipped and comfortable. However, in Amelia's room her cot was broken and collapsed. It was not fit to sleep in that night, and it was now late afternoon. Ada never actually entered the bedroom but stood at the door and looked into it. The viewing lasted seconds. Mrs Brown said that Amelia jumping in her cot broke it, which Ada accepted and made no attempt to probe further. Mrs Brown may well have been telling the truth, but what was striking was the absence of a deeper inquiring approach, which was what the social worker was there to do. This is the same two-year-old child about whom the referral alleged there had been a lack of proper care and it was reasonable to consider that this could be a scenario in which that child was receiving inferior care to her brother and to that which Mrs Brown provided for herself. However, Ada did not incorporate any such hypothesis into a more critical dialogue with the parent. Nor did she show any interest in why Mrs Brown was in her pyjamas and dressing gown at 3.30 in the afternoon when she knew the social worker was coming, the most obvious hypothesis being that this could indicate depression.

On coming downstairs, the worker started to conclude the visit, and was met by another challenge from Mrs Brown:

Social worker:	All right, well, what I'll do is I'll write it all up and …
Mrs Brown:	Oh yeah, I do want to ask you a question now: why do you have to see their bedroom and that?
Social worker:	Oh, we normally do, because what … well, I don't need to look at your bed, it's just the children's, because then it gives us an idea of their home environment and, do you know what I mean? … No, it's lovely, you've got a lovely house.
Mrs Brown:	Yeah I have.
Social worker:	Yeah, a beautiful house.
Mrs Brown:	That's what I have.
Social worker:	Yeah I know, it's really nice.

It is striking how determined Ada was to get her positive evaluation of the home across to Mrs Brown. She then left. The visit lasted just 15 minutes, which is very quick and much less than the typical time taken for initial assessments, which Chapter 2 showed to be in the region of 45 minutes.

Ada's first words on leaving the house were about Mrs Brown: 'She was simmering underneath, I think she was trying to keep her temper wasn't she.' The social worker's view in the car straight afterwards was that the referral information was probably true, which she did not share with the parent. It then emerged on the journey back to the office that Ada did not even know whether the other adult in the house was a man or a woman. I thought it was a man, so I asked her what she made of 'him': 'I thought it was a girl, but then I did look at her legs and they were very, very hairy, and then I thought maybe it is a man. But no, I think it was a girl, but I'm not 100 per cent sure.'

In general, social workers in the research were rigorous in asking for the names and addresses of anyone present in the home who appeared to have significant access to children, so that they could do police checks. So for this to be absent to the extent that the gender of the person was not even clear was a striking omission. When asked in the car straight afterwards whether she had considered speaking to the five-year-old on their own Ada replied: 'But yeah I, I could have done, couldn't I, really? But I didn't think about it at the time because he's only five.' I knew that this worker had interviewed a five-year-old alone in another case I had shadowed her on, so this was not a convincing reason for not doing it. As Ada continued to drive, she must have been silently reflecting on this and, a couple of minutes after this comment, volunteered: 'But I'll be honest, I didn't, I didn't even think about it, I don't know why but I didn't.'

As we travelled at times in silence and the worker thought more about what occurred on the visit she seemed to begin to become mindful of the children and how absent they were from her attention. As she was getting out of the car at the office 15 minutes after the end of the visit, referring to the five-year-old, she said, 'I don't know why I didn't talk to him.' The worker was unable to explain even to herself how she had so totally failed to think about the children and keep them in mind. In the heat of the visit, talking with and other forms of relating to the children became unthinkable and the fact that she had not engaged with them in any way was, at the time it was happening, unknown to the worker. The children had ceased to exist to her, despite being there right in front of her. They were invisible children.

The process of detaching from children and losing sight of them

In its most complete form, social workers' lack of meaningfully relating to children and detachment from parents involves the worker becoming intuitively, cognitively, spiritually and energetically absent. It is a form of absent presence. This results in automated practice within an avoidant pattern of relating. Even their physical presence is limited as the worker spends little time in the encounter and uses their body in rigid, almost robotic like ways that are devoid of flowing movement, playfulness and attunement to the children or adults. This shows how stress and the emotional impact of the work can affect perception and clear thinking and also lead to what Rosa (2019, p 105) describes as a feeling of being alienated from one's own body. The body becomes an enemy or an unknown stranger and how it behaves is not what we intend, by blushing, sweating, belching, refusing to move and so forth (Rosa, 2019, p 105). When they sit awkwardly, don't play or reach out to children, and move fast to escape a home, social workers' bodies are acting against what they intended to do. Workers are also emotionally absent to the children and their experience (and to parents and other carers too), but not entirely to themselves in that they experience intense feelings of anxiety that drive their avoidance and preoccupation with their own safety.

It would be easy to blame individual social workers for such errors and judge them to have failed due to lacking the skills and competence to do the work. But this simplistic interpretation immediately runs into trouble because the same workers were observed on other occasions practising coherently. My argument is that such detachment from children occurs *when practitioners reach or go beyond the limits of anxiety and complexity that it is possible for them to tolerate*. They are overcome by the sheer complexity of the interactions they encounter, the emotional intensity of the work, parental resistance and the tense atmospheres in the homes. Such avoidant practice is deeply non-reflexive in the sense that, while the worker may be reflecting superficially on what is going on, there is no self-monitoring or critical thinking being practised that results in them adjusting their approach in light of the experience they are having and the reasons they are there. So thorough was this with the Brown family that the work seemed driven by an (un)conscious intention to get through it and back to the office as quickly as possible. This is not so much the 'Start Again Syndrome' that involves practitioners failing to recognise and take into account past experiences with the family (Brandon et al, 2008) as a pattern of *Never Properly Getting Started At All*.

Practitioners' skill levels, knowledge, their energy and aliveness, or flatness, do matter (Handley and Doyle, 2014). But situations in which children are lost sight of and unheld are best understood in terms of a process of invisibility and non-holding that arises from the interaction between organisational influences such as lack of resources, limited or no staff support, and workers' skills, qualities and lived experience. It can be understood through careful analysis of what occurs through the various stages of the Practice Cycle. I will make this argument by focusing in even greater detail on the Brown family, as it was an encounter in which full invisibility and lack of holding of children occurred.

Time and organisational culture

Figure 4.1 shows the journey that was taken around the Practice Cycle, summarises what occurred at each stage and the cumulative effect of the various stages and how they produced automated avoidant practice.

At stage 1, organisational culture first comes into play in relation to the definitions of need and risk to children that are operating and the time available to practitioners to respond to them. In the bigger scale of the child protection work that went on in my research studies the Brown referral was at the lower end of risk. This could have resulted in the worker feeling under pressure to go through the motions and get out as soon as possible so as to be able to return to the office and deal with more serious cases. The worker could even have claimed to have performed the key tasks of child protection: the children were 'seen', the parent(s) spoken to, the home inspected, although these were done in a superficial and ineffective manner. This shows the inadequacy of relying on the visual terminology of 'seeing the child'. Children must of course be seen – 'laid eyes on', as some social workers express it – but they must also be *held*. This may involve the worker using touch and engaging in physical contact

Figure 4.1: Automated avoidant practice

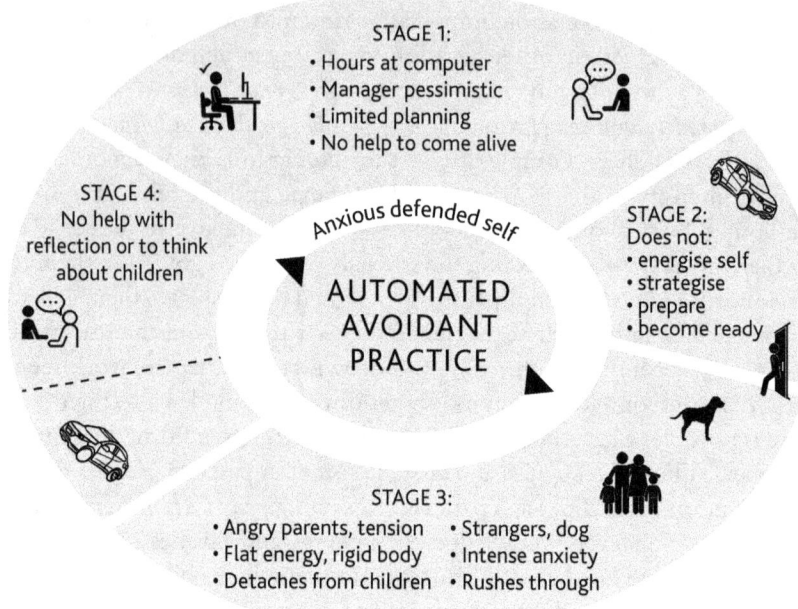

with the children, by picking babies and younger children up, for instance. But where the circumstances are deemed to not require such tactile relating, the children need to be held by the worker in another sense, in *mind*. Central to this is the making of practice in which both worker and child are 'touched' by the encounter, and an energetic connection and attunement occurs that vibrates with resonance (Rosa, 2019). This creation is the worker's responsibility and more broadly that of their organisation. Organisational and systemic factors are particularly influential in how, in general, small amounts of time are spent with children, such as when they are seen on their own. Sometimes this is sufficient to establish how safe children are, but often the time spent is dictated more by organisational requirements, workloads and timescales than the amount of time the worker needs to spend with the children to try to fully understand and meet their needs. A key dynamic, then, in how some children become overlooked is the systemic pressures practitioners feel under to get through their work and the limited time at their disposal to make *any* children 'visible' and held.

These general dimensions of organisational culture are played out through the dynamics of social workers' experience directly prior to (and after) the visit. In this case, the social worker had been very busy on the duty desk during the almost seven hours (8.30–3.30) that separated the start of being on duty and the visit. I observed her and she was sometimes on the phone doing checks with other agencies about new referrals, and mainly on the computer, typing up case notes or on email. In Chapter 1 I referred to the vital role managers need to play in helping practitioners to be prepared and in a state of readiness to engage in an alive, fully present, meaningful way with children and families. This social worker did have a discussion with her manager whose dominant attitude was one of cynicism about Mrs Brown. She had not responded well to previous referrals and the manager said she expected Mrs Brown to be out in order to evade the planned social work visit. This sent the worker on her way with a high degree of pessimism about what she could expect and achieve, which may account for at least some of the low energy and flatness to her demeanour. Nothing was done to help her get out of her bureaucratic, non-relational state of mind and body, what in Chapter 1 was referred to as her 'duty head', and to loosen her rigid body and *come alive* for the encounter.

The use of transitional space

The social worker's state of mind and lack of readiness was compounded at stage 2 of the Practice Cycle by poor use of transitional space. On the way to the visit, Ada spoke about how difficult she found it making the transition from office duties to family homes:

> Sometimes you do go out feeling a bit unprepared, because you're busy doing other stuff and then suddenly you think: 'Oh now I've got to go and visit.' And so you jump up with your paperwork that's sometimes, to be honest, occasionally we're sat outside the house reading it. I mean I did read this, I did read this this morning, on duty, but if I hadn't done it then … so I know what it's about, yeah, I know it can be difficult. … It's like when you get engrossed in things, doing the CP [child protection] checks on other children, and then suddenly you think: 'Oh no!' So you've got to change what you've been thinking about and suddenly you rush out the door.

This preoccupation and lack of prioritising of the impending face-to-face encounter with the child and family bears out what is known about how organisational pressures lead practitioners to have to take risky shortcuts (Broadhurst et al, 2010; Murphy, 2022; Pascoe et al, 2023). In this instance the worker managed to read the referral earlier, however she had not figured out any coherent plan for the encounter, either by herself or with the help of her manager. Nor while transitioning to see the family did the worker do any of the kind of critical thinking and strategising – the car therapy – I referred to in Chapter 1. On arrival at the home, the social worker's state of mind and body were therefore still in the detached state brought about by spending hours at the computer and feeling rushed to get back to the office to continue being on duty. She was in a *bureaucratically preoccupied* state. Although she didn't recognise it, in her mind she had not really left the office. Her heart never seemed to be in it.

Emotional and interactional dynamics

The state of mind and body that social workers bring into an encounter is crucial to the quality of their work. How practice is done is further shaped by stage 3 of the Practice Cycle: the emotional demands, interactional dynamics and visceral impact of the encounter with service users and, in this instance, the home environment. This social worker immediately had to contend with Mrs Brown's 'simmering' anger. Unlike in some other casework covered in the book where workers felt affected by poor home conditions, dirt and disgust, in this case the home was 'lovely'. Therefore, it was fear and anxiety about her own safety and well-being that were a key source of the social worker's automated practice. In my experience of situations in which children were inadequately seen and unheld, anger, resistance, hostility and physical movement by parents and family friends played a significant intimidating role in the encounter. As Figure 4.1 seeks to illustrate, agitated, menacing atmospheres in the home can cause a social worker's already anxious, bureaucratically preoccupied state of mind and self to become further detached and defended. The anxiety becomes unbearable, and defending themselves from having to think about and feel it results in them emotionally disassociating from and not thinking about the children or in many respects the adults who they are there to engage and assess. An automated form of practice results that is driven by avoidance and the desire to flee.

Reflection and decision-making

The full extent of this dissociation became obvious when it emerged afterwards that the Browns' social worker did not even know whether the other adult in the house self-identified as a man or a woman and she was unaware that the children were invisible to her. A crucial opportunity to identify and correct such avoidant practice arises when the worker arrives back at the office. Ada put her head around the manager's door and said 'She was in', to which the manager replied 'Oh, right', and the social worker then went back to work on the duty desk. Nothing was done to help Ada make sense of her experience and bring the children to mind. The lack of holding for the children mirrored the absence of a 'holding environment' for the worker which could have helped her think critically about and process what just happened.

    It is not the role of a researcher to act as a case supervisor but the analysis illustrates how, through the posing of open-ended questions during the research interview in the car straight after the visit, the worker's awareness of how she had ignored the children began to change. A similar kind of debrief with her manager on her return to the office could have had a similar effect in bringing these invisible, unheld children fully to mind.

Conclusion

Observing such practice where children have not been sufficiently engaged with to ensure they are safe raises ethical issues for researchers. I subsequently satisfied myself that the worker had completed follow-up work to check on the children's safety in greater depth. Crucially, the events covered here were not the only actions taken in the cases. This chapter focused on the interactions that occurred before, during and after a specific home visit and has not provided an analysis of all the work that went into the entire case after it. The aim has been to begin to show the processes and interactional dynamics that result in different degrees of visibility and detachment from some children on particular occasions.

Key learning points

- How children become invisible – and, as I have framed it, 'unheld' – is not reducible simply to 'bad' practitioners, but must be understood in terms of the interaction between a range of variables and their cumulative impact (see Figure 4.1). This chapter has demonstrated how the various stages of the Practice Cycle and their interconnections come together to shape the lived experience of the work. These elements significantly affect practitioners' energy, abilities to 'see', move, physically approach, hold and meaningfully connect with children.

- A crucial takeaway is that avoidant practice happens when practitioners reach or go beyond a level of anxiety and complexity they cannot tolerate and they lose their capacity to think clearly and act skilfully, creatively and authoritatively. There is a striking flatness and lack of energy, or attempts at attunement in how workers conduct such encounters.

- Workers get into this kind of disengaged, automated state due to a combination of things. Lack of organisational support with preparation for the encounter leaves them lacking in readiness and limited or no critical reflection on the experience after it provides no help to think about the children.

- Whatever personal qualities, skills at relationship-based practice and creativity they have drain away and they are unable to interact with children or connect with them and enter their world in the intimate way necessary. This also affects their capacity to relate to parents and be present in an empathetic, authoritative way. They are unable to manage the intensity of the visceral and emotional experience and high level of anxiety in the moment of the encounter.

- The place where the encounter occurs and its atmospheres has a big impact on the worker's emotions and the quality of their attention. This is especially the case with the family home because of all the distractions – such as strangers, some of whom are intimidating, pets, especially dogs (Turner, 2025), and the hubbub of family life.

- Workers who are caught up in these kinds of casework situations do not make child protection in any constructive, purposeful sense, but make a dangerously non-relational version of it. Responsibility for children becoming invisible and unheld lies as much, if not more, with the organisations that compel professionals to work under stultifying conditions as it does with individual practitioners.

- Where social workers fail to engage with children or challenge parents, it is not because of a 'rule of optimism' but rather a mixture of fear, helplessness and hopelessness born of intense emotions, disturbing sensory experiences and organisational constraints. We have seen how everything is affected, right down to social workers asking leading questions, the short answers to which enable them to get the encounter over with more quickly. Far from being optimistic in these cases, social workers experience pessimism about the parents and view their stories with scepticism.

- In child death inquiries and much child protection literature, unsafe practice is said to occur due to reasons that are exceptional, rather than it being part of the fabric of the work (Cooper, 2005). Yet my observations indicate that the processes and events that lead to children becoming invisible and unheld in child protection work are in fact routine and everyday ones. Solutions therefore lie in addressing these everyday issues and barriers.

The next chapter will aim to deepen further understanding of avoidant practice and how personal, spatial, emotional and organisational forces interact to hinder practitioners' ability to effectively relate to children and parents. Fully grasping these dynamics is crucial to improving child protection practices.

5

Disorganised practice: chaotically thought about and unsafe children

Having begun to show how avoidant patterns of child protection are made, this chapter takes that analysis further by focusing on what I call 'disorganised' practice. Here children are not completely invisible and unheld but are related to *up to a point*. The interactions are fitful, disorganised and of limited value. While the last chapter showed that automated practice involves workers getting out of the encounter as quickly as they can, disorganised practice involves them staying longer and oscillating between sporadic attempts at relating to children and not relating to them at all. The primary case example in this chapter focuses on child neglect, highlighting the visceral and embodied nature of practice, including the impact of sensory experiences like smell. This shows how disorganised avoidant practice emerges from the intense engagement of all the senses and the experience of powerful emotions, such as disgust. To help understand how this happens, insights from studies of culture and the body will be used, especially Mary Douglas' (1966) work on dirt as 'matter out of place' and what Julia Kristeva (1982) calls experiences of 'abjection'.

A degree of avoidance and detachment from children will be shown that became so total that the worker could not respond to a child who was in front of them literally crying out for attention. Such responses may seem unthinkable and bizarre on a rational level. This is why psycho-social thinking, which allows us to delve beneath the surface and analyse the interior worlds of the practitioner, the organisation, the family, and the home or other places where encounters occur, is crucial for understanding how children become invisible and unheld. Once again, the aim of drawing out the nature and dynamics of these avoidant patterns is to raise awareness of them and identify ways in which they can be prevented.

Stepping into fear and complexity

The main case study around which this chapter is built involved 'Ray', a lone-parent father of two sons: 'Steven' (14) and 'Sam' (10). The referral was made by the police after they had been called to the home late at night to investigate reports of shouting and things being smashed. The police described the house as 'dirty'; there was dog poo on the floor and it was cluttered with bikes and empty drink cans. There was a plastic bag filled with vomit by the sofa and the house smelt of alcohol. The father was asleep on the sofa under what was described as 'a very dirty' duvet and he was clearly under the influence of alcohol and/or drugs and when stirred was aggressive to police officers. Ten-year-old Sam told the police that just before they arrived 'some horrible men' came to the house and threatened to punch his dad and that the vomit was Ray's. While the police were at the house, a group of five teenagers arrived with cans of lager to have a house party. Sam was taken by the police to relatives several miles away and seemed relieved to leave the home. The children were on Child Protection Plans some time previously for 'neglect' and there had been some sporadic social worker involvement since then. The case was officially closed four months prior to this referral because, I was told, of the 'father's refusal to engage'.

On the way to the family in the car the social worker, Melissa, spoke of finding it hard to adjust from being on duty and busy at deskwork to doing the home visit. She did not feel in a good state of mind: 'I am not being myself; I'm not, I'm elsewhere I think.' Soon after she began to drive, Melissa explained what she was thinking:

> I'm planning in my own head and thinking: right, where do I start, what do I say; will the children be there, won't they? You know; will they be at his mum's or, I guess, well, I want to have a look around really. I want to see, I think the state of the house is going to say a lot, so that will be, that will be something. ... So, I guess all this is going through my head: what do I want from today and what am I going to, what am I going to say to him?

She was feeling a bit better about the visit because she had spoken to Ray earlier on the phone and he sounded fine with her visiting. Melissa said she felt anxious partly because 'as a rule' she didn't really like initial meetings with people and 'I don't like dirty house ones because I just don't feel confident with them really'. She feels embarrassed about pressing people to talk about the state of their home and related this dislike, in part, to how her own mother kept their house spotless when she was growing up.

As she arrived at the home, the social worker's feelings were: 'Okay, I feel [*pause*] nervous in my belly, you know. I'm like, I do feel awkward and uncomfortable.' The social worker parked 60 metres away from the home and as we walked and approached the house two tall young men were outside it walking towards us and one of them was holding a large stick. As the social worker was expected I fretted silently to myself about whether it was a baseball bat and these men were there to beat the social worker (and me) up. Then the man threw the stick down and they passed without any problem. But this was an intimidating moment for the social worker, as she mentioned after the visit.

On arrival at the front of the house, Ray let us in and directed us through the kitchen and dining area and into the sitting room, where 14-year-old Steven was sat on the armchair in the corner, watching television. Sam was present too. Without any prompting Ray spoke about how messy the house was, blaming it all on his sons. The social worker suggested she and Ray sit outside in order not to discuss things in front of the children and he declined because he didn't want the neighbours to hear it, which Melissa conceded was a 'good point'. The social worker put the concerns about neglect to Ray who said that on the night in question he had a few friends over and 'a few drinks'. Sam was much more forthcoming than his father:

Sam:	When I came home from my friend's, because we're just going down town to the park, I came back at something like seven o'clock, yeah. Daddy …
Father [*interrupting*]:	It's all right.
Sam:	Daddy was asleep, yeah. These boys were outside smashing it, yeah. And I told them to stop, and they said, 'Why?' I said, 'Because of the noise and the neighbours and social services.' And then Daddy woke up, said they should go, and then this boy said, get these 'naughty word' inside or I'll punch you.
Social worker:	To who?
Sam:	To Dad
Social worker:	How did that make you feel?
Father:	Upset.
Sam:	I cried and I was angry. Scared.
Social worker [*Eight-second pause and then speaking to the father*]:	Any problems at the minute? Any drink or …?
Father:	No.
Social worker:	No issues?

Here was an immediate indication that the social worker was struggling in that she didn't acknowledge the child's feelings of fear and anger. Rather, she took a full eight seconds to think of a question which she directed at the father, moving attention away from the child. This set the pattern for the entire visit. Sam kept trying to be heard and 11 minutes into the visit asked the social worker to take him to McDonald's, a request his father said worried him in case it was interpreted as meaning that he was not feeding his children.

Melissa did not manage to see the children on their own. This was despite Ray, in one of his few moments of overt co-operativeness, asking her if she wished to. Unusually, Melissa turned down the opportunity – another early sign that she was struggling and that her plan for the visit was disintegrating. She then proceeded to timidly give 14-year-old Steven the choice of talking on his own:

Social worker:	What about Steven when he's at home? Do you want to tell me. Do you want to chat? How do you feel about stuff?
Steven:	Fine.

Social worker:	Do you want to talk alone, or do you want to talk with the group? Yeah?
Steven:	No, I'm all right.
Social worker:	Group, yeah. How do you get on in general?

Ray kept interrupting Steven's monosyllabic replies and there was little virtue in the social worker giving him a choice in front of his father to talk alone, an offer he was never going to accept. Steven would have picked up from the tentative way Melissa made the offer that she was not really receptive to hearing anything difficult or painful. In fact, the social worker's line of questioning gave Ray the opportunity to challenge Steven to name how he (Ray) might need to change:

Social worker:	If you could change anything about living here, what would you change?
Steven:	More things to do round here.
Father:	What about me? What would you change about me?
Steven:	Nothing.
Father:	What about me?
Steven:	Nothing.
Father:	What about me, Steven? What about me?
Steven:	Nothing.

The situation became even more uncomfortable when Ray forced Steven to stand up to show Melissa how big he was getting:

Father [*shouting*]:	Stand up. Stand up. Please!
Steven:	No.
Father:	Come on, Steven. Stand up a minute and then you can lie back down. He's 14. [*Steven stands up*] He's my size already. Look at the size of him. Sorry, sit down.

Steven appeared embarrassed and humiliated by his father's controlling behaviour and this added to the growing climate of despair in the room. Ray said that Steven was doing 'good' at school and to prove it he showed Melissa his school report. She managed briefly to explore some areas that are standard in assessments, such as what social support they had and the children's health. She also asked if Ray had cleaned the house knowing that she was visiting and he replied: 'No, hardly. Only small bits. The kids actually messed it up a minute ago, and that's all I was doing.'

The social worker then asked ten-year-old Sam: 'If you could change anything, what would you change?'

Sam:	I'd rather change. … I would rather change [*quietly*] let me think – I would rather change who's on the throne. I would rather be on the throne. I'd rather change [*pause*] the house.
Social worker:	Yeah. What would you change about the house?
Sam:	I would be the king and then I'd have a lovely palace. I'd rather like a mansion or a nicer house, because the walls are destroyed a bit.
Father:	Say that again.
Sam:	Because the walls are destroyed a bit on that side.
Father:	They're not all, but that's you with hammers and things. I've got to re-plaster that.

Sam could be interpreted as using his imagination to state his unhappiness with his father's leadership as the 'king' of the home and his desire to live in a better environment, however the social worker offered nothing in response. Sam was now standing on the coffee table with a cuddly dog he'd brought in and Melissa showed some interest in his things, complimenting him on his creativity and lively imagination. The room's sparse appearance, with sections of wallpaper torn off and some plaster missing, suggested poverty. The room also seemed uncared for, given that surfaces were covered in dust and the floor with dirt and the unpleasant odour – which the social worker referred to a lot in our later discussions.

Ray's behaviour oscillated between brief moments of acceptance at the social worker's presence and periods of belligerence and indignation. He was restless, moving around more often than he was seated. This included patrolling up and down in front of the fireplace and at times using a dustpan and brush to sweep the living room directly in front of the social worker. In these moments, he seemed more vulnerable and fearful, no doubt anxious because his parenting was being scrutinised. However, the edgy movement was both agitated and *agitating*, like it was part of an attempt not merely to defend himself but to dominate the encounter. When he sat down, it was on the bench shelf that ran across the room each side of the fireplace, always sitting directly in front of the social worker, always looking right at her. He regularly took drinks of water from a bottle. At one point Steven fell asleep. The atmosphere was a strange mixture of frenetic energy, aggression, stupor and melancholy.

After 35 minutes, Melissa managed to ask if she could see upstairs and Ray, who was pacing to the right of the fireplace, grunted 'no', that it wasn't very clean. Melissa kept quiet and there was an awkward silence. He then disappeared without explanation, after which the noise of him upstairs (tidying up, presumably) could be heard. Although this left the two boys in the sitting room without their father being present for seven minutes, the social worker just sat quietly without relating to the children directly. Sam continued to be very playful and, after 90 seconds of complete silence, asked her if he could read to her. But she showed no interest and he didn't get to do it.

When Ray emerged again in the sitting room, breathless and sweaty, Melissa asked him: 'What do you think?' and he said, 'I suppose you can go up there. I just don't like people, you know, going up there.' So, 43 minutes into the visit, she got to the bedroom where she was told Sam slept and found bunk beds that had dirty, urine-stained mattresses stripped bare and no bedding. There were two pillows/cushions on the bottom bunk which were deeply stained. There were no carpets or other floor covering. There was a TV monitor but no games or toys, no ornaments or signs of anything that was a child's. The floor was scattered with bits and pieces of paper and other small objects of dirt but had the appearance of some effort having been made to clean it. The door into the room was not on its hinges but leaning against the bunk bed. Melissa asked where the bedding was and Ray said it was at his mother's being washed. She did not directly take up with him her concern about what she told me afterwards she regarded as conditions that amounted to child neglect.

What she did ask Ray was 'If you could have help with anything, what would it be?' and he couldn't answer it, describing himself as an 'independent person'. She asked about where the children's clothes were and he said mostly among a pile of washed stuff which he kept in his bedroom. Melissa did not ask if she could have a look in there. Nor did she check out other rooms upstairs and it dawned on her afterwards that she did not even know how many bedrooms there were. This raised the question of where Steven was sleeping. The social worker did not find out. The only discussion of sleeping arrangements and care concerned Sam. As the example of Jim in Chapter 2 illustrated, when assessing 'neglect' social workers tend to examine all the bedrooms, bathrooms, toilets and kitchens and often check in cupboards and fridges for food and drink. The intrusiveness of such thorough investigation often makes social workers uncomfortable, yet it is generally considered acceptable to them in probing potential neglect. The absence of this rigour on this occasion was significant.

On going downstairs, the angle of arrival in the kitchen/hall area rendered visible a deeply soiled pillow on top of a pile of clothes which was not there when we entered the home. It must have been Sam's, put there by Ray when he did the quick clean up. Melissa said afterwards that she strongly suspected that he had put everything from Sam's bedroom into his own – which raises again the question of why she didn't check it? In the car afterwards she ventured that she didn't want to push the father too far on this visit and would look in all the bedrooms next time she visits. Postponing seeing the totality of children's living conditions was not what would have been expected by her organisation. Much more likely is that the worker avoided going deeper into the home and the issues because the anxiety she already felt was unbearable and seeing more of the home would only make it more so. The deeper practitioners go into the intimate 'private' spaces of individuals and families, the deeper they are forced to go into themselves and their own interior worlds and emotions are affected. There is a strong likelihood that defences against anxiety will be activated, leading to avoidance.

Disgust and the smell of child protection

How can a practitioner become so immobilised and ineffective, so disorganised and detached in their interactions, that even when the dominating parent is upstairs and not in the room with them, they are unable to connect with the children, even when one is crying out for attention? This encounter had some similar features to the case study in the last chapter, but in this instance the experience was of what social workers typically refer to as 'poor home conditions'. The first thing Melissa said to me when she walked out of the home was:

> As soon as I walked in the house I just felt utterly uncomfortable. I don't know. There were lots of things I didn't say or do that I think, I think the dirty house just kind of overtook me, to be honest. I'll have to go back because I don't believe half of it.

The immediate disgust she felt and visceral effects of the home were also apparent in her experience of sitting:

> The seats were all right, weren't they, but when I sat down I felt like my bum was wet ... and I thought to myself: oh, have I sat in something wet? I did. And it [the referral] did say about dog poo, but I got so panicky about everything, but I couldn't even find the things I was trying to find to read.

The feelings of anxiety from the intimidating father and atmosphere and the fear of contamination from dirt and disgust at the smell led to what Rosa (2019, p 105) describes as bodily alienation, where the body feels like a stranger and is no longer under control. This experience paralysed her, affecting her mind, ability to think, as well as body, to the point where her eyes couldn't focus and she was unable even to read the referral sheet. As she reflected afterwards, she began to realise the inappropriateness of speaking to the children solely in the presence of their father and acknowledged that she avoided challenging him about what she regarded as neglect:

> I thought it wasn't like a kid's bedroom at all, it wasn't, it was bare, dirty, smelly, there was nothing there. It was, it was not at all loving, was it, or would make you feel wanted or, there was no value put to that bedroom, nothing, I don't think. You know, no effort had gone into that room, not at all. And he said he had lots of toys and stuff, and I looked around and there was just nothing there.

The worker defines 'neglect' in terms of the complete absence of any signs of love, care or effort to provide the children with comfort or playful things. This fits with a theoretical perspective on everyday 'things', developed in anthropology, that analyses what objects symbolise and the meanings they carry. Ordinary things, including relatively inexpensive objects that, for instance, personalise a child's bedroom, like pictures, decorations, toys, are understood as being vital to showing love and sustaining relationships (Miller, 2008). Professionals need to recognise the constraints poverty imposes on parents' ability to materially provide for their children (Gupta and Blumhardt, 2017). Nonetheless, it remains appropriate for social workers to seek and expect signs of parental love and care being expressed even in modest material possessions.

A significant aspect of Melissa's narrative afterwards related to her own childhood experience of being brought up by a mother who insisted on tidiness. Melissa described her own home as 'spotless' and how 'it makes me feel a bit crazy, you know, a messy house ... [and] if you've got a clean house and things are clean, then my life's organised and that's the way that I feel about it'.

> I just felt uncomfortable in the situation. I'd already wound myself up before we got there about this dirty house, and then I've gone in and, and it's just like, it was like, you know, squalor, squalor I thought. You know, there were kids hanging around everywhere [outside], we went in, and ... and then I just lost my, the normal pattern of any assessment has kind of gone out the window.

She could recognise how difficult things got before she even entered the home and that the effect of her reflection on the car journey was not to calm her or help her readiness for the family encounter but to 'wind' her up. She knew that she was being ineffective and halfway through thought about leaving: 'And even with the child, I was aware that I couldn't focus on him, because he was chatting about his toys and his teddy, and I'm thinking, I was just, my mind was just [*makes noise*] tricking everywhere off, thinking: "Oh, what do I say?"'

While she could barely talk in coherent sentences, she did manage to move physically to go upstairs, but her thinking wasn't purposeful and her overall practice lacked follow-through. Her state of mind mirrored the domestic chaos she found herself in: 'It made me feel rubbish. Just a rubbish situation really, that I've done a really, a really poor job. I don't know how I'm going to, which is bad, I don't know how I'm going to write an assessment about this when I haven't got anything.' Despite her deep desire to defend herself against the 'rubbish' she abhors, the worker became tainted by it and now felt dirty and ashamed.

Abjection, disorganised practice and chaotic thinking

What Melissa, like all social workers, had to grapple with was what the anthropologist Mary Douglas (1966) famously referred to as dirt being 'matter out of place'. Dirt, she argued, does not have a universally fixed meaning. What is considered dirt differs across cultures and is defined by cultural norms. Shoes, for example, are dirty when placed on the table in Western societies because they are expected to be on the ground. These classifications still matter and I have found that, just like people in general, social workers have deep emotional investments in them. At an experiential level this is about what Kristeva (1982) calls *abjection*. Abjection refers to aspects of experience that unsettle bodily integrity and make us go 'yuck!', such as fluids, orifices, defecation, vomiting, blood, death and decay. As Tyler (2013, p 26) explains, abjection 'expresses the subject's response to that stuff which threatens to overwhelm their body border and their attempts to turn away and distance themselves from the "flow, discharge, haemorrhage" which threatens to engulf them.'

Foul smells, pets in places where they are deemed unhygienic, rooms without doors or doors that are there but off their hinges, clothes and all manner of things on floors, or on tables, are just some of the 'abject' experiences I have seen threatening to overwhelm practitioners' body borders and lead them to detach themselves from children and families. This could easily be taken to mean that social workers crudely impose middle-class values onto people living in poverty and confuse poverty for neglect. A very important 'poverty aware' perspective has developed in recent years that seeks to sensitise workers to the risks of such class-based prejudice (Gupta, 2017). I have been in situations where I concluded that oppressive classist practice occurred, but it is vital to grasp the impact abject conditions can have even when poverty awareness exists. As another social worker remarked after a home visit:

> [I]f the smell is really bad in the house you don't want to stay in there very long, I don't, so I think that makes your visit shorter when the smell is overwhelming and it can sting your eyes and catch the back of your throat, that can be quite difficult.

Remember, too, the experience of Christina, the social worker in Chapter 3, when she said she could taste the smell of the cat urine and lack of care and hygiene in that home. Aspects of this can also be seen in Melissa's plan to deal with the impact of the visit discussed earlier on herself:

> I feel like the clothes should be straight off! 'Right, these will definitely need a wash! I won't wear those trousers a second day in a row!' [*Laughing*]. They'll go in the wash, and yeah, no I feel like I need a clean, I'll go in and wash my hands and everything! [*Laughs*]. That's naughty. But yeah, no I'll do that, make sure I'm clean.

Many social workers have spoken to me about the unpleasant lingering smell and the need they feel after such visits to go through what can be called a process of 'cleansing'. I frequently engaged in similar rituals of cleansing after home visits when I was a social worker and as a researcher have often been uncomfortably aware of the unpleasant smells on my clothes and felt the need to remove them and my shoes as soon as I arrived home after a day of shadowing home visits. Melissa's self-recrimination for making a 'naughty' comment about feeling contaminated shows the taboo there is in social work about admitting such things. Humour is an important way in which talk about families and homes being dirty is legitimised in social work's organisational culture. When a social worker and I were leaving the office to visit a family their colleague quipped 'You've got your jeans on so you're ready for the visit [*laughs*]' – meaning that she was going into a dirty house.

Jo Warner (2015) has shown the ways in which moralistic representations of 'disgusting families' by the media and politicians serve a social and political function by drawing a line between undeserving and deserving families, rendering the 'dirty dysfunctional families' totally responsible for their misfortune and deserving of punishment. This prevents serious consideration of the conditions of racism, sexism, poverty and disadvantage that pervade the lives of struggling families who are impoverished by low pay and insufficient benefits. However, sensitivity to power and not being seen to judge already marginalised people and communities should not lead to a lack of attention to the sensory and emotional dimensions of social work. As this chapter has demonstrated, child protection is a 'fleshy' activity that fully engages all the senses and practitioners can feel disgusted. There is no contradiction in workers from such a humane profession, which promotes poverty awareness, finding the lived experiences of some homes and their inhabitants discomforting or even disgusting. It is vital that there is honesty about such feelings and experiences so that their effects in causing children to be related to as literally untouchable and their lived experience avoided can be identified and addressed.

The making of disorganised practice and avoidance

This chapter has illustrated how a disorganised pattern gets made, where the practitioner's thinking and actions are chaotic. The children are seen in the sense of eyes are laid on them but relating with them is at best fitful, reflecting how the self of the worker is deeply defended and detached. The absence of a capacity to relate and the desire to avoid can be so extreme that the workers cannot even respond to children who cry out to be related to, recognised and held.

Figure 5.1 illustrates how as the worker travels round the Practice Cycle every stage contributes to them becoming more anxious, defended and ultimately disorganised and avoidant. They leave the office feeling unprepared, having received little support with planning the visit or managing their feelings from their manager. In the car on the way to the home, rather than using the transitional space in a thoughtful way to enhance readiness for the encounter by tuning into the tasks and challenges that may lie ahead, the worker becomes more anxious as she anticipates what she might find. This could be mistaken for the process that I have characterised in the book as 'coming alive' and getting 'energised' to be relational with the child and family, which it isn't. This is because the worker, in her own words, 'winds' herself up into a state of heightened anxiety which ended in emotional overload. The necessary aliveness involves practitioners needing to cultivate composure through a finely tuned, regulated awareness of their emotions, body and mind, channelling the

Figure 5.1: Disorganised avoidant practice

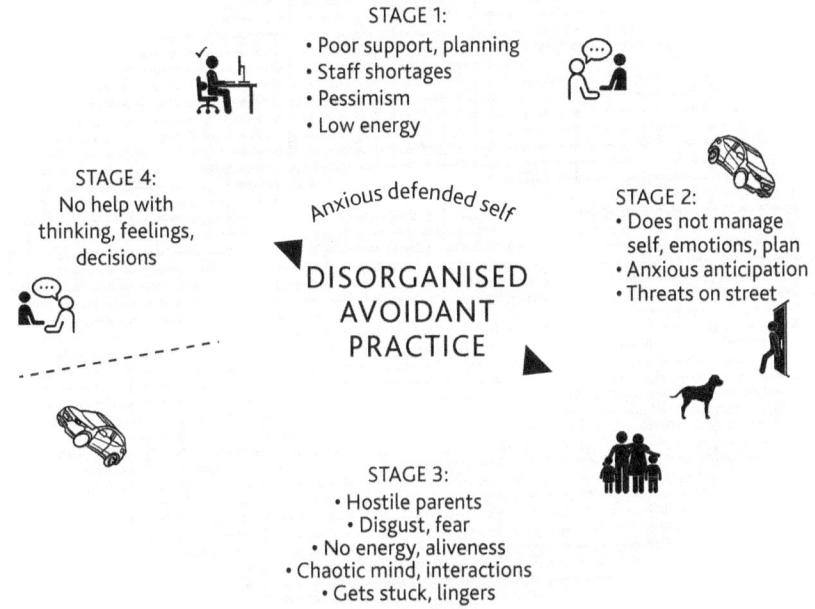

arising feelings and energy in purposeful ways, that doesn't cause overwhelm. Achieving this is helped by meditative reflection while walking and in the car while driving and 'live' supervision and support from managers, both in the office and outside of it while on the move – that was shown to work so well for Jim in Chapter 2.

On arrival in the neighbourhood Melissa's anxiety and fear levels shot up still further as there were frightening looking men on the street. On stepping into the home she became overwhelmed by disgust and never recovered from that state or felt bearably comfortable in it. This anxiety was compounded by the father's belligerence and aggression throughout, using his body to move around in front of the social worker as well as his voice (denials, veiled threats) to communicate a hostile message. He was allowed to control the visit. The social worker could not adapt to the different messages she got from the two children: the enthusiasm of ten-year-old Sam to engage with her, while 14-year-old Steven was passive and withdrawn to the point of falling asleep and painfully controlled by his father. The disorganisation in the pattern lies in the fumbled attempts to connect with the children and how the social worker swung chaotically between some efforts to get closer and total silence and non-relating. The worker struggled to manage her emotions and compose herself enough to engage in an intuitive, improvisational and intimate way that kept the children in mind. Even by the time she was upstairs and out of his presence Steven was forgotten as she never even asked where he slept. Her chaotic thinking reflected the chaotic conditions and atmosphere she was in.

Melissa's dislike of initial home visits, especially to reputedly 'dirty houses', makes the manager's decision to send her out on the visit highly questionable. We will return to the question of personal preferences in terms of relational styles in Chapter 10. What can be said at this point is that I observed Melissa practice with more skill and confidence in some other casework that did not involve this level of complexity and alleged neglect. However, her energy levels and presence always came across as somewhat flat and lacking in enthusiasm. This attitude and her relational style and (self-declared) limitations contributed to the avoidant disorganised practice. But this was far from being her responsibility alone. Organisationally, due to a stretched workforce, managers felt they had little choice but to allocate her the family. She was 'dropped' (in it) rather than held.

Conclusion

This chapter has shown that the disorganised practice pattern is best understood in terms of how it is made cumulatively through each of the stages of the Practice Cycle.

Key learning points

- This cycle begins with limited managerial support to plan and become energised and there is pessimism about the family and the work. Transitions to see the child and family are not used to further enhance readiness and tune into the tasks and challenges. Instead, the worker becomes even more anxious. If the practitioner can become aware that they are about to turn up to the family in this state, then seeking live supervision from managers and the support of peers is crucial.

- The impact of the encounter and environment where it happens adds further to the anxiety and emotional overload felt by the worker and erodes their composure. All the senses are in play and when poor home conditions generate feelings like disgust and are added to intense anxiety this creates a chaotic state of mind. An absence of authoritativeness, skill and purpose takes hold. Sporadic, incoherent, ultimately disorganised relating with children results, even when the latter clearly signal their desire to connect. The pattern is further compounded back at the office when practitioners receive limited engagement and support from managers to reflect on the encounter and bring the avoided children to mind.

- In the disorganised pattern the worker does not seek to flee the home and encounter quickly, as we saw occurs in the automated pattern, but they become stuck – in a sense trapped – and stay for a relatively long period. In the case study of Ray and family it was an hour. They lose the capacity (and desire) to reflexively respond to what they find, which further compounds their anxiety and defensiveness and lack of focus on the children.

- To recognise and correct for disorganised practice that detaches from children and parents it is essential for managers to critically reflect on the centrality of their role in it and the Practice Cycle and to seek to alleviate all the factors that can contribute to it.

- The chapter has also taken forward a key aim of this book, which is to go beyond the prioritising of the visual ('seeing children') to explore the total multi-sensory nature of child protection work and how it is experienced in real time. This includes how matters of smell, dirt and cleanliness directly impact on the bodies, perceptions and states of mind of practitioners. Recognising this enables better understanding of how information passes into the mind and body not just via the eyes but through the nose, the ears, hands, the feet, and the skin. While the primary example used in this chapter concerned child neglect, a disorganised state of mind and avoidant practice can occur in response to work with other harms and risks to children.

Having spent this chapter and the last one identifying avoidant patterns of child protection work and how to spot, prevent and learn from them, the book will now explore in depth relationship-based practice that is intimate and focused on keeping children safe and helpful to parents and families.

6

The intimate pattern: seen, heard and held children

So, what does practice look like when it gets close to children and families? This is what I refer to as intimate practice, which fosters holding relationships for both children and families. I define intimate practice as meaning practitioners *having authentic, close relationships with children of the kind where they see, hear, touch and sense the truth of their experience and are able to act on it and achieving appropriate closeness with parents, other carers and family networks*. This chapter will show how intimacy with children can be achieved not just through conversation, but through tactile contact, play and other forms of movement (like walking or driving). Equally important is the aura of workers, their energy and the kind of presence they embody. This is conveyed by their aliveness, ability to energetically attune to both children and parents and desire to have relationships that are close and that resonate with meaning and connection (Bloom, 2006; Rosa, 2019).

An in-depth case study will be used to explore what intimate practice with children involves. Further insights will be given into themes the book has opened up, especially in Chapter 2, concerning how the first meetings with children and families demand sophisticated relational skills and how it is possible for real closeness to be achieved within minutes of meeting children. We will see how the Practice Cycle can be negotiated in ways that are very different to what occurred in Chapters 4 and 5. Each stage is worked through in ways that ensure the worker comes alive relationally and stays that way. By not only seeing children but holding them practitioners provide them with a closeness and *nurture* that can have therapeutic benefits. This raises important questions about the purpose of child protection, as my argument about holding suggests the need for a mindset that is not just about completing tasks such as assessment, but also about the therapeutic value of providing comfort through relationships.

Casement, a psychotherapist and former social worker, captures well a key dilemma that practitioners face in how close to get to children and families:

> Therapists have to learn to remain close enough to what the patient is experiencing for this to have a feeling impact upon himself [*sic*] while preserving a sufficient distance to function as a therapist. But that professional distance should not leave him beyond the reach of what the patient may need him to feel. A therapist has to discover how to be psychologically intimate with a patient and yet separate, separate and still intimate. (Casement, 1985, p 30)

Professionals like social workers face the dilemma of determining how physically as well as emotionally close or distant to be with service users and deciding what are appropriate boundaries.

Intimate practice in initial encounters with children

Closeness through being tactile is not the only or necessarily the main way practitioners achieve intimate practice and relational connection. A scene that exemplifies this was a 42-minute home visit during which a mother sat on the sofa with her 12-month-old son on her knee with the social worker never closer than four feet from the child. It was the first visit and due to concerns about domestic abuse. While conversing with his mother the worker spoke to the child on 12 separate occasions and also connected with him through smiles and other gestures such as clapping her hands in unison. He smiled a lot and moved excitedly. There was no suggestion that the child may have experienced physical harm and the approach seemed proportionate. This was effective relationship building which had an emotional feel to it that Bloom (2005, p 58) has called 'non-physical touch, through energetic attunement'. This idea of practitioners and service users attuning to one another 'energetically' speaks in part to experiencing rapport and an emotional connection. But it goes beyond that and is a way of capturing the demeanour and attitude of the worker and the service user. If we think back to the avoidant practice that featured in Chapters 4 and 5 it involved practitioners who were energetically flat, dull, strung out, pessimistic and devoid of hope. As we shall see, a very different energy typifies intimate practice – that I call resonance.

In some casework touch as well as play and talk are used to get close to children and communicate care. A case study that illustrates these dynamics and how physical and emotional intimacy and energetic attunement occurred very soon after meeting children involved a White British social worker, 'Jessica', and a five-year-old boy, who I will call Anton, and his seven-year-old sister, Nikita, being cared for by a lone-parent mother, Jade. Jade is Black British and the children of mixed heritage, their estranged father being White British. The concerns surrounded neglect and emotional harm. Social care had been involved on and off for several years, most recently through family support services visiting the home. Jade had stopped allowing them to go upstairs to check on home conditions and there were concerns about how the children were presenting in school, 'dirty' and exhibiting disturbed behaviour and control problems. A new boyfriend was thought to be on the scene and there had been historical concerns that a previous boyfriend may have sexually abused the children. This meant that the social worker also needed to find out about the new boyfriend and establish if he is safe to be around the children. I shadowed Jessica on her first visit to the family home; she had previously met Anton once, in school, and had never met Nikita before.

The worker's plan for the visit was:

> I feel really it is just a basic put your head round the door to get a feel for these home conditions. But it'll be interesting to see my observations of what the bedroom is like and the house, the home conditions. And also to see if Anton, the boy, remembers who I was from school. I'm quite prepared for Nikita, apparently she is quite distant and not very talkative and obviously her speech is very poor, so it will be nice to see with my own eyes what the assessments are about her, her speech. … I'm quite looking forward to doing the observations in the home over the next couple of weeks, like in the very early morning or quite late in the evening just to see how they function at home.

The dog was barking as Jade answered the door and Anton immediately jumped into the social worker's arms as she stood on the doorstep. Jessica hugged him into her and playfully carried him into the house while saying: 'This is cool! Woo-hoo!' and put him down in the kitchen. On seeing Nikita, Jessica said: 'Are you Nikita? Wooh, I've been excited about meeting you.' A minute later Nikita announced that she was going to her friend's to play and her impending absence led the social worker to ask her in an enthusiastic way if she would show her her bedroom and when Nikita said yes Jade agreed it was okay. Jessica held Nikita's hand and spoke to her as they walked up the stairs.

There were dog faeces on the landing and in the children's bedrooms, which contained urine-stained mattresses, no curtains or light bulbs. The landing had underlay but no carpet and was covered with debris and paper. In Nikita's room there was a pile of clothing and no cupboard. It had a television which she said didn't work and the social worker told her: 'Well, perhaps we could have a look to see if we could fix that for you. Shall we? Yeah.' Anton's bedroom was barer than his sister's room. The floor was cluttered with clothes and other things and there was no sign of any toys. Jessica was very thorough in her inspection. When she looked under Anton's bed, she found a urine-soaked school shirt. She picked it up and showed it to Jade, asking if the dog was responsible, and Jade blamed Anton.

Jessica not only *saw* the home conditions but *experienced them in depth*. She checked the locks on windows in all the rooms, including the bathroom, to make sure they were safe. Despite Jade saying Anton had toys Jessica kept looking and never found them. Anton eventually said his mother had thrown them out. The social worker asked Anton where he brushed his teeth and when he led her to the bathroom he put his hands in the toilet, which the social worker told me afterwards had faeces in it.

Having spent 13 minutes upstairs the social worker went back to the kitchen where Jade was cooking and playing loud music. This three-minute spell included Anton asking Jessica to take him into her arms and she warmly did so and danced with him in tune to the music, saying: 'Oh ho-ho! What a lovely dancer you are! What a lovely dancer you are, Anton! I still haven't found them toys.' The worker praised Jade for the nice food she was cooking and told her she was very concerned about the state of the bedrooms.

On returning to the sitting room, 23 minutes into the visit, Jessica went straight to the family photographs which were on display, telling the children how lovely they were as babies and engaging Jade about the wider family members featured. Nikita never actually left the home, which wasn't surprising given how the social worker was with her. She asked Nikita who gives her a bath, who brushes her teeth and who washes her hair, telling her what lovely hair she has, touching it several times as she said it. Jessica then invited the child to feel her own hair, which Nikita did.

Social worker:	And who washes your hair?
Nikita:	Me.
Social worker:	You wash your own hair? Can I see the back of it? Oh, it feels lovely. … You have lovely hair. She's got hair just like me. Feel my hair. It's very like yours, isn't it?

Jessica then dropped down to the children's level on her hunkers, and then fully on to the floor, skilfully explaining what her role is as a social worker, checking out whether Nikita understood.

Social worker:	So I'll come and see you next week, yeah? Do you know what my job is? And you know [family support worker's name] that you have as well? I'm like [family support worker], okay, and I'm called a social worker. Yeah? Do you know Tracey Beaker on the telly?
Nikita:	Yeah.
Social worker:	She's a social worker, and what my job is, I have to make sure that you are, and these are what I have to do: safe, I've got to make sure you're happy, and if you're not, I have to do things to make sure that you are safe and you're happy, and I am Nikita's social worker, and who else's social worker?
Nikita:	Anton's.
Social worker:	Anton's, yeah. And some mummies and daddies, or aunties and uncles, sometimes they find it really hard to be a mummy, yeah? Sometimes it's really hard to be a mummy, and sometimes they need some extra help, yeah? So that's what Jessica's doing, and that's what [family support worker] has been doing, isn't it? Yeah? So sometimes you'll see me talking to mum, sometimes you'll see me talking to [Jade's boyfriend] because he comes to your house.

	And I need to see you at school, that's when I talk to you about how you're feeling and if there's any jobs, sometimes you can give me lots of jobs you want me to do. So it might be you want me, one job I'm going to do is try and get you new curtains. So that might be a job we could do, is to get your curtains, because it wasn't very nice to have them curtains pulled down, so that might be a job that we could do together and get some help with, okay? So that's what my job is. So, let's see if you've really listened. What's my job?
Nikita:	To make me happy, happy and safe.
Social worker:	Good girl, wow, how clever are you! Well done, Nikita, I didn't think you would remember all of that. I thought you were just being nice and saying, 'Yeah, yeah, yeah.' But really you listened, didn't you? You are a very clever girl. Very clever. And what about if I come and see you at school? Let me see when I'm coming to see you at school [*looks in diary*].

Jessica negotiated when would be best to visit both the children in school and concluded by pointing out in child-friendly language that it will be 'five more sleeps, five more sleeps and I'll come to breakfast with you at school. Is that all right?' To which Nikita responded: 'Yeah.'

Anton was on the periphery of the social worker and Nikita's interaction because he was constantly active in different parts of the room, including falling. Jade's new boyfriend, 'John', arrived and sat down on an armchair. Only now, half an hour into the visit, did the social worker sit down for the first time, on the sofa. Jade went back to the kitchen to prepare the tea. Anton positioned himself beside the social worker on the sofa or more often on top of her. He sat astride her and leaned back with Jessica holding his hands, in a see-saw motion. While the social worker spoke with John, Anton became active again and fell off the television stand, hard on to the floor, and the social worker rushed from the sofa to help him and rubbed what she called 'magic dust' onto his hurting knees with her hand.

Social worker:	Quick, before the magic dust goes! Quick, Harry Potter's going to get the magic dust, come over to me! Where did you hurt yourself? … Good. [*Rubbing Anton's knee*] Does that feel better?
Anton:	Yeah.

Anton was restless and in an almost permanent state of movement, alternating between climbing over furniture, falling off it and sitting beside or on top of the social worker. At one point he tore out of the front door and his mother had to chase after him to get him back, a common occurrence apparently. While the social worker was discussing with the boyfriend, John, arrangements to see him on his own to find out more about him, Anton was now stretched out on the sofa lying beside her, with his head touching against her hip. While writing down the boyfriend's details using her right hand, the social worker began stroking Anton's face and hair with her left hand:

Social worker:	Okay. What day is best for me to come out to see you?
John:	Any day, really.
Social worker:	Any day. You know [*stroking Anton's face and hair*], you are beautiful, you are beautiful [*sing-song voice*]. You are beautiful. Now [*to John*], let's have a look. Well, I'm coming out to see …
Anton [*interrupting*]:	I'm stupid.
Social worker:	You are beautiful. You've got beautiful big brown eyes.
Anton:	I'm stupid.
Social worker:	You're not stupid.
Anton:	[*Laughs*] Yeah!
Social worker:	You're not, you're not. I'm not allowed to tell fibs. You're not stupid. Who told you that?

Anton did not say. This phase in the sitting room lasted 26 minutes and the social worker then went into the kitchen to see Jade where she spent another 12 minutes telling her how concerned she was about the home conditions and checked the fridge and cupboards and found there was plenty of food in. She said her goodbyes by asking Nikita: 'How many more sleeps until you see me?' and Nikita said five, to which the social worker replied: 'You are the most cleverest girl I know! [*Looking at mother*] She's clever, isn't she?' Jessica then empathised with Jade about how hard it is having a social worker visit and left.

Responding to children's needs in the moment

The social worker's plan for the visit – 'just a basic put your head round the door to get a feel for these home conditions' – had to be revised from the moment she got there because of what she found. She improvised in creative ways and clearly got very physically and emotionally close to the children and very quickly. She did this by speaking to them in a clear and accessible way, such as when explaining her role and relating to them with passion and excitement. She expressed excitement about coming to see them, oozed relish and joy in being with them, and expressed a deep desire to get to know them. Note, too, that prior to the visit she expressed how she was looking forward to seeing and getting to know the children. In short, Jessica's attitude and energy were immensely positive and relational.

Also significant in this were the ways she went beyond talk, skilfully using touch and play and moving with authority around the home, seeing and feeling what it was like to be the children living in this place. So playful and full of aliveness and body confidence was she that she was prepared to dance with the child, in full view of the parent (and me). Nikita's delight at being told she has nice eyes and lovely hair and having it touched and being able to touch the social worker's hair was plain to see. When Anton jumped into the social worker's arms on the doorstep, she could have carried him into the house in a dutiful way and put him down immediately in the hallway, but she did it playfully and for longer than she needed to, which shows the ease with which the worker greeted him in his physicality and accepted his neediness. When he was stretched out on the sofa with her, she did make it clear in a polite playful way that there are limits and boundaries, like the moment when she jokingly pointed out to him that she'd rather not have his 'smelly feet' literally in her face! Still, the social worker embraced and held him, in every sense. She imaginatively used the 'magic dust' to rub and heal his hurting leg and soon after stroked this five-year-old boy's face and hair as he lay on her lap, while telling him he is 'beautiful'. This shows a social worker who was not only willing to use touch but to *be touched* by accepting the children's physical contact. And she was willing and able to tolerate being touched by Anton knowing that he had put his hands into the toilet bowl that had faeces in it. In total, the social worker's positive energy, skill and desire for relational closeness and resonance vibrated powerfully through the encounter, generating emotional connection and hope.

I asked her in the car afterwards if this kind of tactile intimate practice comes easily to her.

> It's with different children. Those children [who we've just been to see] are children that really crave it and actually I knew he would probably be quite in your face and kinda wanting a lot of, I mean even though he smelt and his trousers were wet and his hands smelt and he was putting his hand; the only time I kinda pushed him away he was putting his hands in my mouth, and he put his hand down the toilet at one point which I knew had got faeces in it because I saw it and he flushed it. But just after he did that, after he put his hand down the toilet [10 minutes later] he has his arms around me. I couldn't push him away. It was difficult, you know, because he doesn't get much affection or love. Whereas some social workers that are in this building [*pointing at the social work office*] there is no way they would even pick up a child. And again I always find it's a good reason you know when you are tickling just to observe any injuries.

The worker was able to work through her disgust and resistance to being touched by a child who was dirty and 'contaminated' and embraced him and his needs and trauma. Her relational style is clearly deeply intimate and relational and she is critical of colleagues she says she knows who do not hold children. This kind of use of movement, voice and especially touch clearly takes intimate practice to the limits of what is ethically acceptable behaviour. The social worker's rationale for it was essentially therapeutic – although she did not use that term. She explained after the visit that she was very aware of the children's neediness and desperation for closeness, which she consciously gave them:

> Those kids, I mean I've not had the case long, but I know that they don't get very much physical affection so that's why the stroking of the face is, and you could see as you stroked his face or gave him some magic dust, like a cat or a dog would kinda put their head towards you, he had that little bit of emotional comfort there and that's how he responded. So there is that. And that positive praise about actually 'you are beautiful', 'you've got lovely hair', 'you've got nice eyes'; good things about them. Whereas all they'll probably hear from mum, especially Anton, all he gets from his mum is negatives.

For this social worker, practising in this intimate and nurturing way enabled her to give comfort to children and enter their inner worlds in a manner that being less physically close probably could not have achieved. It created space for a deep relational connection between worker and children to occur, which enabled her to help them therapeutically. The combined rhythms of her soothing, calming voice and stroking of the face led Anton to disclose something of how he saw himself – as 'stupid' – and gave an early sense of the kinds of emotional harm he had endured. By telling him he is 'beautiful' the social worker was willing to talk the language of care and love as well as show it. Casement (2006, p 87) describes the need for such holding in terms of how as children we all need 'significant others, especially parents, who are able to manage what we are not yet able to manage in ourselves. This includes our anger, our destructiveness and our hate'. The worker provided this kind of containment by holding him, both physically and emotionally, giving Anton a nurturing experience of feeling unconditionally accepted and cared about, which led him to begin to trust that she would be willing and able to bear for him that which he could not bear within himself. Such intimate practice creates vital therapeutic moments for children.

The social worker explained to me before and after the visit that Jade was known for withdrawing and rejecting workers and refusing access to the home and children if she felt criticism of her was too harsh or overt. So, if she was to engage, challenges and strong uses of authority had to be balanced with some praise or recognition of her strengths. This was the balance the worker sought to find with Jade, whose willingness to continue working with Jessica in the ensuing months suggests that she found it. This is a powerful example of the use of what I call 'good authority' in action. The social worker acknowledged Jade's vulnerability as a lone-parent Black-British woman, facing the challenges of a hostile neighbourhood where she endured racist abuse, while struggling to care for two children on her own on a very low income. Periodic relationships with men suspected of being abusive further heightened her and her children's vulnerability.

There is a risk that in providing such skilled care and nurture for children in front of a parent the worker becomes seen as the 'better parent' in contrast to the actual parent(s) who have not been able to provide it. This may be unavoidable to a degree when the aim is to meet children's immediate needs for closeness and nurture and improve parenting. Workers need to explain to parents why they are relating to their children in these ways. Such intimate practice with children in front of parents is acceptable within a plan to ultimately support the parent in being the better parent, rather than undermining or replacing that role.

From engagement to immersion in children's lives

What is common to all the examples of intimate casework I have seen is that from the moment they entered their lives, the social workers immersed themselves in the children and families' worlds. I think the language of *immersion* captures this better than the commonly used term 'engagement' because achieving an intimate relational connection draws on all the professional's senses and their emotional capacity as well as requiring an ability to communicate and problem-solve on their feet. In this example, we see how this was done by showing pleasure and delight at seeing children, being respectful and at the same time very challenging to their parents, while entering their most intimate spaces. Intimate practitioners not only inspect bedrooms but spend enough time in them and elsewhere upstairs to gain a sense of what it is like to be a child who lives and sleeps in this bed, in this room, in this home. This distinction between inspecting children's living conditions to check on the standard of care and *gaining a lived experience of them* is important. The former is often done quickly, while the latter involves spending time in rooms to gain a feel for what they are like and the presence and state of objects in them (beds, curtains, lightbulbs, toys), in the way Jessica did. Here again we see how sensing and absorbing what Hicks (2020) calls 'the feel of the place', its atmosphere, really matters.

In this intimate pattern, communication and understanding of children and relationships were enhanced by skilfully utilising objects, such as photos, that adorned the children's and family's lives. Additionally, such workers brought toys and other items to the home (Jessica's car boot was full of them), to use to further deepen the connection. This closeness to the home and other objects was not incidental but central to the intimacy that was achieved (Scholar, 2017). It confirms Miller's theory that 'usually the closer our relationships are with objects, the closer our relationships are with people' (2008, p 1). This is supported by other research into interactions between social workers and children that shows the importance of using worksheets, games, colouring pens and paper, toys, puppets, sand play and other activities (Ruch et al, 2017; Whincup, 2017). The more practitioners creatively engage with the home or other environments where they meet service users and utilise a variety of available materials, the more intimate and effective their relationship-based practice will become. Practitioners also need to make wise assessments of when the home isn't the best place to meet children alone or should not be the only place they are seen. Instead, social workers use schools, cars, cafes or outdoor spaces like parks and walking interviews to connect with them.

The ethics of intimate practice

An important question that arises from all this is how acceptable and ethical it is for social care practitioners to use physical touch with children, to pick them up, hold them, play in tactile ways, hug, caress and comfort them? I have presented some of the research examples of tactile intimate practice featured in this book to many hundreds of professionals at workshops and lectures. Some agree with the way the social worker Jessica used touch with Anton and Nikita and say that it reflects their own attempts to get close to and nurture children, while others are critical of it because they regard it as overstepping a boundary. The big fear that many workers express about getting physically close is leaving themselves open to allegations of child sexual abuse. Men in particular say this, but some women do too. Some workshop participants go so far as to vehemently criticise this kind of affectionate, tactile behaviour because they regard it as similar to the grooming of children by sex offenders. The fear is that a worker being so familiar and tactile with children, especially so soon after just meeting them, means they are unwittingly making them more at risk by modelling unacceptable adult behaviour and giving the message that it is okay for complete strangers to touch you. This would then make the child more vulnerable to seeking and accepting intimate contact from inappropriate people.

Professionals who take up this detached position often say they immediately stop children who get physically close to them when they climb on them, by distracting them or even, as I have observed, scolding them. They regard themselves as using 'role modelling' to try to teach the child and parents a lesson about boundaries and what they – the worker – regard as good behaviour. Some workers also argue that it is more ethical to remain physically detached from children until the relationship and trust have become established. But as this chapter has shown, workers can use touch in ethical ways and emotionally attune to children within minutes of meeting them for the first time. 'No touch until trust is established' narratives can be a cover for other reasons for staying distant, like those practitioners who have described themselves and their relational style to me as 'not touchy feely' and said they avoid tactile contact in their personal as well as professional lives (see also Chapter 10).

The counter-argument is that the provision of nurture and intimacy by professionals seeks to meet the child's immediate needs and is more likely to reduce the risk of children seeking it from strangers. Sophie Hallett's research with young people who had experienced sexual exploitation found that their view was that 'had their needs been acknowledged by significant others, they would not have been in these sexually exploitative situations' (Hallett, 2017, p 100). The most vulnerable children are those who have not received love and care from anyone. How these dilemmas are resolved depends in part on the extent to which children are regarded as having agency and the capacity to understand the difference between trustworthy, safe people and those who aren't. We saw how the social worker explained to Nikita who she was and her role and the child confirmed for her that they understood it. She had already done this with Anton on the one previous occasion she had met him, at school. Consideration must be given to children's ability to perceive and intuit who is truly genuine, all while helping them to understand the social work role and what they are doing – as Jessica did so well. The quality of this social worker's presence and relating had resonance. Being there, I could sense the wire that connected the children and the worker vibrating powerfully and feel how they were all touched by the interaction, feeling moved and changed as a result (Rosa, 2019, p 179). It is within the safety of a trusting, caring relationship that professionals can help children to learn how to keep themselves safe and distinguish who is trustworthy. In the absence of such a relationship they can't learn and the way to begin to establish such a relationship is to (literally) embrace and accept them for what they are at the outset. This means not pushing them away or diverting them in order to 'role model' but receiving their tactile contact and giving them what they need in return.

It must always be borne in mind that some children and young people do not want physical closeness or to be touched, such as some who have been sexually abused. And that even if they did accept touch, or wish for it, it may be inappropriate. As Lefevre (2018) argues, the appropriateness of touch must never be based on the worker's needs but always on the help the child or young person needs. The social worker showed Anton what Carl Rogers (1961) called unconditional positive regard. Rogers meant by this accepting and valuing a person without judgement, regardless of their behaviour or circumstances, encouraging them to express themselves and to grow. In a similar vein, Page (2018) speaks of people who work with young children needing to show them 'professional love'. Jessica allowed Anton to enact his chaos upon her, and embraced and held his awkward, sometimes aggressive, in some ways repulsive and needy physicality. Role modelling could be addressed later; the immediate need was to offer comfort and acceptance in the moment, as the social worker did when the child expressed feeling he is stupid. Jessica subsequently told me about how she gradually tried to place boundaries around Anton's behaviour by modelling, but only after she had provided for him a foundational experience of unconditional acceptance and nurture. Crucially, this very quickly led the child to trust that she would hold for him whatever he needed to disclose and rid himself of.

The social work office had closed by the time the home visit was completed and the following morning Jessica had a long meeting with two managers. A plan of intensive home visiting by the family support worker and social worker was put in place. This included providing resources like beds, curtains, toys, toothbrushes that made the children's lives and their mother's more comfortable.

Jade was helped to develop her relationships with her children and improve the standard of care for them. Jessica continued to work directly and therapeutically with Anton and Nikita, alternating between doing so in school and at home. Over time, there was marked improvement in their well-being.

Intimate practice with older children and teenagers

Obviously, the older children become, the less possible and appropriate it is to provide nurture for them by picking them up and holding them in the way one would a baby or younger child. Five-year-old Anton was close to the age limit for being picked up. Yet the need to feel cared about, held, loved remains throughout the life course. As Lisa Warwick's (2021) research shows, close physical contact and hugs between teenagers and staff in residential care is common and often welcomed by young people. Hugs from social care workers, always risk assessed and given with the young person's consent, should be an option. I have also heard social workers use the language of love. Katie (17) had the same social worker, Monique, for two years and was still considered very vulnerable to child sexual exploitation. On a home visit Monique told her, 'We want someone who is kind and not abusive like [name of one previous boyfriend] was', and added, 'It's because we all love you.' Having seen and felt the closeness in their relationship I could tell Monique's expression of professional love towards Katie was genuinely meant.

Connection with young people is forged through talk and text – literally in the use of messaging by phone, email – and through play, such as bowling, pool, on digital devices, and activities such as gaming. Some teenagers favour remote communication on video or voice calls and the more practitioners are prepared to mix digital and in-person encounters the better (see also Chapter 11). Some young people also value getting close through objects, such as the shared intimacy of viewing photographs and other personal things, in their bedroom or elsewhere. Also appreciated is togetherness through car rides, going on walks or to cafes. As social worker Lily put it, 'Yeah, older children I will take out, go to McDonald's or go down to the park and kick a ball, I like going, you know, going somewhere where we can get out of the home, away from others.'

Achieving intimate practice through the Practice Cycle

Summing up, we can see how in the intimate pattern, the stages of the Practice Cycle build cumulatively into purposeful, agile, emotionally and energetically attuned practice and relationships (see Figure 6.1). Before the visit the social worker developed a clear plan for the encounter, which took account of existing knowledge about the family (Jade's dislike of harsh criticism and bedrooms being inspected; Nikita's delayed language skills). She was supported in this by her manager and in ways that helped her to mentally leave office duties and bureaucratic preoccupations behind. This enabled the social worker to come alive, it energised her, making her feel positive and even excited about meeting

Figure 6.1: The intimate pattern

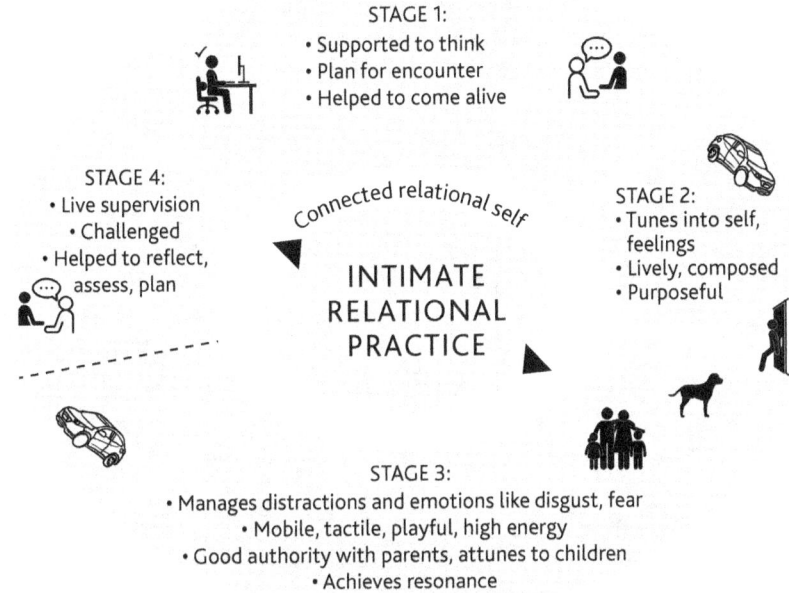

the family. The worker was already on their way to being fully emotionally, intuitively and energetically present for the children and parents.

In the next stage of the cycle, transitional space on walks and in the car was used productively to further this process by tuning into the self, emotions and being ready for the encounter. Once in the interaction with the children and adults the social worker showed a strong capacity for improvisation and creativity, having to immediately think on her feet about literally how to handle a child who jumped into her arms on the doorstep. Home conditions and her immediate concerns about the children's well-being, especially Anton's, were worse than she expected and her improvisational skill enabled her to revise her plan as she soon realised this was not going to be the kind of relatively relaxed introductory visit she anticipated.

Jessica exemplified how practitioners in the intimate pattern put their whole professional selves and bodies into the encounter, being prepared to use movement, play, touch and even dance to enter children's worlds, provide comfort and create resonance and therapeutic moments. They practised intimately by not only seeing and hearing the children but immersing themselves in their world and holding them. It involves putting concerns openly and directly to parents while working hard to bring them along by balancing the use of empathy, compassion, challenge and control to achieve good authority. Finally, back at the office the Practice Cycle was completed by Jessica's managers providing reflective space that helped her to think about the encounter, assess the risk, and decisions were made about what the children and family needed.

Conclusion

This chapter has argued that closeness and meaningful relationship-based child protection requires practitioners to have authentic, close encounters with children of the kind where they see, hear, touch and sense the truth of their experience and are able to act on it.

> ## Key learning points
>
> - Such closeness can be achieved with some children through talk, play and creating an energetic and emotional connection. In some situations, however, the humane use of touch is vital to having meaningful relationships and ensuring children are safe and helped. Assessing the appropriateness of physical closeness on a case-by-case, moment-by-moment basis is crucial for ethical practice.
>
> - The attitudes, personality and relational style of individual practitioners significantly influence the intimacy and closeness of their practice. Every manager and practitioner needs to ask themselves: how close and intimate or distant is my relational style? How might I incorporate physical closeness as a crucial aspect of child protection work? If I am not comfortable with physical closeness or it does not feel appropriate in a particular encounter, how will I connect intimately with children in non-physical ways?
>
> - The capacity for playfulness is of crucial importance, both as a form of communication in child protection and to enable children to experience moments of happiness (Steggall and Scollen, 2024, p 2136).
>
> - The quality of a practitioner's energy is vital in conveying to children that they are welcomed and that their disclosures are valued. How will I practise in an effective relationship-based way with children that fosters a resonant connection that makes them feel worthy, cared for, and even loved? What needs to happen for me to be able to show genuine interest in and enthusiasm for being with children and parents?
>
> - As was the case in previous chapters, there is a systemic foundation to this relational pattern. The level of energy, playfulness and intimacy practitioners have with service users is shaped by experiences within each stage of the Practice Cycle. What can managers do to provide the release from thinking about bureaucracy and the emotional support that will enable practitioners to come alive and be as fully present as possible with families in the encounter? What needs to be done

to open up and encourage discussions with individuals and within teams about touch, closeness and their boundaries? Having 'no-touch' policies is unrealistic and unethical, as they deny children the physical comfort they need.

- Education, training and leadership need to develop the workforce to be ready and able to provide intimate child protection practice. How can educators, leaders and managers do this, while ensuring that the impact of inequalities on families are as far as possible addressed and social support provided?

The next chapter will delve deeper into these questions and intimate child protection work by focusing on relationship-based practice with babies and younger children.

7

Hands-on practice: making relationships with babies and young children

When I worked as a child protection social worker many years ago I was involved with the Lewis family due to concerns about five-year-old Jack. Mr Lewis was on probation due to petty crime and Mrs Lewis was pregnant. Soon after Mrs Lewis and her baby girl went home following the birth I received a phone call from Maria the probation officer saying 'I've just been to the house and the baby's got a hole in her head'. I rushed round only to find the baby was fine. I could make no claim to being an expert on newborns, but I did know that all babies are born with two soft spots on their heads, known as fontanelles, where the bones that form the skull haven't yet fused together. I knew because my youngest sister was born when I was 11 and my brother came along three years later and I was fascinated by the softness of their fontanelles and the way they pulsed. Had it not been for that experience there's every chance I'd have been as clueless as that probation officer. The simple reason for this ignorance was that the professional training we had did not prepare us for knowing enough about babies or working with them.

This chapter develops the theme of intimate practice by focusing on encounters with babies and younger children under three. The core question it poses is how do professionals in child protection have a relationship with a baby? It departs from the approach of analysing casework as it negotiates the Practice Cycle and instead uses case material to explore the theme of working with infants in a more general way. Relating to children and keeping them safe requires different knowledge and skills depending on their age and developmental stage. The casework examples featured in the book were chosen to provide insight into the safety needs and practice with children of different ages and developmental capacities. However, professional training and the child protection literature do not serve children of all ages equally well, with the least focus on babies.

In the last 20 years there has been a significant growth in understanding and training for professionals on child development, attachment and infant brain development. Infant mental health services have developed somewhat and in parts of the UK infant development expertise and infant–parent relationship specialists offer training and support to child protection professionals (Parent-Infant Foundation, 2023). Efforts have been initiated to enhance learning in work with babies and young children by synthesising findings from serious case reviews (Murray, 2023; Child Safeguarding Practice Review Panel, 2024;

Derby and Derbyshire Local Safeguarding Practice Review, 2024). Despite these signs of progress, much more consideration needs to be given to how professionals actually interact with babies and how they *should* relate to them to ensure they are safe.

Working with babies demands detailed attention, especially since children under 12 months old are the most affected age group in cases of serious harm or death from abuse or neglect. These are children who have 'endured shocking, almost indescribable, violence and maltreatment' (Child Safeguarding Practice Review Panel, 2024). In 2020, 37 per cent of serious incident notifications that were examined by the national Child Safeguarding Review Panel in England were about children less than a year old and in 2022–2023 it was 36 per cent. In other official data, of the 50,780 children on local authority Child Protection Plans in England at March 2023, 1,310 were unborn, 4,170 under one (8 per cent of all children) and 11,380 aged between one and four (22 per cent of all children). Collectively, approximately 25 per cent of children on Child Protection Plans were aged 0–4 (DfE, 2024). In at least one-third of the cases I have observed in my research into everyday practice, the children were too young to communicate verbally with social workers. They were not seen on their own but along with their parents or other carers. In light of this, what skills and attributes do practitioners need to relate effectively with infants both as individuals and in the context of their relationships with carers?

The baby blind spot: in search of infant voice and experience

There is extensive literature on 'direct work' with children and young people and facilitating their meaningful participation in meetings and decision-making processes (Lefevre, 2018; Diaz, 2020; Dillon, 2021). Karen Winter (2011) provides valuable research-based insights into working with younger children, although less so with babies. Winter et al's (2017) observations of practice showed how social workers sometimes held babies, with parents' consent, or related to them by making eye contact and talking in a 'sing-song' voice, while touching their hands, arms, legs and feet (see also Bernard and Greenwood, 2019). Important research has been done into pre-birth assessments of risk to the unborn child (Critchley, 2020), socio-legal issues in the removal of babies from their parents (Masson and Dickens, 2015; Broadhurst et al, 2022) and how to prevent them (Keddell et al, 2023).

Karen Broadhurst and Clare Mason's ground-breaking research has shown the high numbers of repeat removals of infants from the same mothers, their vulnerability and the additional devastating trauma losing their babies causes them. Ward et al (2012) carried out a detailed study of 57 infants who were referred to social work for child protection concerns before their first birthdays and followed 43 of them until they were three, focusing on risk assessment, family work and long-term outcomes. Attention is now also being given to the lived experience of babies in foster care and their right to have contact with their birth parents (Miron et al, 2013). Critchley et al (2022) show how, once in care, the baby's lack of access to breastmilk is ignored in policy and practice. Noting how the experiences and rights of infants removed from their birth families tend to be overlooked, they follow Gottlieb (2000) in asking: 'where have all the babies gone?' (Critchley et al, 2022, p 6).

Where, indeed? Whether intended or not, the commonly expressed notions of 'communicating with children', 'giving the child voice', gathering 'their wishes and feelings' assume that the children involved can talk and walk and play with the worker. It may also be assumed that because babies lack these capacities there may be little point in communicating with them. But as McFadyen et al (2022) argue, 'Babies have their own minds and have things to communicate about their experiences, views and needs' (see also Elwick et al, 2014). Vivid visual evidence of the communicative skills of infants and pre-verbal children is provided daily in the social media posts (Twitter/X, Bluesky, LinkedIn) of Dan Wuori (and see Wuori, 2024).

The literature on child deaths contains many tantalising examples where social workers and other professionals were in the presence of babies and children under three who at the time were seriously injured or emaciated but it was not discovered (Derby and Derbyshire Local Safeguarding Practice Review, 2024). It was in part because they were not engaged with in any physical way, such as being picked up, that their injuries and suffering were missed. The national Child Safeguarding Practice Review Panel in England recently identified the 'emerging theme' of needing to recognise and respond 'to the vulnerability of babies' (2024, pp 81–105; see also the Child Safeguarding Practice Review Panel briefing [2022b]). Their analysis emphasises that parental and family stressors are the most critical factors contributing to an increased risk for infants, alongside the effects of parental mental health challenges and trauma. Many tragic cases involve men who were violent and abusive towards both women and children. However, due to poor inter-agency communication, social workers were often unaware of the criminal backgrounds of these male perpetrators. The report suggests safe sleep assessments and discussions with parents about this were often missing. A recurring theme was the reluctance of parents to engage with services, with some displaying hostility. However, while identifying these patterns and dynamics and pointing out that 'such young children have no voice of their own', the report has little to say about how the infant's voice can be heard and what direct practice with babies needs to involve.

Concern is also emerging that infant voice is absent within early childhood studies and practice in settings such as nurseries (Wall et al, 2019; Guard, 2023; McFadyen et al, 2022). Gaps in workforce training, knowledge and confidence relating to work with babies and toddlers are widespread (Hogg, 2021). As Caroline Guard (2023, p 607) observes, even research that does advocate for listening to the views of children aged under two 'has seldom generated evidence of how voice materialises, opting to privilege the spoken word'. Sally Hogg (2021) refers to the 'baby blind spot' and argues that the common language of referring to 'children and young people' is no longer adequate and the term 'infants, children and young people' needs to be adopted. A momentum has gathered on social media using the hashtag #babyblindspot. As Karen Bateson, Consultant Child Psychologist and CEO at the Oxford Parent-Infant Project puts it, '"Infants, Children and Young People". Or "Babies, Children and Young People". Take your pick, but if you don't include infant/babies, chances are you're maintaining a cognitive bias that focusses on children over five AND perpetuates the #babyblindspot in policy and practice' (Karen Bateson, Twitter/X, 27 June 2022).

While the work of the researchers cited earlier suggests that infants are not totally ignored in the literature, to a very significant extent the #babyblindspot exists in child protection work, policy making and discussion. But where infants are at risk of child abuse and neglect, the argument of this book is that it is not sufficient to listen to 'infant voice' in the literal sense of the sounds they make. Babies also need to be *enabled to speak through their bodies*. They need to be directly engaged with, picked up, physically held, and held 'in mind' through closely observing them and how they relate with caregivers. Voice is not enough (Lundy, 2007). It is important therefore to insist on a concept of 'infant voice' in child protection that is not just about expression through sounds and communication through the gaze and 'facework', but 'voice' as a metaphor for the totality of embodied interactions with infants and young children that includes holding and practice that is nurturing. Practice must be hands-on.

How babies get overlooked in practice

I have observed many instances where practitioners were in the presence of babies, usually on home visits. One pattern is for the baby to be looked at, partially seen from a distance, but not held, or observed in meaningful ways that give clues to their well-being. This is typified by a visit to a family in which the concern surrounded child neglect:

> Michael, the father, and the three younger children were present in the sitting room. The social worker sat on the sofa beside Michael. The baby was close by asleep in his cot and two minutes into the visit the social worker got up from the sofa, walked over and looked briefly into the cot at him and then sat down again. For the next eight minutes the social worker interacted with the father, exploring issues around the baby's health and how he was coping with the three children.

When I asked her afterwards about how she interacted with the baby the social worker said, 'I always like to make sure they are breathing'. However, a brief look from a distance to establish that an infant is alive is insufficient.

Among the other influential experiences I've had that have shaped my understanding and views on this was a home visit I shadowed to a family where there was a four-month-old baby, Megan, who was on a Child Protection Plan due to having suffered a broken arm when ten days old. The social worker related to the parents but never once related directly with the baby or her 19-month-old brother, Nathan. Megan was awake and alert, spent time on her back on the floor and being nursed by her mother and father and the worker did not directly acknowledge the baby's existence by interacting with her. Nathan was active in the room and equally ignored. Afterwards when I asked the social worker about how she related to this baby today and in the past she told me that in the four months she had been involved she had never held her, picked her up or had any real direct interaction with her. So here was a baby who was regarded as at such high risk that she could only live at home with her parents if they agreed to another family member being present all of the time, yet the social worker did not have a relationship with that baby. Nor did her managers seem to notice or challenge her to have such a relationship. The worker could say that the baby was 'seen' in the literal sense of being there in front of them and such observation does provide some valuable information for assessing infant well-being and parent–child interactions and relationships. But the infant was not held, either physically or connected with emotionally or energetically. The infant's voice was silent/silenced. The vision of intimate practice that I am proposing in the book of workers having authentic, close encounters and relationships with children of the kind where they see, hear, touch and sense the truth of their experience and are able to act on it was not realised in practice.

Developing relationships with babies and young children

So, what does good practice with babies and young children look like? Based on insights from observing practitioners, building relationships with babies and young children can involve non-physical closeness achieved through emotional attunement, as well as physical holding. Chapter 3 introduced the story of the Nicholls family – mother Maria, father Patrick, and baby Isabelle. Maria's children were taken into care some years ago due to her drug addiction and abusive partner. She became pregnant again with a new partner, Patrick. A pre-birth assessment determined they could provide adequate care for Isabelle, who went home after birth. On most of the (seven) encounters between the family and professionals that were observed, the social worker, Shelly, gave quality attention to both parents and to the baby. We can now examine these interactions in more depth. For example, on one visit when the baby was six months old Shelly held her for 12 minutes, having asked Maria if she could. On being handed Isabelle, Shelly nestled her in her arms, placing her in front of her, making eye contact, smiling and talking to her, very gently bouncing and jiggling her. The baby responded pleasurably, holding the worker's gaze, while smiling and wriggling. In this way the worker established a relationship directly with the baby, by holding her and making contact through facial movements, the eyes and voice. Isabelle was a professionally *held child*, both physically and emotionally. There was a palpable sense of a vibrating connection between the baby and the social worker who were clearly touched and affected by one another and their interaction had the responsiveness that is at the heart of meaningful relational encounters that resonate (Rosa, 2019, p 179).

Experiencing vibrant, emotionally connected interactions and relationships, particularly with primary caregivers, is crucial for the well-being and development of babies. The absence of such connections causes significant distress. This is demonstrated in the classic 'Still Face' experiment, where mothers remained expressionless towards their young infants, who quickly intensified their efforts to elicit responses from their mothers, seeking the facial gestures, mirroring, touch, energetic connection and signs of love they normally received. Without their mothers' usual responsiveness the babies quickly became distressed (Tronick et al, 1978). The need for such responsive, caring connection is deep and it continues throughout the life course. Its absence can literally kill people, as shown by anthropologists who have found instances where communities have imposed social death on people by ignoring them and they died (Rosa, 2019, p 172). From birth to death, engagement and change occur within a dense, interactive field of relationships. Babies can only thrive psychologically within this relational field that provides love, consistency and secure attachment (Bowlby, 1973). Social workers routinely intervene into families where attachment is problematic and relationships often harmful. They need to be part of a relational field that supports parents and other carers to provide good enough care and attention and, I am arguing, be prepared to provide it to service users themselves.

Translated to child protection work this means professionals providing infants and children with encounters and relationships like Shelly did for Isabelle. Workers need to get close enough to connect with the infant through facial gestures, talk, play, and possibly touch and physical holding. There are various forms that touch and 'holding' can take. As Shelly demonstrated, it can involve cradling the entire infant in one's arms. Alternatively, it might involve sitting or standing beside a parent who is holding the baby, offering a finger for the baby to grasp, stroking their head and admiring its softness, all while maintaining an animated expression and seeking eye contact. Through such physical and emotional connection the baby enters the professional mind and heart and becomes real. Such holding practices have a role in assessing the infant's safety and well-being, as well as helping to establish a meaningful connection and relationship that benefits them.

Meaningful intimate interactions between workers and infants can occur through non-physical connection. Communication between adults and babies is often subtle and nuanced. Babies make sounds and so do adults, often it seems in an unconscious way. This can be illustrated by the responses of a social worker when she was on a first visit following the birth of a baby. Social workers became involved with 19-year-old 'Adele Harris' when she was expecting her first baby and was regarded as very vulnerable due to mental health problems and Jamie, the baby's father, was known to have been violent towards previous partners. Adele was reticent about social care involvement because she knew they regarded Jamie as high risk and their unborn baby was placed on a Child Protection Plan. The family lived in a small bedsit and on the first home visit after the birth Adele was in bed with the baby, Ralph, and Davina the social worker sat on the bed alongside Jamie (I sat to the side on the floor). Davina said 'Congratulations, the baby is beautiful, you must be so proud' and watched as both parents nursed the baby, telling them: 'You are both very natural with him.' Five weeks later, on another home visit, Davina took along a colleague to introduce them as Adele's new social worker.

> Adele opens the door and smiles at seeing Davina. As we enter the [bedsit] room Adele goes and sits on her bed while both social workers sit on the floor, Davina closer to Adele. The baby is five weeks old now and asleep in the Moses basket. After they settle in, Davina asks Adele how she feels about attending the [domestic abuse survivors] programme and she says she isn't keen. She doesn't like going to groups and Davina offers to ask the person running it to speak to Adele beforehand and they could get Mary the Family Support Worker to take her to the session. … The baby wakes and Adele takes him from the basket into the bed and nurses him. Davina immediately moves [from the floor] and sits beside Adele on the bed and talks to the baby. She is so warm and friendly, sounding genuinely delighted to see him. She makes appreciative humming 'ahhh' sounds as she gazes at him and says 'He gets more beautiful every time I see him.' Adele beams at this.

This illustrates the way in which the social worker was developing a relationship with the baby through her gaze, tone of voice, sounds and by moving to be close to him and delighting in his presence. This movement from sitting on the floor to onto the bed once the baby had been taken there was a key improvisation that signalled the social worker's intent to have a relationship with the baby as well as his mother. The humming gave voice to the vibrating wire of connection between them that Rosa calls 'resonance', that is relating that is full of 'relatedness' (Rosa, 2019, p 167). These heartful moments of connection enable workers to think in meaningful ways about children and internalise their interests. Davina had an intimate relational style and liked to get physically close to young children and the 'cuddle' she told me straight afterwards that she was keen to have happened on another visit soon after.

This scene also shows the impact of space, in this instance the small bedsit, on how the interactions took place and the challenges involved in conducting the work when seating options are limited to the floor or the service user's bed. Practitioners frequently grapple with how physically close to service users and their things – including their bed – it is ethical and useful to get. Here, again, we see that the ways in which workers position themselves, decisions about whether to sit, stand, hunker down or move, and how close they physically are to service users, fundamentally shape the quality of the encounter and attention they can give. This shows again how child protection work demands movement, alertness and total sensory engagement, requiring what can be described as high-quality 'embodied attentiveness'.

With younger children who are mobile the dynamics are often different than with infants because they can move to get close and initiate physical contact. One social worker spoke of this in terms of those 'who climb on your head when you first walk in the door. We need to find ways to be with them without them climbing over us so much'. Another experienced practitioner shares that, 'Children who are experiencing trauma look for people who are kind and if you can't get close to children why are they going to trust you?'. She gives a moving example of a three-year-old child she had taken into care due to serious neglect and how 'on the last visit the little boy came to me and took my hand as if to say I'm ready now. ... They wanted comfort and reassurance from me'. This shows how it is not just babies who require careful sensitive handling and tenderness, but toddlers. If children's emotional needs are not being met by their parents/family, they may act out some of what they need. As one social worker put it, 'if the child wants to sit next to me or on my knee, I'm not going to turn them away. If children aren't getting that support in the family home I'm not going to reject that'. Another refers to children who are more subtle and gentle in their approach than climbing, 'they just get up against you, lean on you to show you something or lean on your knee'. This resonates with how, in Chapter 6, the social worker Jessica tenderly responded to Anton's hyperactive agitated behaviour of climbing over her by sensing his need for comforting therapeutic touch and gave it to him. What social workers provide young children with during such moments and relationships is nurture.

Thinking about the rights of babies and hands-on practice

Achieving such intimate practice with babies and young children can be very difficult, ethically fraught and requires careful negotiation with the child's caretakers. What to do for instance when, like in the case illustration given earlier, the baby is asleep on the visit? Unsurprisingly, workers feel very uncomfortable about asking the parent(s) to wake the child so that they can properly see and perhaps hold them. And an abruptly awakened baby is likely to express their displeasure. Resolution of this depends greatly on assessed risk to the child, expectations and how the worker's role is defined and understood by the family and by the worker themselves.

It is important to distinguish between babies who are at serious risk of harm or have already been harmed and are subject to Child Protection Plans, and infants at lower risk who receive family support from social care workers and social workers. In child protection work the need to see the children on every visit is non-negotiable. In the messiness of everyday life, however, this does not always happen: one of the children may be at a friend's, the baby may be out with one parent or grandparent and so on. The key thing is the need to keep the baby and their rights and voice in mind in ways that carefully considers when they have been seen, *how* they were last seen (awake, asleep) and the nature and quality of the connection that took place with them in terms of physical and emotional closeness. These are also questions for the network of agencies involved with the family and it is vital that professionals communicate clearly about what hands-on relating with the baby has and has not been done.

A crucial issue is how proactive and purposeful practitioners feel they should be and are able to be. I have discussed with many social workers and operational managers the question of how close they get to children and whether or not they seek to hold babies. As the book is showing, I have observed some doing it and many not. Some regard holding – 'cuddling' – babies as a key way to relate to them and part of keeping them safe and they will initiate it, either by just doing it, or by asking parents if they can do it. Others say that they will only hold an infant if the parent(s) invite them to, that they would not be proactive and initiate it by asking to. A third group do not want to do it under any circumstances. As discussed in the last chapter, gender often influences how comfortable practitioners feel about getting close to children, due to fears of being perceived as behaving inappropriately and facing allegations of sexual abuse. While some women are affected by this, it particularly troubles some men. These fears can be even greater when race and ethnicity are considered. For instance, media reporting of child sexual exploitation and politicised commentary have aggressively depicted it as a problem solely perpetrated by gangs of migrant men from countries such as Pakistan (Gill and Harrison, 2015). Consequently, male social workers of South Asian heritage have told me they will never be alone with teenagers, in their home or in the car, and are very wary of getting physically close to children of any age. This is due to how their identity has been racialised and this racism distorts perceptions of their motives. These issues and relational styles are explored in greater depth later in the book (Chapter 10).

Central to amplifying the voice and experience of infants is considering their rights and imagining what they would express and choose if they could articulate their wishes. Do they really want to be picked up and held by this (strange?) professional adult who enters their home and world every week, two weeks, or even only monthly, and who either upsets, angers or uplifts their carers? Supporting parents to be the primary providers of care should be central to child protection work. But as I am arguing, social workers and other professionals have a potentially important role to play in providing at least some nurture. As one team manager put it:

> Generally we try to get the parent to do the parenting and try not to take over. ... Emily, one of my social workers went to see a family and focused on routine and meal prep, so took a back seat and the parent was doing something and said can you just hold this baby and she did. And we discussed it and Emily felt the baby was distressed and needed comfort and it was the right thing to do for that baby at that time.

Babies are physically vulnerable and need to be very carefully held. The sensitivity and tenderness required and some of the tensions involved are identified by Greta, a very experienced social worker and team manager.

> With babies, you have to be very sensitive of the parent, especially with newborns. You can go on a visit where you're desperate to hold the baby because you have a relationship with the parents, but you almost have to wait for permission. I would often just wait and hope the parents would ask. In cases where you're concerned about physical harm, and the baby is in a Moses basket, that doesn't tell you much in a CP case but if the parent is handling them, that can. Every case is different. When social workers come back to the office and have held a baby it's a topic of conversation, there's a lot of excitement, we're all jealous. Miranda comes back beaming from visits with the baby who's almost adopted – she had a picture taken with him when she was holding him.

This speaks beautifully to the important influence of organisational culture in the particular needs of babies being recognised and them being relished. Workers are much more likely to hold babies and listen for the infant's voice if it is openly recognised as a valuable part of practice and professionally a potentially pleasurable thing to do.

Also important is whether workers feel confident enough and qualified to handle the physical vulnerability of babies. Some managers recognise that some social workers, as one put it, 'haven't had a lot of experience with young children so don't really know what to do'. One of this manager's social workers 'would almost encourage it, she's very vibrant and out there and wants to play. One of my newly qualified social workers has a baby on his case load and has never held a baby so that's something we've talked about'. Another manager suggested to their social worker that they should go to 'health visitor drop-ins to get experience of babies and she has'.

In 1989, Olive Stevenson wrote of how the university social work department where she worked had just initiated a 'nursery' placement for all students intending to work in statutory child and family work. This was to fill the palpable gap in many students' personal and professional experience of babies and children. Stevenson wrote that:

> Initial resistance by some students has been overcome and there is universal acknowledgement of its value. As one young male student put it: 'it was the first time I had spoken with a person under five.' Thus, social unease, even embarrassment, may have played its part in the failure to relate adequately. (Stevenson, 1989, p 170)

I actually worked in the same university department that Olive Stevenson was writing about and when I arrived there in 2008 the nursery placement she spoke of no longer happened and was never mentioned. In fact, I have never heard of placements dedicated to working with babies and young children being systematically provided for all social work students happening anywhere. This is not unique to social work. Research by the Parent-Infant Foundation into mental health professions found significant gaps in workforce training, knowledge and confidence relating to work with babies and toddlers (Hogg, 2021). While I am suggesting that there is a great deal that social workers can and need to do in relating with babies in everyday child protection, it is very important to recognise the limits to what they are trained to provide. Lucy Morton, a highly experienced child protection social worker and parent–infant relationship specialist, argues that where there are complex risk and parent–infant relational issues, infants at risk of harm and their parents have a right to specialist infant development expertise and therapeutic relational support (Personal communication; see also Parent-Infant Foundation, 2023).

In social work in the UK and Ireland the closest to specific input on babies and toddlers appears to be on human development across the life course modules, with a particular focus on attachment theory (Bowlby, 1973). However, the amount of teaching social work students get on it and whether it is always taught accurately, critically and in culturally sensitive non-oppressive ways is debated (White et al, 2020; Foster and Duschinsky, 2025). On some social work programmes, a small minority it seems, students undertake a period of infant observation. The theory, supported by research, is that silently observing the infant and its mother interacting in their home for an hour every week over an extended period helps students/practitioners to learn how to think about babies and hold them in their minds. It also enables better understanding of the mother's mind and the challenges and rewards of parenting and relationships (Hingley-Jones et al, 2016; Parkinson et al, 2017). This learning opportunity needs to be widely adopted. However, it is not sufficient because social work in child protection involves more than observing parent–child interactions. Practitioners need concerted preparation for direct interactions and hands-on practice, including holding babies and playing with younger children, which demands confidence, skill, the desire for relational closeness and connections that resonate with meaning, and the ability to engage both body and mind.

Intimate practice with babies and children is about meeting their needs but, as mentioned in the last chapter, it also often involves an element of modelling close relating for parents who struggle to provide good enough care. Social workers worry that parents will interpret them picking up and holding their baby as intrusive and undermining. A common thing I have heard professionals who are themselves parents say is that they would not like someone coming into their home and picking up their baby. Ironically, these child protection professionals may overlook what their baby might prefer, require and have a right to, such as safety. Nor should it be assumed that parents will always regard social workers holding their babies and children with suspicion and negatively. One social worker I shadowed asked to hold a baby and a few weeks later its mother told her how pleased she was about this because 'no one ever asks to hold my baby because of the neglect'. Showing an interest in, relishing and caring for babies by seeking to hold and connect emotionally with them is a way of showing respect towards the parents as well as the child. All parents like their children to be admired and those who are struggling to provide good enough care need the opportunity to feel like their children are loveable. Holding babies can vicariously help some parents to feel cared about, loveable, and symbolise the care and nurture being provided for the family.

Conclusion

This chapter has sought to build on the emerging awareness of the need for 'infant voice' and younger children's experiences to be articulated and worked with in child protection.

Key learning points

- Child protection has a baby blind spot which I have argued needs urgent attention. The question that must always be on the minds of practitioners and managers and the inter-professional system is what kind of relationship do I/we have with this baby/young child? And what needs to be done to develop it and make it good enough?

- A deep knowledge of babies' physical and emotional development, their capacities and how to communicate with them is essential – including of the fontanelle. Every student and professional must ask themselves: how can I best have conversations with parents about babies, and give voice to those infants in ways that includes having a direct hands-on relationship with them?

- Guard's (2023) research with early childhood practitioners in day nurseries shows that recording and reviewing videos of interactions with babies can empower practitioners to recognise infant voice and agency. This method allowed practitioners to see the sophistication in babies' actions and enabled the workers to reclaim and develop their communicative skills. Although video methodology is expensive and hard to replicate widely, universities and social work training should as far as possible adopt this approach.

- Systematic efforts need to be made to ensure that at the point of qualification all social workers have completed infant observation training and had some experience of interacting with babies and younger children. Qualified practitioners need the opportunity to develop their skills and confidence at hands-on practice with infants and play through ongoing continuous professional development.

- Reflective supervision and case recording should also include the infant's perspective (O'Keefe and MacClean, 2023; O'Keefe et al, 2025).

- While I have argued that there is much of value that child protection workers can do in relating with babies, they and families need access to infant development expertise and infant–parent relationship specialists for support with complex risk and relational issues (Parent-Infant Foundation, 2023).

- Recent government guidance in England (Department of Health and Social Care, 2024) provides conversation prompts for practitioners to explore parent–baby relationships, such as asking parents to describe the relationship and identifying sources of joy. While this is a start, much more support is needed for child protection professionals, especially in how to work with babies whose parents are involuntary service users. This includes having conversations about creating safe sleeping plans due to the risks of bed-sharing.

- The commonly expressed language of 'communicating with children' and everything that is described as for 'children and young people' needs to be reframed as 'with infants, children and young people' and explicitly incorporate being skilled at more than talk.

Good enough child protection practice involves meeting the needs of babies, children and young people through relational and hands-on intimate practice. The next chapter will take this further by delving deeper into the process of developing holding relationships with families, exploring in detail how they foster change and provide therapeutic benefits to both parents and children.

8

Holding relationships: helping parents, families and enabling change

Previous chapters have shown some of the key dimensions of short- and long-term relationships, in both their avoidant and more intimate forms. This chapter will consider in much greater detail how close, intimate practice can be made and sustained over the longer term, through what I call a 'holding relationship'. This takes us into considering not only how safety is provided for children but how parents and families can be helped to change and how change happens. As I argued at the start of this book, while there is a great deal of valuable literature on the need for relationship-based practice in helping service users, it is not just the existence of a relationship that is important, but the type of relationship and the kinds of interactions within it that truly matter. The psychotherapist and academic Jonathan Shedler is critical of what he calls 'platitudes like the relationship heals': 'You need to articulate *how* the relationship heals, and *what kind of* relationship heals, and *what exactly* therapist and patient *do* in the relationship that is healing, and *why* it is healing, and how a therapist goes about *creating and maintaining* a relationship in which this can happen' (Shedler, Twitter/X, 21 June 2024, original emphasis).

This chapter takes a similar approach, illustrating how help is provided and change is facilitated in social work and child protection by expanding on the concept of a holding relationship. It will show that holding relationships have five key components: reliability; ethical holding; emotional holding and energetic attunement; physical holding; and immersion in service users' day-to-day existence and life skills.

I have intentionally chosen the tactile metaphor of 'holding' to convey that while some physical contact may be involved, fundamentally the holding lies in its psychological and emotional dimensions. It reflects how children and families are 'held in mind' through the relationship, in ways that provide significant therapeutic benefits. Social work literature focuses a great deal on what social workers *cannot* do due to bureaucratic preoccupation and having limited time to spend with service users and the book has shown that these are highly legitimate concerns. However, a core aim of this book is to go further by examining and reaching understandings of how social workers can use the time they *do* have to relate to children and families. If practitioners had all the time they need to conduct good practice what would it involve and look like? As this chapter will show, social workers have a significant amount of involvement with some service users some of the time, and the holding relationships that are made can have a transformative impact on their lives.

From the Practice Cycle to the seasons of child protection

The analysis again draws on psycho-social theoretical work on the self, emotions and relational dynamics and the influence that power structures and organisational systems have on relationships. This will take further the arguments of Chapter 2 about containment (Bion, 1962) and the Winnicotts' theory of how the holding that occurs in professional–service user relationships is similar to how parents provide a mindful, secure, reliable relationship for their infants (C. Winnicott, in Kanter, 2004, p 152). Shadowing encounters between social workers and service users from week to week, month to month over the course of a year (Ferguson et al, 2020a) enabled me to identify the presence of such reliability and holding and their meaning and importance.

The concept of the Practice Cycle has to be used somewhat differently as an analytical tool for making sense of long-term work. Practitioners have to complete the office–journey–practice encounter–office cycle many times across months and even years. This means that close-up analysis of particular home visits and other interactions on singular journeys around the cycle are no longer such a priority. Instead, a more summative approach to identifying patterns of relating over time is needed because there is so much more practice to be considered, while at the same time incorporating examples of typical interactions, practices and organisational dynamics. The approach is still forward-facing and focused on the making of practice as it unfolds in real time. But the visual representation of the cycle that featured in earlier chapters is no longer offered. Instead, we can more productively think in terms of phases of time and how life and relationships are not fixed but change, ebb and flow, what can be thought of as 'seasons of social work' (Ferguson et al, 2020a). The language of 'phases' and 'seasons' helps to connect practitioner–service user interactions to the rhythms and emotional texture of life and relationships as they are influenced by the vagaries of organisations, staffing, practitioners' skills, knowledge, vulnerability and relational styles and the vulnerabilities and strengths of service users. Sometimes it is families who are in crisis, or a practitioner is struggling, or it is the social work organisation that is going through disruption, or it can be combinations of all of those.

Understanding this requires wisdom about relational complexity, human vulnerability, the capacity for mistakes, love and hate, and cycles of co-operation, crisis, rupture, rejection, reclamation and how helpful relationships work. This includes practitioners having a *capacity to be hated and not retaliating*, what in Chapter 2 I called being a *reliable hate object*. Within the phases and ebbs and flows of relationships an overall consistency in patterns of relating over time can be identified, such as where the family are always reluctant and it's a 'hostile relationship' (see Chapter 9), or, as this chapter will show, where co-operation, mutual respect, intimacy and relational depth prevail.

A case of holding relationships in practice

A case study that illustrates the nature of a holding relationship and its impact involved a social worker, 'Miriam', and the 'Clarke' family. 'Samantha' and 'Oliver' were both White British and they had a baby son, Louis. Some 69 encounters took place between the family and professionals during the 12 months it was observed, 17 of which were home visits by social work and 41 by family support services. Fourteen of these encounters were observed and audio-recorded by the research, one staff supervision, and the parents were interviewed once.

Phase 1: In care

I first met Samantha and Oliver on a social work visit shortly after Louis was removed from them at birth. The first phase of casework involved parenting assessments and decision-making about the child's future. It was 18 months since Miriam took Samantha's older child, Daisy, into care due to drug and alcohol abuse and the serious domestic abuse she suffered which the child was traumatised by. At that time Miriam said she 'disliked Samantha intensely': 'She was vile when I met her, aggressive, vile, wouldn't let us in the house, the most difficult person we had to work with.' Samantha had already been through a programme for women survivors of domestic abuse four times and the outlook for the baby being returned to her care was regarded as hopeless. The emotional intensity of the work often disturbs social workers' sleep and Miriam described how Samantha and her family had so permeated her psyche and inner life that one night she kept hitting her partner in her sleep, saying 'We've got to get out of the house!' over and over due to fear of this mother.

By month two Miriam told the social work team meeting that Samantha was co-operating with the parenting assessment, seemed motivated to change and that she was starting to think that perhaps Louis could be returned to his parents. She now felt that keeping the baby in care was 'so punitive' and questioned the perspective of some social work colleagues who believed Samantha was displaying 'disguised compliance', suggesting that her apparent changes in attitude and co-operation were not genuine (Leigh et al, 2019). By month three Miriam was even more convinced that the baby should be allowed to go home, even though in the social work team 'everyone's against me'. Then, in supervision, her manager fully supported the case she made for Louis to be returned. At a meeting in the office at this point in month five the social worker and parents discussed the plan for court and Miriam offered lots of praise and reassurance. The court social worker rejected the proposed reunification, but the judge was happy for it to go ahead. At court 'Samantha and Oliver are obviously delighted – they are both smiling so much' (field notes). Samantha told the social worker that 'no one has ever stood up for me in the way you have', and Miriam said in a research interview after the hearing that she sensed how the parents 'felt empowered being beside me in court'. Opposing the court worker's position in order to stand up for the relatively powerless family was a crucial act of 'ethical holding' by the social worker.

Phase 2: Reunification

Louis was returned to his parents at the age of six months. An extensive visiting plan was put in place, with the intensive family support service going in daily and the social worker, initially, visiting most days. The first home visit that I observed occurred the day after the baby had spent his second full night at home. Louis was present with his father, Oliver, while Samantha was at therapy. The visit lasted 32 minutes during which Miriam interacted with the baby on seven occasions. The following scene conveys the essence of how the social worker practised:

> Miriam touched Louis on the face three times while his father fed him in a high chair. He takes Louis out of the chair and onto his knee. The social worker touches Louis on the foot twice and encourages Oliver to be more self-confident. He smiles and agrees he needs to be. Miriam gives her finger for the baby to hold and says 'Hello' when the baby looks at her. She suggests that Oliver changes the baby's nappy and takes the changing mat and puts it on the floor. The change complete, Oliver lifts the baby off the mat and kisses him. Miriam is now sitting on the sofa and asks for 'a quick cuddle'. Oliver hands Louis to her and Miriam stands the baby on her knees and holds one hand around his knee and bottom and the other under his arm. She begins jogging Louis as he stands on her knee facing her and they gaze into each other's eyes.

The worker's intimate relational style and the 'energetic attunement' it produced is evident in her use of her gaze, voice, touch and playfulness, and how she built a resonant, highly responsive relationship directly with the baby. The combination of empathy, compassion and practical advice and support she gave to the father typified how she helped both parents to develop their parenting skills and confidence. She explained afterwards in the car and on numerous subsequent occasions that touch was, for her, an essential tool in working with children. It allowed her to assess their well-being and safety directly, get a feel for how they are, and experience a crucial emotional connection with the child through holding.

The combined efforts of the intensive family support service and social work was vital during the early reunification period. This scene in month six, three weeks after the child went home, is taken from my field notes and is typical of their approach:

> Samantha is sat on the floor and talking about her expectations of group work, Miriam affirms how painful it can be to dig deep. The doorbell rings, Samantha answers it, it's Susan the family support worker and as soon as she comes in the positive energy increases further. Samantha admires Susan's appearance and

sits on the floor again and is showing Miriam and Susan the workbook on her therapy. She speaks knowledgeably, including about 'disassociation'. Susan tells her 'I feel really proud of you and I am rooting for you'. Samantha is so open and genuine, there are real relationships here. Miriam says, 'I'm really chuffed and proud with how the three weeks of reunification have gone'. ... Susan turns to me and is telling me that she has known Samantha for a long time and says out loud how wonderful it is to see how much she has changed and tells me about how angry Samantha has been. Samantha agrees and says in the past she hid things. Both Miriam and Susan are still sat on the sofa leaning forward, a body position that signals their interest and positivity. Miriam stands up and coos at the baby. Susan gets up from the sofa and stands beside Samantha and touches her on her arm, tenderly.

We see here the reach and power of the holding environment coming alive: Samantha speaks of the therapeutic effects of the group psychotherapy, while experiencing the strengths-based, emotional holding work of the social work and family support service. It is also becoming evident how good Samantha herself now is at co-creating a holding environment.

By month seven the social worker regarded Samantha as seeming 'much more relaxed now'. One effect of the development of trust and their close relationship was that from early on Samantha phoned Miriam nearly every day. But however much the relationship was based upon care, worries about power and control were ever present for Samantha. In month seven she expressed fear to Miriam that while social care are involved 'then he's only half mine. ... If I was having a bad day, I'd worry that you'd come and take him away from me'.

Phase 3: Going deeper

By month eight the intensive family support package was complete and the social worker and family support worker who was based in the social work office settled into a routine of fortnightly visits. The ten home visits that were observed in the six months after the child returned home lasted an average of 45 minutes (the longest was 60 minutes, the shortest 22). On all of these the child was awake and interacted with by the worker. The interactions mostly took place in the same space – the sitting room – and always on the same sofa. Most of the time was spent seated on the sofa, although Miriam always had periods on her feet and sometimes on the floor with the child. The social worker's mobility and willingness to move in order to play, touch and physically hold the child were central to her relational practice and effectiveness (Ferguson, 2018b). On all the visits she was observed on, the social worker was tactile with and held the child, typifying how the holding relationship was built on physical and emotional closeness and certain actions being repeated time and time again.

Louis now being safely settled at home opened the way to a new phase where attention to issues such as the couple's relationship and Samantha's past and identity as a mother of a child in care deepened. These topics and attention to

Louis' health, eating and sleeping patterns would be gone over again and again on visit after visit. This kind of disciplined attention and repetition is a very important aspect of keeping children safe and supporting parents to change. Mini-crises were dealt with: one week it was a Facebook argument, on another visit Samantha showed Miriam a letter about benefit payments, explaining they are 'financially stretched' and she is stressed. Social work managers had the discretion to provide small payments and following this visit Miriam organised this. The mood of visits fluctuated according to how the parents were doing and how social care worked with them. On a visit by the family support worker in month nine Samantha was 'very happy and playful throughout. She expresses her happiness and that she is "doing OK"' (field notes). The visit was a mixture of investigative work – the bedrooms and kitchen were checked – talking about support groups and the drugs service and friendly casual talk about the baby and both parents' joy in him.

In month ten, Samantha was upset by the family support worker making an unannounced visit, fearing this meant an increase in concern about Louis' welfare. Miriam calmly reassured her that it did not represent any change in how she is regarded by social care and reminded the parents that unannounced visits were part of the visiting plan, to see the family as they naturally are and check for signs of drug and alcohol use, for instance. On one of the visits in month 12 the mood was celebratory as Louis had just had his first birthday. He was now crawling at speed – including over to the researcher and climbing up them! On a further visit in month 12 Samantha was feeling sad and again wanted to talk in depth about her feelings about her other child, Daisy, still being in care. She said she and the child could not understand why they cannot now live with her. Miriam reminded Samantha that there was an agreement that the return of Daisy would not be considered until Louis was well settled with her and it was clear that having two children to care for would not put that at risk.

> No one thinks you have given up on the child, no one thinks that, we know that you are there for them 100 per cent. I think it is just very tragic and really sad that that was the situation that we were in and now you know we are in this situation, and you need to hold on to the fact that you have got Louis with you and you do have contact with Daisy. They are really resilient and they are doing really well in school.

After a silent pause Samantha responds that she understands that it is still too soon, but she does want Daisy home eventually.

> Last year before Daisy was taken it was heart-breaking to be fair, it wasn't fun for me or for them. ... Sometimes when you think you are protecting your child the most you are not, you are shutting them away from the reality of what you're feeling which can potentially

> worry them more. … You couldn't imagine me saying this a year and a half ago could you?

The worker is empathetic, including recognising the responsibility of the men who abused Samantha, while not protecting her from the reality of the harm to her child. This is sensitive, skilled work. The social worker's challenge is not to invalidate past problems and Samantha's part in them while holding her as a good enough parent in the present. Miriam was able to hold the difficult painful legacy of the domestic abuse, drug use and removal of her child by tolerating it until Samantha found a way through it and was becoming able to tolerate it herself. Samantha's sense of how she was changing was evident in her comment, 'You couldn't imagine me saying this a year and a half ago could you?' How the social worker holds Samantha and her pain from the past and guilt about her older child helps her to tolerate those feelings and this enables Samantha to create the mental space to care for her baby, and to do it well.

Parental perspectives

I interviewed Samantha and Oliver two months after Louis was returned to them. Oliver said Miriam encouraged him to be involved with the social care plan, but he would have liked this to have happened sooner when Louis was first removed. He now sees social care as supportive and feels they have helped him to see what being a father involves, including the need to play, which has promoted his bond with his son. '[Louis] means everything to me, everything to me. … That is just really why I have always just wanted to be, really just be a father and just do everything that my Dad didn't really do for me.'

Samantha recounted a long history of abuse as a child and lengthy periods in care. She expressed many criticisms of social work, how vulnerable she has been and described herself as having been difficult to work with: 'I didn't have any manners. … I just needed help – I don't like their systems and I don't trust them.' When Louis was removed at birth social workers told her she probably wouldn't get him back. When he was returned to her she found the involvement of so many professionals and daily visitors while coping with a new baby 'overwhelming, stressful'. To prove herself she would clean the house more. She feels she has changed: '[T]he social workers showed me how bad my relationships were.' This has helped her to become a better person, and she has changed so she can fight for Daisy, her other child in care. Samantha felt her relationship with Miriam had changed, improved, and 'I haven't got to be so panicky'.

> I didn't feel obliged to have any manners or respect for them [social workers] to be fair. I am just thankful now that they have finally seen that I am a good mum and it is not the fact that I can't care for my children, it is more the fact of the situations that I have been in. They use a lot of my history but then instead of looking into why

my history is the way it is, and trying to help me do that, you take away the only bit of love and unconditional kind of affection that I have, and that is my kids. So I have always been a bit yes ... I have always kind of held a grudge against the Local Authority because of that to be fair. ... I am still cautious, of course I am. I am still worried about 'right you come in my house you will say something, how do I know you're not going to go back to the office and write something totally different'. But I think being able to communicate with her [the social worker] is a little bit more easier. Since [month four] my opinion of Miriam has changed. She's not the bitch I thought she was, [the relationship now] is a lot better, not so tense, in a way a little bit more friendly as well, it is not so formal. It is more casual when she comes round now and she is a lot more open with me about herself. I didn't even know she had children – she has told me about how one of her children struggled so that was quite reassuring.

Because of her long, troubled history with social workers, her hatred and mistrust in them ran deep. But Samantha had recently changed her opinion of Miriam and trust developed. This occurred at exactly the point at which the social worker was observed changing her mind about Samantha and recognising her potential to care and love – that is, at precisely that point when the holding relationship became established.

The components of therapeutic holding relationships

So what are the key components of these vital 'holding relationships'? The five I have identified are reliability; ethical holding; emotional holding and energetic attunement; physical holding; and immersion in service users' day-to-day existence and life skills. I will now elaborate on them all, beginning with the most important, reliability.

All the casework that was practised through holding relationships involved regular and punctual contact and workers maintaining consistent attitudes towards service users. In effect, over time individual workers and services were *reliable*. As Donald Winnicott put this when referring to psychoanalysis: 'The analyst would be there, on time, alive, breathing' (Abram, 1996). Unquestionably, breathing helps! But the aliveness referred to is a kind of energetic presence where the worker is consistently open, alert to, curious about and receptive of the service users' thoughts, feelings and experiences. It reflects a willingness to hold for them what they are not yet able to bear themselves, as Miriam demonstrated with Samantha. Holding relationships are formed through interactions that maintain a dynamic thread of connection and responsiveness, described by Rosa (2019) as resonance. This resonance involves both the worker and the service user being heard, touched and emotionally moved, creating a bond that has a powerful impact in the moment and that can be sustained over time.

'Ethical holding' was a key dimension in how the practitioners used critical reflection and brought an awareness of power and inequalities into their work. They saw service users holistically and in terms of their capacity to change and develop, trying hard not to reinforce racism, sexism, homophobia, shame and the stigma of poverty, mental health problems and having had children removed by the state. This led the social worker to approach Samantha Clarke with an open mind and to fight hard against colleagues who felt she shouldn't keep the baby because she was using 'disguised compliance'. As Miriam reflected back at the end of the year:

> [I]t really taught me that actually you've got to have an open mind to work with the families, which is hard to do, to kind of switch off what your own prejudices are in a way. It couldn't go unrecognised how much work Samantha had done and all the progress she had made since that point when I met with her in [18 months ago]. I could see that there had been a change, I really, really pushed her, so I made it very difficult and probably quite uncomfortable for her, but my instinct told me that it was, she would, would stick to the plan. I think her desire to love Louis was so huge and the fact that she'd lost Daisy pulled her through to not go back to that lifestyle. I'd done my assessment and I was really clear actually she has done enough. And what I was seeing was that the court was a really punitive system for her. … I'm really pleased for her, I'm pleased for Louis. I didn't even envisage that it would be this positive. Just in a generic way, how we treat families, even though they're doing well, we're still kind of, 'Oh but that's still not good enough'. It really made me realise that we can be so judgmental even though we think that we're probably the least judgmental practitioners. We do look at faults as opposed to successes. I think I listened to her, that was probably the most powerful thing.

The worker listened and followed her 'instincts'; she learned from experience. This meant that it was not just the family who were changed by the relationship but the worker too, a mutual impact that was crucial to achieving closeness and change.

Trust develops through not only feeling listened to, but families knowing that practitioners adjusted their approach in ways that respected their needs (Wilkins and Whittaker, 2018). The workers accepted families' criticisms of past workers and systems and they advocated on parents' behalf, in the manner Miriam did for the Clarkes in the courts, for instance. Social care did this while still placing clear boundaries around parental behaviour and limits on what they were prepared to accept, authoritatively checking home conditions and for such things as signs of drug or alcohol (mis)use. What social workers provide then is not simply what Winnicott (1965) called 'care-cure', but a combination of 'care-control-cure', that represents the use of 'good authority' (Ferguson, 2011; Forrester et al, 2019).

This reinforces the argument I made in Chapter 2 that an important aspect of the complex position and identity of social workers involves them being 'reliable hate objects'. By her own account, Samantha didn't 'have any manners or respect' for social workers, part of her – and at times all of her – hated them. This highlights another crucial aspect of reliability – how service users come to understand what to expect from workers during each interaction, knowing that they will continue to return even when the family is angry, hurt, distressed or rejecting, and without retaliating. Professionals have to carefully manage their own hateful feelings. A year on from regarding this mother as 'vile' the social worker had stopped hating her and now saw her as 'a likable person ... charismatic, insightful, open'. By month eight Samantha was able to say that social care showed her how 'bad' her relationships were and that Miriam was 'not the bitch I thought she was'. Hate was still present for Samantha in terms of fear and suspicion, but so too to a greater extent now were respect, care, love. So, the workers became 'reliable care objects' too.

Social workers are not therapists in the psychodynamic sense of delving into the unconscious or in drawing straightforwardly on Carl Rogers's person-centred counselling approach to practise unconditional positive regard (Murphy et al, 2013). The paradox, however, is that while they are not therapists, social workers' relational, holding work can have direct therapeutic effects. What occurs in holding relationships is in part an unconscious process in which service users experience the worker's mind being available to them and know that it is open to their emotional experience. They feel held in mind by the key worker and the professional network even when the professionals are absent, just like a child does when cared for by a good enough parent (Winnicott, 1971). The professional network provides individual acts of help and holding, but the role of social workers as case managers places them at the centre of this larger holding environment. A reliable holding environment and relationship creates a lived emotional experience of care and security which is pivotal to helping people (like Samantha) for whom those experiences were absent during and since childhood. It also works by social workers forming an idea of the service user and their needs and holding that idea in the relationship so that when they see them the service user can find that part of themselves which they had given the practitioner. A compelling example of this was the way that Miriam held the shame, guilt, remorse, anger and loss that Samantha Clarke regularly expressed about her past and her child being in care.

While it has a psychological basis, the holding relationship also has a literal meaning in the intimacy of encounters and the physical holding of children by professionals. As I have argued throughout this book, the question of what the use of touch means to parents and the children themselves has been peculiarly neglected (Green, 2017). As I argued in Chapter 7, physically holding infants, cherishing and nurturing them are not just central to developing a holding relationship with young children. This kind of intimate practice also seems, vicariously, to help some parents feel held, symbolising the emotional holding, care and nurture provided to the family. Similarly, non-physical closeness and energetic attunement can achieve the same with older children, through activities such as play, car journeys, walks, visits to cafes, or interactions using computers and digital media.

The holding relationship is also made from social care practitioners becoming deeply immersed in children and families' everyday lives. This involves connecting in very practical, 'hands-on' ways with the day-to-day needs of families, helping them to learn the skills of caring, develop self-efficacy and self-esteem and to address their struggles with trauma from abuse, discrimination, poverty, housing and relationships. In research interviews parents have told me of how they longed to have an ordinary, settled life together with their partner and children and the pleasure they got from nights in together by the TV – as Samantha Clarke put it, 'Netflix and chocolate nights' – and accomplishing day-to-day things, like going for walks together and to the shops. Walsh (2018, p 219) refers to this as 'being alongside' service users and 'valuing the seemingly mundane'. Repetition and giving attention to the mundane by going over the same ground from week to week, month to month emerges as a very important dimension of therapeutic work. It is a crucial expression of reliability. In this way good enough practice mirrors the repetition, security, availability and willingness to process difficult feelings that is at the heart of good enough parenting.

Due to workload pressures and bureaucratic demands, achieving such reliability and repetition is a constant struggle. The first home visit Miriam was meant to take me on was the one she did the day Louis spent his first night at home, but she forgot. This was because of the sheer difficulty of being able to think clearly due to how busy she was: '[I]t's been one of the hardest weeks the [team] has had for a long time, 17 new cases.' This typifies the weight of work that was competing for Miriam's attention and the scale of the challenge involved in being able to see families regularly and think clearly about them. The social worker described the relatively large amount of time she spent working with the Clarke family as the 'exception and not the rule': 'I've had to make time. Those first few weeks of reunification were crucial and I found the time. … I had to drop everything else and the [team] noticed, felt unsupported. Daily visits, court cases.'

At times, a holding relationship was sustained with the family despite what went on in the office, not because of it. Miriam sometimes felt let down by management and the organisation due to the sheer weight of her caseload and complexity of her role and on journeys to home visits she would articulate how exhausted she felt. It is very important to recognise the challenge involved for social workers in being reliable and making themselves available, by not cancelling appointments, turning up and consistently having that quality of presence and aliveness that provides quality attention for the family. Miriam managed to do this most but not all of the time for the Clarkes despite the huge bureaucratic preoccupations she faced. As she travelled round the Practice Cycle again and again, more often than not she found time in the office to plan for practice encounters and her manager remained supportive of all her decisions and motivated her. She used the transitional space of the car journey to process her anger with managers, let go of bureaucratic preoccupation, clear her mind and come alive so as to be fully present to the child and family. The social worker's intimate relational style, energy and ethical stance drove her to get close to each family member and have a relationship with the baby as well as the parents. The fact that the social worker described being able to find the time to do this kind of sustained relationship-based practice as the 'exception and not the rule' is a serious indictment of the system. Ultimately, she had enough conviction and support to be able to go against the grain of her colleagues' negative, pessimistic views of the parents, overcome her disappointment about the system and help the family create change.

Conclusion

This chapter has extended the Winnicotts' theory of holding beyond the concept of a holding environment, and Rosa's (2019) theory of resonance, developing these ideas into the unifying concept of a holding relationship.

> ### Key learning points
>
> - The chapter has uncovered important aspects of the complexities of long-term relationships, including their ebbs and flows, the dynamics of love and hate, and the vital role of reliability in facilitating therapeutic change. By adopting a forward-facing perspective that examines the making of relationships as they happen in real time, this discussion has illuminated the skill, creativity, improvisation, courage and endurance required of practitioners and families in their day-to-day interactions.
>
> - Practitioners can provide holding relationships by consistently being reliable, getting emotionally and physically close in ethically appropriate ways, and engaging deeply in service users' everyday lives to help them develop their life skills. Practitioners establish trust and sustain it through consistent engagement. Recognising and learning from the transformative practice already going on helps us to know what good relationship-based practice is, and to reimagine what a reformed system that enables similar kinds of child protection work to happen regularly and be the norm might look like.
>
> - A particularly significant dynamic is the making of social workers into 'reliable hate objects', enabling parents to process complex emotions and past traumas. Over time, these practitioners, along with family support workers, often evolve into 'reliable care objects', offering stability and emotional holding to the entire family.

- As well as with the family as a whole, it has been shown how relational work needs to be done with each individual, helping mothers and fathers to develop their safety, skills and capacities to care and practitioners having close relationships with each child, including babies.

- The chapter has further advanced the argument that the energy practitioners bring to their relating with children and families is vital and takes two forms. It means having the vigour and stamina needed to keep going back and be reliable. And, once with service users, having the vitality, the aliveness, needed to move, play, be still, be attentive, listen, talk, touch, hold and emotionally attune that adds up to being fully present for them. This opens the way for meaningful connections and encounters that are intimate, resonate deeply and bring about change through relationship-based practice.

- It is vital to reflect on what personal and professional qualities help practitioners to have the desire and energy for connection and the capacity to sustain reliability and relational depth in their work. How can organisational structures better support practitioners to feel 'held' themselves and energise and enable them to provide transformative holding relationships? Managers, systems and policies must prioritise practitioners' time and capacity for meaningful connection and sustained relational engagement, rather than bureaucratic demands.

Relationships in child protection often require practitioners to withstand rejection, anger or distress and maintain a non-retaliatory and supportive stance. The next chapter will examine this huge challenge in depth by considering 'hostile relationships' and how they can be sustained and overcome.

9

Hostile relationships: conflict and good authority in working with involuntary service users

In child protection work practitioners are urged to strive for relationships with parents and families that are empowering and based on mutual respect. While the literature and policy stress the importance of such 'user engagement' and working in 'partnership', some relationships are not like that but are transacted through mistrust, fear, hostility and even hate. Empowering reciprocal relationships are thought possible and even to be the norm because it is too often assumed that service users are voluntary and want a service (Barber, 1991). However, 'the reality is that most social work relationships are involuntary' (Smith et al, 2012, p 1462) because the person receiving the service does not freely enter into it. As Donald Forrester (2024) argues, this means that challenge and conflict are at the heart of everyday practice. How professionals can have a relationship with someone who does not even want to be involved with them is one of the most pervasive, difficult, important and yet under-analysed dilemmas in child protection work.

We even lack an agreed language to refer to people who don't want a service (McLaughlin, 2009). Beresford (2005) suggests the term 'service refusers' might be most appropriate, even though the statutory intervention of child protection still has to be provided. As people who have no desire to use a service are not service 'users' in any meaningful sense, the term 'involuntary client' seems more honest and accurate. Recognition of involuntary clients and the complexity of working with what Laming (2009) called 'resistant and deceitful parents' and elsewhere have been termed 'families whose engagement is reluctant or sporadic' (Child Safeguarding Practice Review Panel, 2022a, p 88) has grown in recent years (Calder, 2008; Turney, 2012; Tuck, 2013, Trotter, 2015; Rooney, 2018). In such high-risk cases intimidation and physical violence by family members towards social workers is quite common (Stanley and Goddard, 2002; Littlechild, 2005). The emotional complexity of working with strong feelings and dealing with aggression and hostility has also gained recognition (Hunt et al, 2016; Smith, 2018; Cook, 2020). Notions such as 'respectful uncertainty' (Laming, 2009) have been coined to try and capture the delicate balance of trust and doubt that professionals need to achieve. Models such as Signs of Safety include valuable techniques for advancing such work through strengths-based practice (Edwards and Turnell, 1999; Turnell and Essex, 2006). Similarly, 'restorative practice' usefully sets out an approach based on 'high challenge – high support' (Finnis, 2021).

Yet little attention has been given to what 'involuntary' relationships look and feel like *in practice* and how they are actually conducted in real time. This chapter shows how such relationships are formed and sustained over time or break down and argues that the concept of a 'hostile relationship' is needed. These relationships involve complex emotional dynamics and power struggles that sometimes result in workers becoming hateful and punitive towards families (Winnicott, 1949). The chapter explores the nature and experience of hostile relationships and how they can be worked through with parents and provide safety for children. At the heart of this is what I will call 'Practice by Negotiation' as part of using what I call 'good authority'.

Involuntary relationships

Some families who do not want a service reconcile themselves to the inevitability of statutory involvement, are not overtly aggressive towards practitioners and try to make the best of things to get them out of their lives. Some parents, however, are extremely unhappy, often hostile and remain that way. This hostility is not solely a result of parental attitudes or personalities, it is also shaped by professional attitudes and a product of how interactions between families and professionals evolve into hostile *relationships*.

For example, the concerns about the Newman family surrounded neglect of the three children, aged six, eight and ten. Social workers always undertook joint visits and the 11 encounters that were observed for the research were characterised by anger, acrimony and frustration. At meetings and on home visits the parents attempted to take charge by interrupting, shouting and making accusations – that social workers are liars, inconsistent, hypocritical and 'in cahoots' with other professionals. Social workers at times raised their voices and argued with and talked over the parents, which only made their hostility worse. After a period of involvement, things got so bad that having let the social workers into the home the parents walked out and hovered around outside the front door. The practitioners tried to relate to the children in the home and saw them at school, but the parents eventually blocked that too. The awkwardness of these encounters was painfully obvious; contempt and hate filled the air. When interviewed Mrs Newman was scathing:

> [I]t was uncomfortable and it has got worse and worse the longer it has gone on. We felt like we were being judged obviously, which we are, nothing has properly been explained to us. We have been lied to actually from social services, blatant lies to our face so there is definitely no trust or anything there. They seem very aggressive, and very argumentative and sometimes patronising. ... From our point of view it seems like they are trying to pull the whole family apart. All of the experiences so far have been very bad and they keep

> coming round and saying, 'Well, we are here to help.' Well, no, you're not because you're just causing problems and making everything a lot worse and worrying people and stressing people out rather than actually doing anything to help anyone. It has caused a load of stress, headaches, made us sort of feel ill in ourselves.

The social workers, meanwhile, regarded the parents as being responsible for the lack of co-operation and saw this as further evidence of their problematic parenting.

A second example is the Lewis family. They were seen 24 times by social care over the course of the year that we shadowed and 15 of these encounters were observed. The Lewises also prevented and avoided more visits. There had been significant concern for the two children, aged four and five, from early in their lives due to their father's drug addiction and violence towards their mother. The social worker, who had known them for over two years, was so used to the family pretending not to be in that she no longer waited for them to answer but would knock and immediately walk into the house. The parents – Ron and Angela – didn't like it, but it enabled the worker to see the children, who always seemed glad to see her. Three months after the research got involved, there was yet another incident of Ron, the father, being found to be in the home, despite being told he was too big a risk to be there, and the social worker, Rebecca, made a home visit:

> Although there was a polite greeting there is an intense atmosphere. Rebecca in particular seems really angry with Angela and Ron, she doesn't hold back as she notes Ron's presence and the complete lack of engagement with the Child Protection Plan. Ron barely acknowledges the conversation initially, although it's largely aimed at him. Angela obviously does not see the problem with having Ron in the home. Both deny it and Rebecca threatens to do spot checks in the middle of the night. Ron leans back, puts his arm behind his head and splays his legs. Angela continues to have her feet up, snuggling into the sofa. There is a remarkable contrast between Rebecca, who sits rigidly and tensely upright on the sofa, and Ron and Angela who give off an air of not caring. Rebecca raises her voice to talk over them, she talks about the concerns of nursery. Ron, who was so placid and uncommunicative earlier, begins to seethe. He demands to know what the nursery workers are saying about him, complaining that there are never any concerns when he picks up [youngest child]. Ron begins to raise his voice, he waves his hand around in a gesture of frustration, raising his voice louder still. Rebecca tries to bring it back to Angela and Ron's relationship, but they don't understand what she means. ... Ron paces around, in and out of the kitchen and living room. You can feel the anger coming off him, anger with Rebecca and her manager for how he feels he's being described, anger with Angela for seeking to go back to court [because of his violence] and complaining no one helps him.

In forcefully challenging the parents, the social worker did not disguise her annoyance with the lack of progress and ongoing risk to the children and she just about maintains her composure in the face of the father's behaviour. In working with ongoing hostility, social workers face huge challenges in maintaining their professionalism by having empathy for service users' fears and not retaliating.

While these examples illustrate how social workers may consciously channel their anger and frustration into challenging parents, the danger is that they unconsciously project their own hate and return the hate service users have projected onto them. This can lead to practitioners becoming punitive without realising it – an occurrence that Winnicott (1949) referred to as 'hate in the counter-transference'. All the parents who were interviewed for the study who were involuntary clients felt social workers and other professionals crossed the professional line and were punitive and persecuting. The threat by the social worker to do spot checks in the middle of the night expressed her commitment to checking on the children's safety, but because it was so unrealistic it could be construed as retaliatory. Nothing changed and by the end of the research the children had been removed from their parents. These skirmishes, the anger, threats and walk outs, all delivered in highly personalised ways, show how incredibly emotionally and intellectually demanding these hostile relationships are for everyone concerned (see also, Robson et al, 2014). But because of the child protection concerns, neither families nor social workers can walk away, and somehow a relationship based on hostility has to be sustained.

Sustaining hostile relationships over time (or trying to)

These, then, are some general characteristics of the hostile interactions between social workers and involuntary clients. But how do hostile relationships develop over the course of a year and how are they experienced? As in the last chapter, the concept of the Practice Cycle now has more to do with phases and 'seasons' of practice and relating. The issue becomes not just what happens on one or a small number of circuits of the cycle to complete assessments and short-term work, but the cumulative effect of what practice and relationships become over time. The form of relating that emerges – in this instance 'hostile relationships' – is shaped by the ongoing interactions between systemic, organisational and individual practitioner and family influences.

Phase 1: Difficult, hostile beginnings

'Roberta Dixon' had two children, both of whom had been resident with their fathers for the past two years and she saw occasionally. They had previously been on Child Protection Plans due to concerns about physical abuse. Roberta was now pregnant and described in the referral to social work as having a history of violent and abusive behaviour. In the 12 months covered in the research there were 68 face-to-face encounters between social care and the family. Some 30 of these were done by social workers and their managers, the rest by family support workers. Most of this work was done in the second half of the year, after the baby was born. Despite her overt hostility to social care, Roberta consented to being part of the research and 21 of her encounters with professionals were observed. Roberta was also interviewed on three occasions during the year: in months six, eight and 12.

The initial social work response to the referral was to ring Roberta who replied that she does not want anything to do with social workers and angrily said she would search their name on the internet and hung up. The first home visit was done by the team manager, Olivia, due to the social worker Susan's unavailability. From the start social workers always visited in pairs because Roberta was regarded as potentially dangerous. Roberta showed her feelings as soon as the two social workers arrived and were parking up, by standing on the doorstep and forcefully slamming the door shut. They eventually managed to negotiate their way inside: 'Seven minutes into the visit … it feels like she is very angry. The atmosphere feels incredibly tense. Olivia still seems nervous, she talks quietly. Roberta is much louder and really dominates the room.' Roberta queried and denied everything.

In a staff supervision session a few weeks after this visit, Olivia and the social worker, Susan, agreed that Roberta was preventing the pre-birth assessment by refusing to co-operate. They were alarmed by her aggression, mental health problems and history of alleged violence:

Susan:	I'm really concerned about this baby, really concerned … I'm really worried about this baby … [I] can imagine her hitting the baby that cries.
Olivia:	100 per cent just losing it. You only need to say one sentence—
Susan:	And whack!
Olivia:	And straight away [*makes hitting noise*].
Susan:	And I really, I really feel worried.
Olivia:	If she's not working with us and we can't get into the home it's not safe enough for her to take that baby home, end of story. So, we seek legal advice before if she's not working.

Although Susan had some telephone contact with Roberta, she had not yet met her face to face. It is striking how these two colleagues wound themselves up into a kind of frenzy about Roberta's dangerousness, including imagining and enacting the 'whack!' of her assaulting the baby. A vital function of supervision is for managers to support workers emotionally and to get them to critically reflect on their feelings of anxiety, fear, dread and their impact on perceptions of service users and relationships (Davys and Beddoe, 2021), but it didn't happen. Olivia had borne the brunt of Roberta's anger and was already deeply emotionally enmeshed, which prevented her from achieving the detachment needed to think clearly about the work and relational dynamics, or to support her supervisee, Susan, in doing the same.

Prior to the birth, two case conferences took place, at the first of which Roberta expressed huge anger towards all the professionals, and her unborn child was placed on a Child Protection Plan. The decision was that it was highly unlikely that she would be allowed to keep her baby and Roberta stormed out before the end of the meeting. In months five and six, a pre-birth Parenting Assessment was completed by an independent social worker that involved four home visits and over the same period two home visits were undertaken by Susan, the family social worker. As time passed, Roberta became more co-operative with professionals and was seen in a very positive light by the independent social worker. The statutory social workers recognised that Roberta seemed different – as Susan put it, 'she's a changed woman' – but their narrative remained negative, that she was manipulative, hasn't really changed and that it was 'disguised compliance'. As I argued in Chapter 8, this notion of disguised compliance is highly problematic because it places the service user in a lose-lose position where they can never prove their sincerity or worthiness as a parent (Leigh et al, 2019). The social worker and manager were very annoyed by what they saw as the independent social worker's overly positive assessment, implying that tough questions about Roberta's anger and alleged violence had been avoided. It had a significant impact at the second case conference and the decision that Roberta would be allowed to keep the baby, who would remain on a Child Protection Plan.

It is possible that by being co-operative Roberta was showing a capacity to respond to the empathic approach of the independent social worker, whose report did indeed give limited attention to the risks she presented. Statutory social workers, on the other hand, by seeing Roberta through a lens of dangerousness, did not relate to the caring, loving side of her. What seemed to be occurring here is the psychological 'splitting' into 'good' and 'bad' objects, as outlined in Chapter 3. This process functions as an unconscious defence mechanism for managing intense anxiety and other unbearable feelings (Klein, 1946). Cooper (2018, p 32) describes how individual professionals and whole systems can 'lose their heads' with anxiety, become reactive and stop thinking, and how 'case dynamics become split very quickly'. From the outset the child protection social workers internalised a view of this mother as a 'bad object' and projected their fear and other unbearable feelings into her. Meanwhile the independent social worker related to Roberta as a 'good object', reached positive evaluations of her, idealised her and could not see the danger others were preoccupied with. This splitting into love and hate was also evident in Roberta's narratives when interviewed for the research as she expressed her complete admiration for the independent social worker and her intense dislike of the statutory social workers, especially Olivia. When such splitting occurs, both relationships and the quality of work are adversely affected. Sound assessments and decision-making rely on practitioners and the entire system being attuned to the full range of emotional dynamics and connected to the complexity of humanity – the 'good' and the 'bad' within us all (Cooper, 2018, p 32).

Phase 2: The baby arrives and avoidant practice

Roberta's baby, Amy, was born in month six and much more regular social care contact followed. Four home visits were made by social workers in the first few days after Roberta and Amy went home from hospital. The visiting pattern then settled into weekly home visits, some of which were announced and others unannounced. A visit that Susan and Olivia made in month six was typical of the pattern of relating that became established:

> Roberta leads us into the kitchen. Amy is in a car seat under the sink in the gap where a washing machine usually goes. Roberta is cooking and Susan tells her how gorgeous the baby is. Olivia and Susan ask Roberta lots of questions about the practicalities of baby care. Seven minutes into the visit Roberta moves forward and picks up the baby. Susan steps to her right to allow this and suggests they move to another room and Roberta leads the way despite saying there are no seats in the sitting room. Roberta sits on a stool. There is in fact a sofa and other chair but they are covered in stuff, so Olivia and Susan remain on their feet and stand for the entirety of the visit. Susan offers financial help while benefits are being sorted to take account of the baby's arrival. Her tone is genuine as she strongly encourages Roberta to accept help.

Here Susan was meeting Amy for the first time and while she made statements that acknowledged the baby's presence, she did not get physically close to her, or connect with her energetically, which I had observed her always doing on visits to other infants. During month seven another social worker co-worked with Olivia because Susan was unavailable and on their first visit there was nowhere to sit and after two minutes she got down on her hunkers. This worker showed no excitement or pleasure at meeting the baby. In fact, she didn't properly meet Amy at all in the sense of going up to her and attuning to her by looking into her eyes, smiling, providing a finger to hold. The infant's voice was silenced.

Phase 3: Removing the baby

Social care and other agencies then became worried about an apparent downturn in Roberta's mental health and her capacity to care well enough for Amy. Nine social care visits were carried out in the first half of month ten alone, when Amy was four months old, mostly by Susan. The dynamics of visits continued to be tense and conflict laden. The pattern was for social care workers to ask Roberta questions about baby care and other practical things like housing, with little attention to her feelings about and relationship with the baby. On most of the visits Roberta sat on the stool in the living room holding the baby and there was nowhere for practitioners to sit. This meant they usually stood for all of it or crouched on their hunkers, which they repeatedly described – afterwards but never in front of Roberta – as awkward and painful. When interviewed for the research around the same time Roberta admitted she deliberately covered the seating to prevent professionals from sitting down, orchestrating their discomfort. There is nothing surprising about families who do not want social workers involved using such tactics to keep them at a distance or drive them out. What is striking is that the social workers did so little to try and work through these barriers, most obviously by asking Roberta to clear a space on the sofa for them to sit on. It seemed like their anxious state of mind was such that unconsciously they colluded in their own distancing and avoidance because they did not want to be there.

Then, in month 11, at a multi-agency meeting, Roberta aggressively challenged everything Olivia said and – as Olivia put it – 'exploded' with rage and threatened her. Afterwards in the office Olivia said she was not happy with how she handled the meeting because she felt stressed due to pressure of work and now could see that not enough attention was given to Roberta's views and feelings. After this meeting the professionals feared that Roberta would act out her anger on her daughter. Olivia was very upset by Roberta's threatening behaviour and cried at her desk. On a home visit a few days later Olivia was still feeling traumatised by Roberta's attack, couldn't stop crying, felt ill and stayed in the car while Susan and I went into the house.

Olivia was observed in supervision that week with her senior manager, who recognised that she was upset but did not pursue this with her, instead moving on to address other high-risk cases and staff performance issues in the team Olivia managed. This lack of attention to the social workers' emotional experience and the dynamics of encounters contributed to their relationship with the child remaining detached and avoidant. As Susan explained at the end of the year of research, this was the first baby she had worked with in several years as a social worker who she had never got close to, touched or held as part of forming a relationship. This shows how even in long-term work where such children are regularly 'seen' by practitioners, they can be kept at a physical and emotional distance, avoided and be invisible unheld children.

By month 11 of the fieldwork the cumulative concerns about Roberta and her parenting resulted in the local authority trying to remove five-month-old Amy from her. This was averted in court, in part by Roberta agreeing to the intensive family support service working with her. In her final research interview (month 12) Roberta still had custody of Amy and regarded the attempt to remove her as a persecutory, punitive response. While there is no doubt that Roberta could be a frightening person and that she and her child were vulnerable, the possibility that she was right and that at an unconscious level this was a retaliatory act cannot be ruled out.

The relational dynamics of hostility

Many parents begin by disliking, fearing and even hating social workers. As Chapter 8 showed, empathetic, reliable, authoritative practice can enable parents to engage and feel held. Through this support, some, like Samantha Clarke, are helped to transform ambivalence and hostility into a capacity for co-operation, care and love, allowing them and their children to thrive together. But for some others the hostility persists and comes to define the relationship. It is vital to understand the mutuality of this dislike. It is service users who typically are characterised as 'hard to reach', 'resistant', 'difficult', but social care staff are also often emotionally detached and unwilling or unable to tolerate and 'reach' the parents and children. As Brett Kahr (2020) shows, when Winnicott (1949) first published his work on 'hate in the counter-transference' there was considerable resistance to it within psychoanalysis and the idea that therapists sometimes hated their clients, but this is now a fully accepted part of psychotherapeutic knowledge. The same cannot be said for social work, however, which urgently needs to confront the harsh realities of hate and hostile relationships for children, families and professionals.

Visits to families where there are hostile relationships are consistently fewer, more infrequent and shorter than where long-term relationships are co-operative (Ferguson et al, 2020d). The longest home visit to Roberta Dixon lasted 45 minutes and was the very first, as Roberta angrily sought explanations for why social care needed to be involved. After the birth of the baby social work visits lasted between 18 and 33 minutes, which given the high level of concern was short. This reflects how uncomfortable workers felt having to face such anger and aggression (see also Henderson, 2018; Sudland, 2020). While, as we have seen, some parents, like the Newmans and the Lewises, sometimes walked out of their own home when social workers were present, Roberta's avoidance strategies were more subtle. She ensured there was nowhere to sit, leaving professionals awkwardly standing, crouching or sitting on the floor.

Such regular standing contributed to an atmosphere of practitioners not having fully arrived or settled into the visit. Professionals towering over Roberta merely emphasised their dominance and power – precisely that which she most feared. Social workers said they were aware of this dynamic and the need to, as they put it, 'get down to the service user's level'. It was assumed this would create a greater sense of equality in the relationship and was why they crouched for as long as they could physically bear it. It is crucial to recognise, however, the role the service user played in placing the professionals either in an upright, standing position gazing down at her, or crouching or sat on the floor with her gazing down at them. For Roberta, being stood over did not simply signal professional dominance, but because she engineered it, her taking back some power from those she regarded as persecuting her. She told the research she took pleasure in the social workers' discomfort. However, ultimately for her it was the professionals who had the power and they misused it:

> [T]hey have disrupted my family life and they tried to remove the child from me. To remove a child from someone you have got to say that this child is at significant harm, the child is not at significant harm and she hasn't been throughout this whole process, and they thought it was appropriate to lie. … [When social workers visited] they were like standing up in the middle of the room and you know

> sort of like this whole squaring off with me sort of thing. I wasn't given the opportunity for them to understand me properly, I have been to meetings with them and I was told that we can only read out what is important but we don't want to hear from you. This is what I am basically being told by them and this is a meeting about my child and I can't even voice my opinion or even factual information or correct them on information that is wrong, all I can do is basically sit there and get upset. (Roberta, final interview)

Being 'squared off' with by social workers expresses perfectly how parents who are involuntary clients experience hostile practitioners.

When travelling around the Practice Cycle, the office and transitional space of journeys to the home were not used as opportunities for the co-workers to prepare different approaches to engaging Roberta, like the social worker Miriam managed to do in the last chapter. Because Olivia's senior manager prioritised their performance management role by focusing on the need for staff to meet targets for completing work, they gave little attention to the emotional impact of the work or the relational dynamics between Olivia, the social worker and the family (Chapter 13 returns to these issues). This meant that the team manager and social worker just compounded their unprocessed anxiety by talking about how dangerous Roberta is, splitting and construing her as a hate object. As I argued in Chapter 5, this is not 'coming alive' in the way that is needed, but getting wound up into a state of heightened anxiety that leads to emotional overload and the closing down of thinking and reflection. Coming alive and sustaining that energy and focus involves having a finely tuned regulated awareness of the emotions, body and mind that channels the arising feelings and energy in purposeful ways that creates alert composure.

Good authority in working with and beyond hostility

In *Child Protection Practice* (Ferguson, 2011), I outlined an approach to working with involuntary clients that I called 'authoritative negotiated child protection'. I want to develop that thinking by setting out the essentials of using what I call 'good authority', central to which is 'Practice by Negotiation', which involves nine steps.

Step 1: The starting point has to be recognising that power and authority are central to the child protection role and that conflict not co-operation will underpin relationships with involuntary clients. The goal of Practice by Negotiation is to identify opportunities for maximising the freedoms and choices service users have within the constraints that must be imposed due to the risks to the children.

Step 2: Encouraging openness and honest expression of feelings by having 'clear the air' discussions that involve being open about the hostility and the need to work beyond it. This never happened with Roberta, primarily I think because it is a very difficult, often frightening thing to do, as workers worry that encouraging emotional honesty will open the floodgates to them being heavily criticised and verbally abused by service users and give permission for it. So, it has to include the ground rule that intimidating and abusive behaviour is not acceptable and mutually respectful communication is the aim. Parents and families need to be allowed to have what Turnell and Essex (2006) call a 'position' that gives them the right to express openly dislike of child protection involvement and hold to their views on their children and the alleged problems. We saw, for instance, how elements of this happened with Maria Nicholls in Chapter 2 and Samantha in Chapter 8, who expressed their underlying fear and mistrust of social workers throughout. In contrast, Roberta clearly felt that she was not listened to or respected. Giving parents the message that their feelings and views are being heard and taken seriously may clear the way for them to engage more co-operatively and begin to trust. Barber (1991) suggests that professionals also need to be honest about their own feelings and what they stand to gain from a less conflictual relationship.

Step 3: It is then important to identify what the resistance is really about. The overview of case reviews into children who had been seriously harmed or killed in England in 2022–2023 concluded that 'ascertaining the underlying reasons for disengagement or challenges in engaging (and having the skills to respond to this) was crucial but did not always occur' (Child Safeguarding Practice Review Panel, 2024, p 84). An obvious source of resistance is the loss of freedom and choice about having involvement with statutory social work and the fear parents have of losing their children. Showing empathy by openly stating, for instance, that 'it must be very difficult for you to work with me given that you don't want to' can again enable them to feel heard and understood. It is important to explore what else the family fear and object to.

Roberta particularly disliked unannounced visits and the overall tone and approach of social care. She explained vividly in research interviews how she felt persecuted by the surveillance and would be watchful at the sitting room window wondering when they were going to call unannounced again and also fearing the announced visits. The workers were conscious that they were 'monitoring' Roberta's mothering. However, they were not really aware of the effect of this on the mother and baby. Rebecca internalised the anxious surveillance by social care, experiencing it as persecutory anxiety, which in turn made her even more defensive and anxious about their involvement and her capabilities as a mother. It is likely that the nature and style of the social work surveillance contributed to the worsening of Rebecca's mental health and it certainly contributed to her reactions to professionals and the mutuality of the hostile relationship. Open recognition of these kinds of impacts can lead the way to negotiation about them and, for instance, the possibility that Roberta and her baby would not always be seen in the home.

Step 4: As a prelude to such negotiation beginning, the next step is to clearly set out the risks and dangers to the children in terms of the behaviours, attitudes and evidence of harm. This would have required Roberta's social workers to be honest that there was no actual evidence of harm to the child and the perceived risk lay in a combination of previous evidence of her harming her children and her current aggressive, explosive nature.

Step 5: Identifying what is *not* negotiable in how these dangers will be worked with. The most obvious of these is the need for the child to be seen regularly and, if old enough, on their own to explore their lived experience. As I argued in Chapter 7, for pre-school and non-verbal children ways of incorporating their 'infant voice' and experience are essential. This must be through a direct relationship with the baby, by holding them or by connecting through the gaze and sounds. The requirement for children to have developmental or other health checkups by health visitors, GPs or paediatricians must be explicit in the multi-agency plan. Regular checks on home conditions are now the norm. If parents have serious addiction problems, attending treatment is usually considered a non-negotiable, as are checks on their abstinence through regular hair strand tests (Derby and Derbyshire Local Safeguarding Practice Review, 2024). Roberta Dixon stage-managed social work visits by covering seats with stuff to stop them from sitting down, but the social workers never challenged it. An insistence on always having somewhere to sit is a reasonable expectation and non-negotiable because it enables workers to relate and do their job better. Workers can then use good authority by making firm, respectful requests for space to be cleared for them and even helping to do it. Other examples of non-negotiables include working with fathers, whether they are resident or non-resident, and needing to know about all the people who live with or have significant contact with the children. Turnell and Essex (2006, pp 118–119) rightly insist on the importance of professional's safety planning needing to include clear statements to the family about 'who is where in the house, garden, garage, etc., when the children are home' (see also Ferguson, 2011, p 177).

Step 6: Identifying what *is* negotiable can now begin. In several respects Roberta was providing good enough care for her child, but this was not properly acknowledged. While social workers were occasionally encouraging, their energy was flat and Roberta consistently felt they were always looking for her weaknesses and criticising her as a mother. The point here is to openly recognise strengths and encourage the family to think as broadly as possible about the areas where they can exercise choice. From a long list of possibilities, a good example is the scope to negotiate where the children are seen some of the time. As all the casework examples given in the chapter show, the workers seemed to find it unthinkable that sometimes these involuntary clients could be seen somewhere other than in their home. The emotional impact of hostile relationships paralysed workers and organisations, restricting their minds and actions, confining them in highly constricted domestic spaces where they and parents enacted pathological relationships, taunting and punishing one another. Parents should be asked about other places they would prefer to meet, like parks, community centres, cafes, or on walks or drives in cars (Jeyasingham, 2018).

Another negotiable is for parents to be provided with advocates who can support them. This can help to re-balance the power dynamics where parents, who so often are vulnerable lone mothers, have to cope with visits by social care workers, often in pairs. Parents who have lived experience of the child protection system are particularly good as allies because they have genuine understanding, can offer emotional support and enable parents to feel heard, valued and not just 'bad objects' (Tobias, 2013). This can help prevent reactions like storming out of meetings that are easily interpreted as destructive behaviours that confirm professional suspicions about the parent(s). Processes like family group conferences should also be offered, for their potential to involve wider networks of family and friends to provide support and assist in safety planning. There is a strong argument for these kinds of family meetings being non-negotiable and enshrined in policy (Turnell and Essex, 2006; Mason et al, 2017). In England, a process is under way to make family group decision-making meetings compulsory when children are at risk of entering care (DfE, 2025).

Step 7: Having clarified what is and is not negotiable the Child Protection Plan can be drawn up. It must have a clear statement of risks, all non-negotiable and negotiable areas and the forms of help that will be provided. This should be done by social workers and the family in collaboration with all the other professionals involved.

Step 8: Identifying criteria for progress. All assessments of change must be based on direct evidence of children's physical and emotional well-being, not simply on what professionals are told by parents or others. The family need to be in no doubt about what they must do if their children are to be regarded as safe and well. Similarly, it is essential that there is absolute clarity about what professionals are expected to provide to support this change. Parents must retain the right to challenge and engage in ongoing discussions about how they and their children are being worked with. The tone with which Practice by Negotiation is done is crucial. The children of involuntary service users deserve to be treated joyfully and held, and their parents need professionals to be honest, respectful, compassionate, direct and hopeful.

Step 9: The steps involved in practising through negotiation ultimately constitute the use of good authority. However, my earlier conceptualisation of good authority (Ferguson, 2011) did not sufficiently account for the potentially harmful impact of unprocessed anxiety and hate, which can drive professionals towards retaliatory and punitive practices that negatively affect families. The final step then in effective Practice by Negotiation is the need for reliable supervisory support and honest expression of feelings between workers and managers. This is less of a stand-alone once and for all step and more of a process that needs to occur throughout. The challenges of understanding and maintaining torturous hostile relationships are amplified by the fact that workers often have several such cases simultaneously. Additionally, team managers must support their entire team's caseload of involuntary clients, all while juggling numerous other responsibilities. On one occasion when parked outside Roberta's home the team manager Olivia spoke of how exhausted she felt, having the day before responded to 180 emails and covered home visits for absent social workers. With such demanding, complex workloads, giving families the full attention they need and maintaining a capacity to think clearly about them and the dynamics of relationships is enormously difficult.

Olivia was too enmeshed in the casework and a conflictual, emotionally charged relationship with Roberta to be able to provide supervisory support that would help the social worker Susan to think. In the supervision she herself received, Olivia's manager did not provide her with the emotional support that was needed, in part because of their regulatory role. Limited attention was therefore given to what was going on in the relationship, especially below the surface. This meant that as workers went round the Practice Cycle week after week their practice became stuck in an avoidant pattern that at times had the robotic quality of automated practice (Chapter 4) and at other times the fitful engagement of disorganised practice (Chapter 5). This all has its roots in the high levels of unprocessed anxiety that comes from having to keep going back to hostile relationships and not using good authority.

Conclusion

This chapter has identified the nature and dynamics of what I term hostile relationships, and the ways in which they are made.

> ### Key learning points
>
> - Viewing practice with involuntary clients in a forward-facing way allows us to fully appreciate the challenges social workers face when returning week after week to confront resentment, anger, hate and rejection. The difficulties are undoubtedly even more profound for service users, who have to live with the threat of losing their children and constant home visits, often unannounced, where social workers inspect their personal spaces and expect access to their children.
>
> - Hostile dynamics frequently result in relationships that feel emotionally torturous and unbearable for all involved.
>
> - In statutory child protection work, it is unavoidable that constraints must be placed on parental wishes and behaviours to safeguard children from harm. However, the nine steps that constitute what I have called Practice by Negotiation can help transform hostile relationships into ones that are as co-operative as possible, by maximising the choices available to service users within these constraints.
>
> - Other research supports the argument that using good authority is key to effective practice. Forrester et al (2019) found that practitioners

who used good authority were most successful at engaging families and more able to work in partnership.

- Social workers may channel their frustration with families' lack of engagement, aggression or passivity into constructively challenging parents. However, when confronted with hostility they can unconsciously project their own hate back onto service users, causing practitioners and systems to act punitively.

- Much more thought needs to be given to:
  - How training programmes can better prepare practitioners to use good authority by engaging in Practice by Negotiation, so that they can work through resistance, and foster respectful, reciprocal connections with involuntary clients.
  - How professionals can be helped to learn how to defuse conflict, explosive relationships and recognise their own role in co-constructing hostility.
  - The ways supervision can delve below the surface to help practitioners uncover their true thoughts and feelings about families and understand the impact of fear and anxiety, defence mechanisms such as splitting and the risks of hate and retaliation, while ensuring they remain ethically grounded and connected to their humanity during difficult interactions (Trevithick, 2011).
  - The systemic changes that could support professionals emotionally in sustaining reliability and empathy amid challenging relationships.
  - How power dynamics can be re-balanced by lived experience advocates and family networks being included to support vulnerable parents, who tend to be lone mothers enduring multiple inequalities and difficulties.

While organisational and systemic factors influence all aspects, individual managers and practitioners are at the heart of making child protection work. It is crucial, therefore, to understand how individual workers engage in relationships – their personalities, preferences and the extent to which they are willing to connect closely with children. The next chapter will explore this by examining relational styles in child protection work.

10

Close or distant? Relational styles in child protection work

Over the years that I have observed social care workers in practice relating to service users there have been many similarities, but also clear differences between individuals in how they relate. Every person has their own unique way of relating to people and the world, yet it is possible to identify particular forms of relating that I call *relational styles*. In discussing this with practitioners, some describe themselves as 'natural huggers' and 'cuddle monsters', while others use terms such as 'not touchy-feely' to describe themselves.

The existence of these styles and the forms they take has in some respects already been illustrated in this book. There are those practitioners, like Lynne in Chapter 1 and Jessica in Chapter 6, who come alive and light things up as soon as they meet children, who get down on the floor to play, who show relish at being close, who physically hold them and welcome the child's need to touch and be held. They possess a strong presence, exuding positive, motivational energy. They balance authority with compassion, supporting parents through their struggles and suffering while providing meaningful help to the family. Then there are those who are less overtly extrovert, who nurture and hold children by attuning to them emotionally in non-physical ways and sometimes physically. Like Miriam in Chapter 8, they exude a desire to care, persist and work with parents and families in quietly reliable and effective ways. Finally, there are those whose practice is avoidant, who don't get close either physically or emotionally, who dampen the atmosphere and struggle to be relational or helpful in the active sense at all.

There is surprisingly little literature that attempts to explore and understand the nature of these relational styles, or the reasons behind their variations. There are some valuable studies of the characteristics of social workers who stay in the profession and gain satisfaction from it long-term (Astvik et al, 2020). Burns et al (2020) found that when retained beyond the five-year point, social workers' embeddedness in the organisation and community strengthens and they have a stronger sense of professional confidence (see also, Collins, 2008). Some research has also explored the skills, knowledge and confidence needed in relating to children and families (Handley and Doyle, 2014; Forrester et al, 2019). Ash and Grey's (2022) small-scale study examined the influence of attachment patterns on individual social worker–service user relationships. Williams (2022) shows how social work supervisors and supervisees can have different adult attachment patterns and examines their impact on the supervision process. These papers argue convincingly that much more attention needs to be given to the attachment styles of social workers and managers and how they affect relational practice. Training that promotes self-knowledge for professionals and learning about attachment and relational patterns and their implications has been developed by Dr Alice Loving.[1]

There seems to be a general reluctance to focus on individual qualities, perhaps due to concerns that this might expose front-line workers to blame for poor practice and outcomes or a perceived lack of 'resilience'. The focus then is on the impact of systemic factors such as workloads, staffing levels and excessive bureaucracy on practice quality. But individual attributes, the 'self' at the core of practice and relational styles matter (Dunk-West, 2018; Ward, 2018). They are, however, complicated to make sense of because, as I have been arguing throughout this book, the ways in which practitioners relate and make their practice is a product of the complex interplay between systemic and organisational factors and individual experience, skill and creativity. Despite this complexity it is both possible and necessary to identify individual characteristics and particular relational styles and how they contribute to the making of practice, for better or worse.

I define relational style in a manner that takes account of this overall system and the place of the individual in it. It refers to *the characteristics of the individual, their attachment pattern, 'personality', energy and 'presence', the unique self that is at the core of their practice and how this is shaped by professional training, knowledge and organisational and wider cultures.* This intersection of the personal and the organisational creates a 'professional self' that is at the heart of practice. A key question here is what qualities do – and *should* – individuals bring to their profession and the creation of practice and what are the implications of this for staff recruitment, retention, training and the quality of child protection work? I will develop further the argument that the desire and capacity to relate to service users in close, intimate ways, fostering what Hartmut Rosa (2019) describes as 'resonance', is of critical importance.

The embodied self and relational vocabularies

Everyone brings their unique sense of self to their practice and relationships. This includes how they relate to their own body, their comfort with movement, play and touch, and how at ease they feel both touching others and being touched. Being 'touched' also includes the emotional dimension of getting close and being open to and willing to absorb the feelings of others. The 'embodied self' shapes the extent to which practitioners use their bodies to get alongside children and take their hand and walk around their homes, neighbourhoods, or get onto the floor to play with them, hold them, or – as we saw with Jessica's practice in Chapter 6 – to dance!

---

[1] https://www.able-training.co.uk/speakers/dr-alice-loving/

Relational styles are made up of voice, tone, movement, play, touch, the use of empathy and authority. They are also shaped by an overall relationship to the world, in terms of attitudes such as optimism or pessimism, and have an energy to them, such as flatness or vitality. All practitioners and managers need what Bloom (2005, p 58) calls a 'movement vocabulary', that can increase people's understanding of themselves and how they move and provide a language to make sense of it. Bloom shows how our capacities to move and how we carry our bodies, our posture, have deep psycho-physical roots. The idea that our unconscious and how we think and relate is formed by 'attachment styles' and childhood experience is a familiar one in social work. However, the notion that our development from childhood influences how or whether we *move* and physically relate to others is not well known. For child protection work something more encompassing than just a focus on a vocabulary of movement is required. A *'relational* vocabulary' is needed that enhances people's self-awareness of how they are in relationships, their core relational self with regard to preferences for emotional and physical closeness or distance and the energy, or aura, they give off.

Reflecting on my own career in practice several decades ago my relational style was quite avoidant and physically detached. I have no recollection of ever being asked as a student how close I got to the older adults I was working with on placement. Would I place a consoling hand on their hand or shoulder when they were upset or worried, where did I sit when they were unwell and bedridden, on the edge of the bed or on a chair beside it? Nor can I recall when I was a practitioner working with families being asked in supervision about whether I played with children, or how close I got to them, or them to me. I most certainly never ever danced with a child on a home visit or in any other setting, like Jessica did in Chapter 6. My awkward relationship to my own (rigid) body, shyness and embarrassment about being seen to move was such that I found it very difficult even to dance at dances! My experience growing up in Ireland and of Irish men of my generation was that we were brought up to practice and admire a good handshake and I judged those with a weak handshake suspiciously, as a reflection of poor character. Shamefully, through the dominant lens of homophobia at the time, such men, and any displays of intimacy or vulnerability by men, were regarded as weak. I felt very loved by my parents as a child and young person, and as an adult still shared some hugs with my mother in a context where open expression of feelings and showing physical affection within the family was limited. As I pointed out in Chapter 7, I did gain experience of babies and children through having a sister who was born when I was ten and a brother who came along when I was 14, who I felt great love for and enjoyed being with. This equipped me with some knowledge that I used from time to time when I was a social worker.

So, when I started in social work at the age of 22, I brought a quite detached, defended self and rigid socially conditioned body into my work. It went largely unchecked because I was never encouraged or challenged to critically reflect upon it. Therefore, my personal self and professional self overlapped and were largely undifferentiated. This was by no means all problematic as my experience of my family, friends and culture also gave me a strong desire for sociability and connection. My father was particularly influential as I grew up watching and learning as he initiated conversations with strangers as well as acquaintances – not least in the male-dominated environment of Irish pubs. This is not to idealise that male drinking culture, which was deeply sexist as it restricted the freedoms and choices of women/mothers by leaving them tied to the home, domestic duty and caring responsibilities. Indeed, too much drinking went on, leaving painful effects that deepened my sensitivity to family suffering, borne mostly by mothers and children, and to the urgent need for emotionally engaged men and involved fathers. However, I think this broad cultural experience left me with an attitude and relationship to the world that sought to forge connections with people and places and set me up well professionally to have the potential for meaningful relationships with parents and some children. In Rosa's (2019) terms, I sought 'resonance' through relating to others in meaningful ways and I found my way into social work. My social work training helped me to channel this energy appropriately by teaching me what I needed to know about professional ethics and boundaries, such as limited and careful personal disclosure and avoiding friendships and sexual intimacy with service users. But it taught me little about myself as a relational being and how to use my body as well as my mind, to get close to service users in ethical ways through play, movement and touch. I had little relational vocabulary or help to develop one and my practice.

The relational continuum

My research observations and in-depth conversations with practitioners have led me to think of a relational continuum, with at one end those whose relationship to the world is detached and avoidant and at the other end deeply relational and intimate. To bring this to life, let us consider the practice of two social workers: Jackie, who falls firmly on the avoidant/detached end of the relational continuum; and Molly, who is at the intimate/relational practitioner end. Jackie is the social worker I spoke about in Chapter 7 who on the home visit stayed physically and emotionally distant from a four-month-old girl, Megan, and her 19-month-old brother, Nathan. I'm returning to Jackie here because the question of why she related in the ways that she did was left largely unexplored. Megan was on a Child Protection Plan due to having a broken arm when ten days old that was never satisfactorily explained. She was very nearly taken into care and Jackie stressed how allowing her to remain with her parents was a difficult, risk-laden decision. So why was it that in the four months of intensive social care involvement with Megan Jackie never got close enough to touch her or hold her and had never seen her stripped? The same question applies to her toddler brother, Nathan. After the home visit, when asked about how she feels about closeness to such young children, she said:

> Well, yes, it is part of my thinking, but I just find it really awkward to do, to actually go and pick up a baby off someone else's lap, their

> baby. Like this morning I mean how, in fact that child this morning, I only had to look at her in a funny way and she cried didn't she. … So it's very awkward, the social worker has such a sort of, they don't like letting social workers near their children.

It is partly her assumptions about parents' perceptions of the power of social workers that inhibits and prevents her from even trying to get close to children and being tactile. As we have seen, social workers can sometimes feel disgust and fear contamination when on visits to neglected 'dirty houses', but in an intriguing inversion of that here it is the social worker who is regarded (by herself) as untouchable, a contaminating agent, as *repulsive*. She even has the evidence to prove how hateful and shameful she is because she thinks children cry when she goes anywhere near them. This could be interpreted as good empathic social work in that the worker is sensitive to the power she has and the fears this provokes. But this soon breaks down because it results in the power not being used and instead practice that is detached and empty of relational connection.

In detailed discussions with her after observations of several encounters with different families, it became clear that Jackie's preference was for physical distance. She did not take toys, drawing materials or other objects with her to use in her work with children. She confessed that she preferred being at the computer to being with children and families. Her workspace was kept very tidy, ordered and devoid of any signs of *her*. On another occasion she told a story about a father bringing a baby into the office the previous week and she held it while he did something. The baby had thrush and sucked her cardigan. 'You know me with children … I don't normally hold babies. I'm not into touching children', and she went on to refer to 'horrible, snotty … babies'.

Jackie told me that not being touchy-feely included her disliking physical closeness in her private life. Physical distancing and in many respects emotional detachment was at the core of who she is and she brought it with her into her social work training and practice. While Jackie emphasised that it was perceptions of her role that stops her from getting close and being tactile with children, I asked her how much of this might also be about her own make up and temperament?

> I think it's a bit of both really, I think it's a bit of both. And maybe some people would be there to carry it off better than me. I know I've talked to someone who said apparently when she goes round to people she says 'Oh let me have a cuddle', and I thought that sounds a good plan, but I thought I don't think I could carry that off. … I just find it quite difficult to actually say to people let me hold your baby, and because it's something I feel a bit anxious about myself I just think, oh I won't do it.

Molly was just the kind of 'cuddling' social worker referred to by Jackie and her practice can help us to understand relational styles that are intimate, mobile, playful and full of positive energy. She was deeply relational in her work and warm, animated and dynamic in her accounts of it and her relationships. Molly had a way of enabling people into relating through the sheer force of her commanding presence, energy and palpable desire to connect with and help them. She blazed into people's lives, a whirlwind of finely balanced and attuned care and control and professional love. Her energy and presence were entirely different to Jackie's, exuding aliveness, purpose and drive, with an aura that radiated a deep desire to connect emotionally and spiritually. Alongside this was physical and emotional strength and endurance, having the capacity to sustain positive energy and relate in intimate, helpful ways with families over time.

Molly felt it was possible to resist bureaucratic preoccupation and control the work to some extent by deciding to put more time into working qualitatively in particular cases. She said she *makes* time to do the work she feels she needs to. The previous week she drove two parents on a 60-mile round trip to the foster placement on three separate days to have family time with their baby. This was a huge commitment within a busy caseload. She spoke with passion about the trust that has built up between her and the parents, from an extremely challenging starting point when social work removed the baby at birth and she became the family social worker a month later. 'Michelle', the mother of now seven-month-old 'Jake', had experienced very serious mental health problems and prior to the birth there were fears she may kill her baby as well as herself. Michelle's partner and father to Jake had been known to be abusive towards her. Having been taken into care at birth, seven months later Jake was being returned on a phased basis to live full-time with his parents, who had both received significant interventions from a range of agencies. Molly feels deep pride in the relational work she has done:

> Oh, I think the relationship I have with them has been absolutely crucial. That's why I'm so proud of this case, as I feel that I, I have, me personally, have achieved quite a lot with them, because they didn't trust the previous social worker, which led to, which was a factor for a lot of the removal of Jake. They didn't trust professionals at all, and so me being able to build up a relationship where I think, I don't think they trust me completely, I think they'll struggle to trust anybody completely, but we've definitely built up a relationship where I think we understand each other and I can say, I can say stuff to them and more things and it's not a problem. I think they, I think they feel safe with me and I feel safe with them, I suppose.

The mutual sense of safety, care and responsivity expressed here was at the heart of the transformative relationship the worker and family achieved. Molly explains how Michelle's whole demeanour is different and the parents' relationship has improved, in part because she helped them to learn how to communicate and listen to each other. On the home visit I made with Molly, Jake was present and a week later was due to return to live at home full time.

Some 24 minutes into the visit, Michelle (mother) spontaneously thanked the social worker for her help:

Michelle:	It is just scary, you know, I don't want anything bad to happen for Jake to be taken away from us again. Well, not again, but after all the hard work everybody done as well, and you, I just don't want to disappoint you. We don't want to disappoint you and we don't want to disappoint ourselves either.
Social worker:	You two have done wonderfully, absolutely wonderfully.
Michelle:	No, because we know that you've done a good job, we know that you've done a good. Look at him! [*referring to Jake*] [*laughter*]. Yeah, we know that you've done a really good job [*baby cries*]. ... Oh! Yeah, what was I saying? We know that you've done, you've done an amazing, brilliant job, and if we didn't have you as a social worker, I don't think we could have made it [*baby screeching*] I don't think we could have made it.
Social worker:	You're underestimating what you two have done, you've done everything, absolutely everything, you've changed and you've done everything that we've asked, and that's why you've got your son home and he's so happy and, and you two seem so much happier.

During these discussions with the parents, every five minutes or so Molly gave the infant some attention. This included, 19 minutes into the visit, looking at Jake and saying 'I am looking at you!' and 22 minutes in Molly expressing a desire to hold the child: 'I really want to pick you up but I'm not going to' (because Michelle had decided it was 'on the floor time'). This is an important form of intimate practice with infants that gives them voice by not actually physically holding them. It involves expressing a desire to and delighting in their presence, while connecting with their gaze and using the interaction to be explicit about empowering the parents. The social worker did this in the knowledge that she had picked the infant up and held him on a recent visit. Molly then told the parents there would be an unannounced visit by a social work colleague when she is on holiday, which falls after the baby goes home full-time. This shows how the flow of authority/compassion, care/control was skilfully managed to constitute good authority. The process of Practice by Negotiation that I set out in Chapter 9 had been managed effectively and there was mutual understanding of the need for unannounced visits, the baby to be held by the social worker, and so on. This typifies how the atmospheres of encounters in such casework, even when authority was being assertively used, were often positive, caring, creative and joyful.

Relationships to the world: resonance and alienation

Jackie and Molly are representative of different poles along a continuum of relational styles that fall between closeness/intimacy and distance/avoidance. Their differences show that relational styles are not just about the 'mechanics' of 'interviewing', or the techniques of relational practice, but the energy and persona through which care is embodied and communicated. Relational styles are underpinned by people's attitudes, beliefs, gender, culture, embodied self and psycho-physical development. They concern their entire outlook on life and how they 'live' relationships, not only as professionals but personally: *how they are in the world*. Another way of expressing this is through Hartmut Rosa's (2019) concept of 'relationship to the world'. Jackie and Molly's profiles reflect to a remarkable extent the two modes of relating to the world that Rosa identifies as 'resonance' and 'alienation'. As has already been noted in the book, resonance as a concept seeks to capture an experience that occurs when people form a connection and mutually affect one another by responding to each other, while simultaneously maintaining their individual perspectives (Rosa, 2019, p 167). Rosa depicts this through the image of a vibrating wire resonating between and connecting people. Some people seek to relate to the world and live by having experiences and relationships that are infused with the dynamic energy of resonance. In this quest *responsivity* is pivotal, which in the helping professions means *responding* to, not merely *attending* to, people's needs. This responsivity can be seen for instance in Molly's comment about Jake's parents in how 'they feel safe with me and I feel safe with them'.

Rosa argues that individuals who don't live by and seek out the vibrancy of resonance are likely to have an *alienated* relationship to the world. Individuals in a state of alienation experience a lack of connection and responsiveness in their relationships, work and social interactions. The 'resonant wire' that vibrates in satisfying reciprocal relationships becomes rigid and inflexible. Rosa describes alienation as '*a relation of relationlessness*' (Rosa, 2019, p 178, original emphasis; see also Jaeggi, 2014). Social workers relating in ways that amount to relationlessness is a very apt way of describing the examples of avoidant practice given earlier in the book. Jackie's avoidant practice demonstrates this sense of alienation, where she maintained both physical and emotional distance from children and expressed discomfort with closeness. As I argued earlier with respect to Molly's practice, being in resonance creates an energy and dynamic that is self-reinforcing by inspiring more of the same kind of heartfelt connected relating. Alienation, on the other hand, involves a 'dampening' of connection, where the vibrancy of resonance is absent, leading to rigid, robotic and automated encounters where the voices of service users are not truly heard and children are not held.

For those who relate to the world in ways that seek *resonance* and there is that vibrating wire of connection and responsivity, this creates what Rosa (2019, p 178) calls '*relations of relatedness*'. Translated to child protection and social work this is where meaningful connections are forged between worker and service user; they are both being heard, touched, moved – like what occurred in Molly's relating and relationships. We have seen it elsewhere in the book too, for instance in the practice of Lynne (Chapter 1), Jim (Chapter 2), Shelly (Chapter 3), Jessica (Chapter 6) and Miriam (Chapter 8).

Molly saw her professional development as a work-in-progress and was critical of her employers and the child protection system because of how it frustrated and blocked her desire to learn and grow professionally. For instance, she valued the training they had put on a month previously on 'direct work with children', but remarked ruefully that '[i]t would be nice if after we did the training we were actually let loose around some children!'. She meant that the things they were forced to do instead were too often bureaucratic and office-bound, which, on our terms, pushed relating towards alienation and relation-less relations. In many respects the entire system produces alienated relation-less relating. However, Molly was able to experience enough satisfying relational closeness and resonance in her work (and, I suspect, beyond work) to prevent demoralisation and alienation from seeping into her soul and coming to re-define the kind of practitioner she was and her relationship to the world.

It may seem extreme to speak of some social workers as being 'repulsed' by their relationships and work, but, as I have shown with respect to Jackie, it happens. She saw herself as repulsive to children. Another typical example was Simon who struggled to think of a single family on his caseload where he is welcome, which he summed up by saying: '[I]n short, no, I'm not a particularly liked entity.' His whole attitude to social work is negative: '[W]ho wants a social worker? I wouldn't want one, even if they come cap-in-hand, saying, "We'll offer you x, y, z", I wouldn't want a social worker. It's just a stigma of having a social worker, even if they're really supportive, why would you want one?' He too talks about how children avoid him and incessantly about being hated and, like Jackie, has internalised a belief that he and his job are deeply dislikeable, repulsive even. In the observations of his practice I did, he did not get close to children.

Rosa (2019, p 180) makes powerful connections between alienation and a state of depression or burnout. Depression and burnout involve experiencing the world as flat, cold and hollow, with a loss of the ability to move towards people and things and relation-less relations result. I do not know if Jackie was burnt out, she did not complain of it, but she certainly seemed weary and quite cynical after several years of doing the work. She worked hard – she had to as her workload was high and relentless – and with integrity. I have no doubt that the alienation she and many others experienced was, in part, caused by the tough organisational systems, expectations and the broader societal blame culture surrounding social work. If this blame and shame are internalised by workers, they are at high risk of feeling as though both they and the profession are repulsive, a 'bad object'. Over the years I have seen some highly enthusiastic relationally adept workers who after many years of practice and management managed to maintain that energy and spark that Molly has. Then there are those who had it but eventually became exhausted and burnt out by the stress of the work and poor organisational resources and support (see also, Ravalier et al,

2021; McFadden et al, 2024). But there are some who seem never to have had that spark and desire for close connection and resonance. It is highly likely that their detached, non-intimate relationship to the world pre-dated their entering social work and they brought it into the profession with them.

Developing the professional self and relational styles

Recruiting and developing practitioners who are capable of resonant relational work requires educational organisations and employers to reach an understanding of their students and staff and develop their relational capacities. There needs to be an intense focus on enabling students to learn about themselves, their core self and their relational style and similar opportunities for qualified staff through ongoing continuing professional development (Dunk-West, 2018). Professionals, like every person, are positioned on a relational continuum somewhere between avoidance and intimacy; or, between 'not touchy-feely' and being 'natural huggers'. This in turn is influenced by professional training and ethical practice. As Ward (2018, pp 61–66) shows, we all have a 'core self' that is shaped by our upbringing, family, friendships, social, political, spiritual, and cultural associations and beliefs. This core self interacts with an individual's professional training and the organisational culture they work in to form a 'professional self'. Every student, practitioner and manager needs to locate themselves on the relational continuum and identify their relational style and how it is constituted.

This can be done by them reflecting on a number of areas of their lives, relationships and questions. Box 1 covers the kinds of questions that need to be asked by individuals to deepen understanding of the kind of person they are, their core self. These questions can also be asked of them by educators, trainers, coaches and supervisors.

Box 1 Exploring your core self and acquiring a relational vocabulary

- What sort of person am I in my personal relationships?
- Where have my attitudes towards and behaviours in relationships come from, how were they formed?
- Am I naturally shy and introverted, or confident and extroverted?
- Is my attitude to life pessimistic or optimistic?
- What has been my experience of closeness and affection in relationships?
- To what extent has touch and physical closeness been part of my life and experience?
- How comfortable am I with giving and receiving hugs or other physical closeness?
- What influence does my gender, race, ethnicity, body, abilities, sexuality, faith have on how I relate to others and what I feel able and unable to do?
- What influence has any trauma I have experienced had on how I relate to others?
- What has my experience been of power and authority figures and how might this affect my feelings about and use of authority?

Box 2 contains questions that can be used in similar ways to explore how this core self intersects with work roles to constitute their professional self and its implications for the various aspects of relational work that need to be done, with adults, babies and children. Relational styles and their strengths can be appreciated, and the types of experiences and skills that need further development can then be identified.

Box 2 Exploring your professional self

- How do I feel about getting emotionally and physically close to service users?
- How do I feel about using touch to relate to children, such as picking them up and holding them?
- How do I feel about children touching me, hugging or climbing on me?
- How willing am I to play with children and get down onto the floor beside them to do so?
- What experience do I have of holding and interacting with babies?
- What experience do I have of young children and playing with them?
- What experience do I have of older children and relating with teenagers?
- How does my life experience affect how I am prepared to work with service users? For instance, does it make me less likely to want to work with men or women, lack confidence with or feel well prepared for working with children of particular ages?

As well as posing such questions in teaching and training sessions, I have also found it useful to provide vignettes of practitioners in situations where, for instance, on a home visit the young children they are concerned about are climbing on them. I then ask the participants how they would feel about this and what they would do? Elsewhere in that sitting room there is a baby in a cot and they have to think about what they would do to ensure it is safe and well. Such self-exploration is not a once and for all event, but a process that goes on over time, like the duration of a professional qualification course and beyond that throughout a career. The early stages of a career are often especially fertile for learning. Devaney et al's (2017) research suggests there is a 'beginner dip' after social work qualification, as new practitioners learn to integrate both technical and practical knowledge in the real world of practice. But it is never too late. I have found that similar exercises can work well in training sessions with experienced practitioners. It is useful for entire teams and organisations to think together about these questions and the kinds of relating their team and organisational culture produces, whether it nourishes resonance or stifles it.

Charisma and the kind of energetic presence and warmth that communicates the desire and willingness to relate with heart and soul are inherent qualities. But social work is a role and social workers perform it and there is always scope to help them play their part better. Research on the effectiveness of teaching communication skills and empathy in social work education demonstrates that these abilities can be successfully learned and developed, both in the classroom and during practice placements (Trevithick et al, 2004; Luckock et al, 2006; Reith-Hall and Montgomery, 2022). Professionals need to be supported to develop learning about how to interact with children by using their voice, tone and their body to move, play, be still and emotionally attune, and inspire a child's belief in the worker's capacity to be helpful and make a difference (Steggall and Scollen, 2024). They need to know when and how to slip into the role required: showing excitement about a child's drawing, their photographs; getting down on the floor to play; demonstrating understanding of a parent's pain, trauma, loss and sadness; assessing how close to children and tactile they need to be to come to understand and meet the child's needs in this moment. This is empathy and the professional self in action in how it is related to but distinct from their personal core self. As Donald Winnicott observed about the core conditions of psychoanalysis, 'the analyst is much more reliable than people are in ordinary life; on the whole punctual, free from temper tantrums, free from compulsive falling in love, etc' (Abram, 1996, p 168).

The aim should be for each educator, student, manager and practitioner to acquire a relational vocabulary which helps them to come to know their core self. This provides a foundation for critical reflection on the implications of their core self for relational practice and what needs to happen in the moment of interactions to overcome being too distant or close by activating the professional self. Those at or towards the detached end of the relational continuum need to move their professional self towards the intimate end and enact the movement, play, touch and emotional and energetic presence that is required to best meet the needs of this particular child and family. This is what Jessica, for example, did with Anton in Chapter 6 when he was lying beside her and she sensed his trauma and neediness, stroked his face and told him he was beautiful. Those who identify as having an inherently intimate relationship to the world, who seek relational connection ('natural huggers') also have work to do on themselves. They need to learn to carefully risk-assess when it is or is not appropriate to cuddle and use touch and how appropriate boundaries and closeness can be practised. When needed, their professional self needs to be moved in the direction of the detached end of the continuum to a position that meets children's needs through other ways of showing intimacy through non-physical touch. Suzanne Triggs (2024) shows how career coaching is another highly useful form of support. It works by helping social workers develop a professional identity that is flexible and that fits in enriching ways with their values, self and social work persona.

Managers at all levels of the organisation need to pay attention to workers' relational styles and particularly perhaps those that are avoidant. They need to ask themselves what role they and the organisation may be playing in producing workers who have such an alienated relationship to practice and the profession. Teams and organisations are helped by a clear vision of what constitutes good relational practice and how it will be facilitated across the organisation. For instance, James, an experienced social worker, describes himself as 'I'm not a huggy person' and is able to talk about how he tries to get close to service users.

His passion is for working with teenagers and his creative approaches include going for walks, outdoor play in parks, indoors in bowling alleys and connecting in the car. Little wonder that he tended to get the ('most challenging') teenagers on his team while the younger children went to workers who were more drawn to work with them and relationally disposed to do so in intimate ways.

This shows another big gain of relational styles being explicitly known to team members: managers can play to workers' strengths and support them to develop skills and confidence in other areas. For instance, workers and managers with avoidant/alienated relational styles are prone to accommodate comfortably, even enthusiastically, to prescriptive bureaucratic systems that require a lot of time at the computer and to allow these greedy systems to keep them in the office. By knowing about relational styles managers can be much more equipped to try and ensure relational work is not being avoided. Intimate practitioners and managers can have deep systemic impact in how they and their colleagues benefit from a virtuous cycle where the pleasure of knowing they have made a difference through the quality of their relating feeds into their own and the organisation's positive self-image and confidence. Resonance can then form the foundation upon which teams and entire organisations are built, where colleagues align emotionally and relationally and create an environment where mutual understanding, connection and shared therapeutic purpose thrive.

Conclusion

While organisational and systemic factors influence how practitioners relate to children and families, this chapter has argued that individual characteristics matter and that it is important to identify particular relational styles and how they shape different types of relationships and patterns of practice.

Key learning points

- Practitioners have identifiable relational styles and these influence how they interact with children and parents, how distant, or close and intimate they get. This in turn is influenced by the systems and organisational culture they work in and opportunities they get in supervision and training to reflect on how they use their self, their bodies as well as their minds.

- There is a distinction between the 'core self' and the 'professional self'. The core self is the physical and emotional tendencies, perspectives and ways of relating to people and the world that individuals bring with them into their profession. While it significantly influences the ways in which people relate and practise, relational styles are not solely individual attributes. They are shaped by a complex interplay of systemic and organisational factors, professional training and individual experiences that produce a 'professional self', which evolves and develops over time and learns from experience (Ward, 2018, p 64).

- Relational styles are not just about the techniques of relational practice, such as interviewing, but the energy and persona through which care is embodied and communicated. A key goal is to achieve resonance in relationships with service users, which means investing practice with skill, aliveness, positive energy and both the worker and the service user feeling heard, touched (emotionally and sometimes physically) and changed by the interaction and relationship. This contrasts with 'alienation', which is characterised by workers' feelings of indifference or even repulsion towards their work, profession and service users. This can be linked to exhaustion and burnout and can also have its origins in a person's core self and how they relate to the world. Resonant relationships are energising and provide more effective and meaningful support.

- Professional education and post-qualifying training need to use the kinds of exploratory questions I listed in the chapter (see Box 1 and Box 2) to enable practitioners to acquire a relational vocabulary, learn about where they are on the relational continuum and develop their relational style.

- The professional self needs to be adaptable and capable of moving along the relational continuum to meet the diverse needs of service users in ethical and effective ways. This involves practitioners with avoidant tendencies consciously moving towards more intimate engagement and those who are naturally intimate learning to set appropriate boundaries. Managers have a vital role in noticing and understanding the relational styles within their teams and supporting staff development.

- By embracing these learning points, social work education, training and organisational practices can better equip practitioners to identify and develop their professional selves and engage in practice and relationships that are intimate and authoritative and that ultimately enhance the safety and well-being of children and families.

Achieving such effective relationship-based practice also requires also requires careful consideration of the contexts in which the work goes on. The next chapter turns our attention to the impact of various physical and non-physical spaces and how these can be used creatively in making child protection work.

11

Crafting relational spaces: digital, outdoor and mobile practices

The book has already made very clear that the home is the key site where efforts to protect children from harm within the family and provide support are made. This is why so many chapters have featured casework encounters that occurred inside the home and why journeys to and from the home are so prominent within the Practice Cycle. This should not be taken to mean that other places where children are seen – schools, clinics, hospitals, social work offices, cafes, cars – lack importance. It simply reflects the powerful meanings the home has and the dominant 'frame' through which child protection is thought about and done (Tylim and Harris, 2018).

The book has also shown how the home is a highly contested space in how parents and professionals often struggle over right of entry, whether bedrooms and other rooms can be seen, where to sit, stand or crouch (painfully) and how long to stay. These struggles in such confined and highly constricted domestic spaces can have many adverse effects, not least in rendering children invisible. Also deeply problematic is regarding women and mothers as 'homemakers' and natural providers of care and punishing them when they are judged to be not measuring up, while fathers are ignored (Young, 2005).

This chapter aims to build on these insights by enabling greater awareness of spatial dynamics, movement and power within the home and the potential value of seeing service users in places beyond it, at least some of the time. A key question emerges: what are the best physical and non-physical environments that allow practitioners to understand the experiences of parents, other caretakers and children and foster effective relational practice? As I have argued throughout, movement and being able to give full 'embodied attention' (Bloom, 2006, p 14) to service users and communicate energetically in encounters is fundamental to good enough practice. This chapter considers the central importance of mobility, improvisation and creativity in social care practice by focusing initially on the home and then on two very different examples: the use of the digital and outdoor practices. It asks, can child protection get out more? And what happens when families and workers venture beyond living rooms and bedrooms and have more room to breathe?

The home as a space for improvisation and mobile practice

All 'helping' work is carried out within a 'frame' (Tylim and Harris, 2018). In psychotherapy the frame is the 50-minute session in the therapist's office, held at regular intervals, and there is no contact outside of or between sessions. GPs are seen in their surgery, in the UK typically for 10–15-minute consultations. As the book has shown, in social care work with children and families the frame consists of social work home visits, carried out on a weekly, fortnightly or monthly basis, depending upon the level of concern. More frequent visiting, some of it unannounced to check up on families, or spontaneous visits to respond to crises, are also part of the frame. As I have shown in detail elsewhere (Ferguson, 2004; 2011) this dominant way of working was put in place in the early 20th century and while huge technological and organisational changes have occurred, the basic frame has barely changed since then. Little wonder then that social workers typically construct the home and specific rooms like bedrooms as vital spaces in which to do child protection work and see children (see also Jeyasingham, 2014). The creation of the modern home in the 20th century went hand-in-hand with a hardening of ideals of motherhood that saw women as carers and homemakers and fathers as providers bringing in the 'family wage', for whom the home was a place of rest and recuperation. As Iris Marion Young puts it in her classic essay 'House and home':

> [T]he comforts and supports of house and home historically come at women's expense. Women serve, nurture and maintain so that the bodies and souls of men and children gain confidence and expansive subjectivity to make their mark on the world. This homey role deprives women of support for their own identity and projects. (Young, 2005, p 123)

Young was taken into care as a child because her lone-parent mother didn't clean the home, but she did provide love and emotional care. Young regarded this response at the time as punitive and unnecessary and felt the same way decades later (Young, 2005, pp 133–136).

The 'frame' that sets the ethical and practical boundaries within which therapeutic relationships can occur need not be rigid and fixed; it can be an animated structure which changes and adapts over time (Goldberg, 2018, p 99). A significant challenge to the traditional child protection frame has come from increased recognition of extra-familial child abuse and the need for 'contextual safeguarding'. Scholars of child sexual exploitation convincingly argue that there has been an over-emphasis on the home as the key site of harm and where child protection work should go on (Pearce, 2014; Beckett and Pearce, 2018; Thomas and Darcy, 2017; Firmin, 2020). The frame needs to incorporate key contexts beyond the home where young people spend a lot of their lives and sexual and criminal exploitation happen. This spatial shift could not be clearer than in the title of Firmin, Lefevre, Huegler and Peace's (2022) book, *Safeguarding Young People Beyond the Family Home: Responding to Extra-Familial Risks and Harms*. Social work scholars who argue for a social model of child protection also suggest that it needs to be tied much more into wider family and community life (Featherstone et al, 2018).

In child protection work that concerns complex need, risk, harm, abuse and neglect of young as well as older children by parents or other relatives within the family, social workers regard the family home as centre-stage in part because they are directed to by policy. As we saw in Chapter 1, it is typical for the 'statutory visit' they have to make to see children at least once a month only to be legitimate if they are seen on a home visit and the bedrooms checked. The home is regarded as centre stage because it is where most parenting of pre-school and younger school aged children goes on and where workers can observe relationships, standards of care and relationships and the condition of the home itself. There is nothing in principle stopping children being seen elsewhere – and some are, especially in schools. But as has been shown in earlier chapters, time pressures and bureaucratic preoccupation can result in pragmatic decisions to restrict practice to seeing children and parents only in the home.

As a result, navigating home visits requires highly skilled embodied performances. Movement is – or should be – central to good child protection work, including within domestic space (Ferguson, 2016c). I have observed many home visits where social workers did not sit down at all but stood and moved throughout. In Chapter 6, for example, we saw how in crafting intimate practice Jessica spent the first 29 minutes of the visit on her feet. She moved in other ways by getting onto the floor to relate to the children on their level and connected in embodied ways through play and touch. And she had some shorter periods of sitting down engaging in 'interviewing'. Situations where practitioners managed to overcome potential blocks to being with children were characterised by carefully executed and timed movement. On a home visit to a family who disliked and didn't want social work involvement, a key aim of the social worker was to see 10-year-old Kevin on his own:

> Some 10 minutes into the visit all the children began moving around the room and flowing in and out of adjacent rooms and after 45 minutes they were once again in the sitting room where the social worker was with the parents, except for Kevin. Realising that Kevin was next door in the dining room on his own the social worker got up from the sofa and joined him. On entering the dining room the social worker closed the door and immediately got down on to the floor beside Kevin. She engaged him about the activity (drawing) that he was involved in and he spoke fluently. She spent seven minutes alone with him, gave him a smiley-face sticker at the end, and initiated a high five with him.

While the period spent with Kevin was short, given the parents' and the boy's initial reluctance, afterwards the social worker was pleased that she got to see him alone at all and tentative steps towards building a relationship had begun.

This encounter with the child was not only due to the social worker's communication skills, but just as importantly her embodied attentiveness, agility and purposefulness. She was alert, saw an opportunity and moved at speed to prevent a situation where Kevin could have come back into the sitting room. Had she not gone into the room next door, she could have been effectively blocked from seeing him on his own. It can be argued therefore that an enemy of making child protection work is *being still*. The act of moving the body has the effect of activating the practitioner's thinking and sense of purpose and keeps them mentally, emotionally and intuitively engaged. Movement seems to enhance our capacity for alertness. By contrast, the more rigidly stationary the practitioner is, the greater the risk of them becoming immobilised and *stuck*. This can mean physically stuck in the sense of a restricted capacity for movement, a kind of paralysis caused by fear, anxiety and tension. We saw in Chapter 9 how the service user Roberta set the home up in a way that meant that practitioners found themselves repeatedly standing or crouching awkwardly on home visits. Such embodied dynamics contribute to workers becoming stuck in their thinking, which becomes disorganised, and their engagement with children risks becoming fitful or even completely avoidant. This shows how important it is for workers to be seated, comfortable and still in ways that maximise their capacity to be fully attentive and present to the children and parents. Yet at the same time, practitioners are better able to practice with alertness and creatively when they enter encounters with an *intention to move*. Or, more precisely, when there is an alertness and readiness to move when circumstances and the need for improvisation call for it.

Moving can be problematic too. Practitioners can move too much, or too soon and at too fast a pace. Moving quickly within the home can be a form of avoidance and defence against overwhelming anxiety, a way of *not* soaking up the atmosphere, *not* attuning to the child's world and feelings, a way of paving a route to a speedier exit. As Chapter 4 showed, that is what occurs in the automated pattern of practice. Striking the right balance between movement and stillness and the timing of them both is a core skill and component of making child protection work.

Screen relations: digital spaces

I now want to consider a very different form of relating that goes on in virtual space, through the screen. New relational opportunities (and dangers) have emerged with the ever-increasing impact of the internet, digitalisation and artificial intelligence. It has become possible through 'digital casework' practice to supplement and even bypass completely physical presence with service users and the home by using video calling. Media scholars have argued that achieving experiences of closeness through the screen is possible and refer to this as 'digital intimacy' (Andreassen et al, 2018). The emergence of smartphone and mobile technology since the 2010s has created a culture where we are 'always on' the internet and social media and just one click away from being in contact (Cellan-Jones, 2021). Simpson found that digital communication methods were valued by some service users and especially by 16- to 19-year-olds, because they align with their day-to-day use of phone, email, text and personal messaging via social networking sites (Simpson, 2017, p 92). Yet prior to 2020 and the COVID-19 pandemic, digital communications were peripheral to practice.

In all the observations I carried out in the 2010s covering different parts of the country, I never saw or heard of casework being done via video calling, even though some such technologies were available. Face-to-face, in-person interaction with children and families, usually on home visits, was the deeply embedded 'frame', the taken-for-granted way the work was done.

The COVID-19 pandemic and the requirement for social distancing disrupted that way of doing child protection work profoundly. From its beginnings in early 2020, risks of infection from the potentially deadly COVID-19 resulted in 'lockdowns' of the population in their homes, forbidding visitors from entering and imposing two-metre 'social distancing' which effectively banned touch between people not sharing a household. Children on Child Protection Plans and in complex need were visited at home in-person – inside the house, on the doorstep or in the garden – while children considered at lower risk could be seen virtually. Social workers began to see many families by making 'virtual home visits' using video-calling technology (Cook and Zschomler, 2020). Multi-agency meetings, like case conferences, were offered by telephone or video conferencing and in many areas this continued after the pandemic. Court proceedings took place remotely, and there were serious concerns about the limitations this placed on the meaningful involvement of parents and other family in decision-making and legal processes (Baginsky and Manthorpe, 2021; Ryan et al, 2020; Harker and Ryan, 2022). The aim here is not to analyse the impact of the pandemic on child protection work in detail, which has been done elsewhere (Ferguson et al, 2022a; 2022b), but to use aspects of what occurred during it to think about improvisation and the role of digital communications in the future. This sudden and dramatic disruption meant that more than ever social workers and families were required to improvise and draw on their skills, intuition and courage to craft relationships (Ingold and Hallam, 2007; Sennett, 2008).

The purest use of digital technology occurred in cases where the children and family were never seen in person and were only encountered through the screen. The Gonzales family were having 'relationship difficulties', due to having a new baby during the first COVID-19 lockdown (in 2020) and not being able to go out. Mrs Gonzales had mental health problems and they were a migrant family, which contributed to them having limited support networks. Over the two months it was open the social work was all done by messaging and video calls. The social worker explained:

> So this is the baby that I was talking to over video, and I found myself getting really, really close to the screen so my face was really big and making really over-the-top gestures to which the baby really responded and was smiling and babbling away yesterday, and the parents were supportive of that: they held the phone up really close to the baby so the baby could see me. And I think in terms of how I am working with the parents, it wouldn't be any different other than I would be in the room with them, rather than on the end of the phone. But I think [that] with the baby it is all about that facial

expression and the eye contact and the close-up and the, you know, gaining their attention by stroking their hand or tickling their cheek, and I would be more inclined to do that in a home visit and that is the real difference, maybe engage them with a toy.

The social worker is aware of how social distancing was removing the option of tactile contact and play – although she consistently stated that even had she been able to do in-person home visits she was unlikely to have physically interacted with the child. This was because her relational style was non-tactile: 'I am not a huge physical contact person anyway.' She was pleased with the level of 'digital intimacy' she felt she was able to achieve with the baby and the parents through the screen. But she worried about experiencing video calls as more perfunctory and instrumental than in-person relating and was concerned about how not being there physically resulted in a loss of sensory cues.

This casework was also a good example of how digital communication in an 'always on' culture took the service user–professional relationship into a new rhythm of much more regular contact than the traditional norm of the fortnightly or monthly in-person home visit. Some social workers and families were in touch as often as every day, through WhatsApp messaging, texting, video diaries and voice calls. This is what Kong et al (2022, p 2848) refer to as the 'little and often' approach that emerged at this time. This new rhythm is also evident in another form of improvised casework, the hybrid approach, that involves both digital communications and in-person presence (Jeyasingham and Devlin, 2024).

A compelling example was carried out by a social worker, Sandra, with the 'Williams' family. They were White British and three children had been removed from them in the past and Mrs Williams was pregnant again. When lockdown began in March 2020, Sandra had known them for five months, during which she completed a pre-birth assessment. Her view was that their mental health was much improved, they have a good support network and have 'detached from any contact with their family and that was the risky ... bit, their families'. The baby was born at the start of lockdown, and over the subsequent three months Sandra spoke to the parents daily, either on the phone or by WhatsApp video call. She also visited them in person inside the home regularly, including making some weekend visits, wearing personal protective equipment – an apron, gloves and mask. 'I still maintain my distance, when I am in the flat ... but I do come quite close, close-ish to the baby.' When, for instance, the baby was having her nappy changed, Sandra would get 'alongside, it is quite sort of handy to be able to get eyes on completely, but I haven't held her myself'. Two months into lockdown (May 2020), the social worker told me:

> I think it is a good relationship. ... They will you know sort of contact me a lot. ... Shortly after the birth ... they were sending me daily photographs, daily updates [via WhatsApp] ... if they had been unsure they have felt that they could contact me. ... The other weekend ... I think it was about twenty to ten at night [a text] said,

'Oh can you, are you free to call us?' And they just needed a little bit of reassurance and you know some discussion and the baby was absolutely fine ... they just needed a little bit you know to build that confidence and just get a second opinion because they couldn't get hold of anyone on their support network so they are certainly sort of reaching out and working really well with us. And ... the baby is really thriving, she has got a really good bond with both of them. ... If it was normal times I would certainly have had a cuddle by now and sort of been trying to engage with her, get her to look at me and focus on me and see if I could get her to sort of follow my facial expressions or things like that, you know. She does know my voice now though you know, both Mum and Dad have said that when I ring on WhatsApp she definitely recognises my voice, which is nice. ... I would be a bit more hands-on, put it that way, I am not very hands-on at present, and it is very difficult when I am a sort of a natural hugger.

As a 'natural hugger', the worker's relational style is to get close and tactile but social distancing stopped her from cuddling, holding and touching the baby in the way she normally would. Yet the social worker's narrative suggests she did achieve emotional and energetic closeness and established a meaningful relationship with the baby and parents. This was achieved through the use of a hybrid approach combining audio telephone calls, video calls with the family, the use of photos and video films (via WhatsApp) and in-person encounters. While the worker could not hold the baby physically and always felt this absence keenly, through her virtual and in-person presence, her kindness, reliability and skilful uses of non-physical touch, she held her and her parents 'in mind'. This generated a trusting relationship that promoted the parents' self-esteem, developed their caregiving skills and sense of self-efficacy and contributed to some possible resolution of past traumas (Ruch et al, 2018; Ferguson et al, 2020b). A form of 'digital holding' was achieved (Ferguson et al, 2022b; see also Osei-Buapim, 2021).

On-screen relating and the achievement of 'digital intimacy' (Pink et al, 2022) played a role in this. The parents were very positive about the 'really supportive' help they had received and were glad to bring social workers into their world through voluntarily sharing digital content, such as still photos and films of the baby doing things. The family continued to make excellent progress and by the end of the research fieldwork in December 2020, the baby, now eight months old, had come off the Child Protection Plan. Despite and because of all the potential alienating effects of organisational procedures, record-keeping, face masks and social distancing rules, what the social worker and family managed to achieve together were creative, reciprocal interactions that were transformative because they contained *resonance*: listening, empathy, responsivity, the development of parental self-efficacy and an openness to being changed (Rosa, 2019).

Hybrid relating was also used in some situations where families did not want social work involvement but their attempts to stop it were overridden due to the assessed level of risk. A parent who did not want social work involvement but whose caring routine with her children, aged five and seven, who had special health needs was under scrutiny, told the research she welcomed the opportunity to use a video diary to show social workers how she was parenting. It was a way of trying to exercise some control and keep the state at a distance. But where social workers felt that such distancing went too far and physical as well as digital intimacy were needed, they stepped up the frequency of physical home visiting to see the children in person. For some families, then, video calling and messaging are forms of unwelcome digitised surveillance to add to the in-person regulation of their lives.

Beyond the home: walking interviews and out and about practice

Mobile and outdoor working are not entirely new, as social workers have, for instance, long provided families with lifts to appointments, helped with shopping, played in parks and taken young people on car journeys (Ferguson, 2011). However, the use of outdoor practices has increased since the COVID-19 pandemic, which led practitioners to find other creative ways of connecting with children and families that limited the numbers of visits into the interior of homes. Seeing families on the doorstep and in their garden was a key improvisation. Workers went on more walks with young people and sometimes parents and used parks and other open spaces near family homes to walk, play or just be together in. Practising what one worker called 'out and about social work' and using this wider range of environments opens up new spaces and opportunities for resonant connection, discussion and getting to know children, parents and families.

A social worker and co-worker arranged a 'walking visit' with a family they had been intensively supporting via telephone and video call during the COVID-19 lockdown. They walked alongside and spoke to this mother and did the same separately with her two teenage children in a 'woody foresty area' near to the family home:

> We found that with the young people ... they felt more relaxed in that open space rather than sitting in a home and sitting in a living room and you're talking face-to-face with them. I think they felt more relaxed ... didn't feel so oppressed being in the home and the tensions that were in the home. They felt more relaxed being in that open space and they were able to share a lot more.

Social workers explained how walking in open, relatively empty spaces helped young people feel safe enough to make intimate disclosures and reveal risks and harms they previously did not talk about. One social worker took weekly 'quite long' walks in a beautiful park with a child who was experiencing considerable distress after being sexually assaulted. The mental health team were not offering face-to-face visits and the young person was not receptive to video support. The broader range of choices of location and embodied experience of movement through a park directly contributed to the emotional openness, depth and resonance of the encounters:

> We're concerned around CSE [child sexual exploitation] with this young person, and she is part of a group [where many] have had social workers and she was very much referring to her friend saying, 'You know I have told her, this is nothing like what she said having a social worker was like. … She always said it was awkward, you know, she was in a room in school or she was at home … and actually I have found this really easy … and I found talking to you really easy.' We were talking about the differences and she said she felt that being out in the community, being away from school and home gave her the privacy that she wanted to talk, whilst not feeling locked away, not feeling like, you know, when you're in a room, there is only one door, there is one entrance, one exit. She kind of felt more free in herself to be able, you know, she was very much choosing to walk beside me, choosing to sit on the grass whereas she wasn't in a room with a shut door, so I think there is something about what that symbolises for her.

The social worker also found that walking with the child's mother was productive, allowing her to disclose her partner's coercive and controlling behaviour, which meant additional support could be put in place. The father was no longer involved with the family.

Walking alongside children and other family members offers a form of 'side-by-side' communication that is highly productive, mirroring encounters in cars where service users often disclose more when on the move and not being sat directly 'face-to-face' with professionals (Ferguson, 2010). Social workers noticed these similarities: 'Sometimes when you're not just sitting and directly asking kids questions you get so much more. It is a bit like being in the car with children isn't it, when you're not looking at them directly.' Like in cars, there is often more privacy in open spaces like parks and forests than on home visits. As one social work manager saw it: 'Tricksy parents can be got around by getting out of the home.' The therapeutic effects of being directly in nature while walking are also significant. As one social worker expressed it:

> Similar to going for a drive, a walk is an activity in itself, an end in of itself. If you're just sat in a room, the focus is all on the chat, whereas with a walk, it's nice to get out and in itself it's a helpful tool to get them out in the fresh air and sunshine and getting them feeling better, plus you can have a chat whilst you're there … so it's less about them getting grilled, less intense.

Walking was sometimes done with an end in sight, like going to a cafe, but even then the potential value of the journey by foot was recognised in its own right. On arrival at the destination, a hot chocolate was a popular treat of choice – especially with squirty cream! This suggests that, for teenagers, walks and treats can serve both as forms of play and as sources of comfort and nurture. Sometimes the walk is the end in itself, without a clear destination, which invests it with purpose. An important variable was allowing the young person to lead the walk. A social worker took their dog on walks with teenagers, while 'still doing the old McDonald's trip to get a drink or whatever they want'. They found that 'walks can work quite well with some of our young people, being sat down with a young person can feel quite intimidating for them. We use a lot of texting or WhatsApp to talk to them and we use our phones a lot more than we used to'. Moving side-by-side, while walking and connecting by using mobile technology is less intense and intimidating, which enables deeper disclosure.

However, unlike a bedroom or other enclosed space, the 'frame' for outdoor encounters is potentially infinite and this absence of spatial boundaries can create ethical tensions and concerns about privacy and confidentiality. As one worker put it about working with a family outside their home: '[A]s soon as you turn up for one it's like Piccadilly Circus, neighbours and delivery drivers and somebody has then decided to come and wash their car right next you or something.'

An experienced male social worker gave a compelling example of the potential hazards:

> I'd much rather be outside in public than in a bedroom, which I feel is a very personal space. I believe conversation flows much better in neutral spaces. Schools aren't neutral because many children have very complicated relationships to schools. There is only one office base and it's not easy for families to get to, so I have often found myself in Starbucks or McDonald's or just wandering around the shopping centre, community working. But there are shortcomings. For example, a few weeks ago a 15-year-old started to cry and I had to try and get him to hold his serious disclosure of long-term sexual abuse until we got to the car and he disclosed. It was my fault because I asked him about his contact with his dad [who provided access to his male friend so that he could sexually abuse his son]. We were sat in the car for hours. I'd known this kid since [five months ago] and he knew I was leaving to go and work somewhere else and I wonder if that's why he told me. And I was thinking, I've got all this work to do [case recording and so on before leaving post]. And he gave me a [present] which is probably the nicest gift I've ever got. There was some guilt [because he was leaving]. Managing endings is always important but especially when they are for you and not the family, who are mid-crisis.

Afterwards, the worker arranged for tailored therapeutic support for the young person. Their leaving gift to the social worker affirmed the way he worked with him and how with walking interviews and outdoor practice there is 'less pressure when you are out and away from home which is a place of horrendous memories'. He wishes 'there were more spaces we could use for visits, where there are nice things to do, like to play pool'. How to manage privacy and ethical boundaries outdoors is an important skill that can be acquired. As another social worker expressed it: '[Y]ou pick and choose your conversations due to confidentiality, I've been in situations where I've been able to cover everything I wanted to.'

A major issue is that very often seeing children outdoors is not counted as a 'statutory visit' because the family home and children's bedrooms have not been seen. This can result in standardised, depersonalised home visits:

> I recently went to see a young girl. Straight away she said 'Does this mean that you're going to come and see me every ten days and see my bedroom?' I said no and asked 'When do you want to see me?' She was gobsmacked [by being given a choice]. It worries me how prescribed things have become. For teenagers, being able to have conversations over WhatsApp or Teams, I hope those conversations are able to continue. If their siblings or parents were running around [inside the home visit], I wouldn't get the same information out of them.

These mobile ways of outdoor working enable practitioners to be creative in how they use space and movement in ways that empower children and young people and provide the freedom to walk and talk.

Conclusion

This chapter has explored the nature and impact of relational spaces in child protection work, both within and beyond the traditional confines of the home.

Key learning points

- The home has long been, and will continue to be, the primary site of child protection work in relation to the needs and harms experienced by children and young people within the family. Effective relationship-based practice within the home is made through the creative use of movement and stillness, improvisation and skill.

- In recent years new ways of having professional–service user relationships have been digitally created (Mishna et al, 2021; Copson et al, 2022; Fiorentino, 2023). The increased use of digital technologies can never fully replace or replicate face-to-face in-person relating in social work and in high-risk child protection situations they should not seek to.

- However, a necessity for in-person presence should not be used to close off the creative possibilities of digital communications. There is no single model for fitting the digital into child protection work, but rather it comes about as each case evolves and can involve texting, messaging, video call or voice call technologies.

- Hybrid digital/in-person approaches should be a readily available element of practice. Digital casework through video calling, messaging and other online tools can foster 'digital intimacy' and combined with in-person meetings can facilitate more frequent contact by adopting a 'little and often' approach, or even a 'more and often' relationship.

- There is a powerful momentum in the system towards a total reliance on in-person encounters with children and families (Ferguson et al, 2023). This has been hastened by intense criticism of professionals because children died from abuse at a time when some digital casework was practised in order to maintain social distancing during the COVID pandemic (Child Safeguarding Practice Review Panel, 2022a). While being present with families in person is essential to relational child protection practice, a hybrid approach can still have a role.

- Training programmes are needed for practitioners and managers at all levels of the system to consider the evidence about the merits of digital and outdoor communications. These processes need to include users of services, not least because of how the smartphone has become central to how most people live and function today (Miller et al, 2022).

- The home will continue to be the default place where child protection work that concerns need and harm within families goes on. However, there needs to be much more critical awareness of its limitations and risks in how children are unlikely to speak truthfully about their experience if they fear being overheard. National and local procedures need to catch up with practice by formally allowing children being seen outdoors to count as a statutory visit and ensure it is awarded the value it clearly has in practice. Side-by-side encounters through outdoor and mobile practices, such as walking interviews, can create more relaxed and private spaces for disclosure and empower service users.

- Navigating homes and outdoor spaces necessitates a deep awareness of cultural contexts and practices. Practitioners need to recognise that families and individuals from diverse communities have unique needs, values, and beliefs about rooms, buildings and communication styles that significantly affect engagement and trust.

- Actively involving mothers, babies and older children in activities outside of the home – driving, walking, playing – is not only meaningful relational work. It symbolises their rights as social citizens and can help to prevent oppressive practice that regards the home and home-making as synonymous with women and mothering. Involving fathers in child protection work and home-making and care is crucial to promoting gender equality.

Performing child protection in these mindful, creative, mobile ways is not possible unless practitioners have a capacity to think clearly. The next chapter considers the complexity of thinking and the kinds of support and supervision practitioners and managers need if they are to achieve reflective relationship-based practice.

12

Beyond reflective practice: helping practitioners with thinking and non-thinking

At various points in the book organisational issues and the psychological and emotional complexity of child protection and their effects on practitioners and service users have been given some attention. The final two chapters of the book turn the focus in a systematic way onto the nature of the thinking, support and supervisory needs of practitioners and managers. There are many components to making child protection work and having the capacity to think is a vitally important one. Maintaining a space in the mind for critical thinking and reflection is essential to being able to understand and respond appropriately to children's needs and help families. The importance of being able to reflect in the heat of the moment when with children and families has been highlighted in several parts of the book. We saw the presence and absence of critical thinking and reflection in the chapters which showed the avoidant and intimate forms practice takes. It was central to Chapter 10 in the requirement that practitioners think about their relational style, engage the professional self and craft a response that provides children and parents with what they need in the moment.

Reflective practice is a core concept in social work and probably the most well-known theoretical perspective across the entire applied professions of teaching, health and social care. Its origins lie especially in Schon's (1983) formulation of how professionals engage in 'reflection *in* action' by thinking about their experience and what they are doing while they are doing it and afterwards using 'reflection *on* action' to think about and link their practice to knowledge (Redmond, 2006). This chapter will focus primarily on refection in action and the next and final chapter on reflection as part of making sense of practice after it has been done. In this chapter I want to rethink the nature of reflection in child protection. Observing practitioners as they travel round the Practice Cycle, interact with service users and build relationships in real time has highlighted for me the significant flaws in the current theories used to understand practitioners and their work. It is vital to have a sophisticated understanding of how the mind and thinking work and a theory of the self that is true to what happens on the ground.

The dominant narrative in much of the literature is highly rational. It suggests that all practitioners need to do is decide to take a particular course of action, then think about whether it is working or not, revise it (or not) and then carry it out. This is illustrated by the highly influential inquiry into the tragic death of eight-year-old Victoria Climbié in England, which resulted from horrendous abuse. The inquiry report concluded that preventing such deaths hinges on 'doing the simple things properly' (Laming, 2003, p 105) and that 'Doing the basic things well saves lives' (Laming, 2003, p 69). Laming is referring to tasks such as sharing concerns with other professionals, writing up case notes, reading files, engaging with the child, challenging suspected abusers and doing home visits – none of which were adequately done for Victoria (Ferguson, 2005). But as this book is showing, what appear from the outside to be apparently simple things are not simple at all. Explaining the unexplainable requires looking closely again at the too often neglected systemic and psycho-social dynamics of child protection work, which this chapter will do by focusing on states of mind, emotion and the nature of thinking.

I will argue that practitioners are able to think about some aspects of what they do while they are doing it, but there are limits to how far reflection in action is possible and even the right thing to do. The demands of face-to-face work can be so great at times that workers cannot think about or feel that complexity while they are in it. This non-thinking and repression of emotion can in fact make it possible to focus to at least some extent on service users' needs. Non-reflection arises to protect the worker from unbearable levels of anxiety and is rooted in what, drawing on psychodynamic thinking (Briggs, 2005), I will call the *defended nature of the self*. Becoming aware of these defences and the importance of being able to maintain a space in the mind for thinking is crucial to effective relational work and being able to hold children 'in mind'.

Thinking about reflection

Social worker: Um, when I'm actually in it, it's alright because you're not thinking about how you're feeling ...
Harry: The theory books say you should be reflecting.
Social worker: What, at that point?
Harry: Yeah.
Social worker: What, when you're there?
Harry: Yeah.
Social worker: Um, am I reflecting? I'm aware of everything because that bloke came in and you know her thing and now like okay she's a bit, I'm going to have to manage this, d'you know what I mean. You are obviously taking in everything and trying to respond in the correct way, d'you know what I mean, what you've got, but I'm not sure whether that's conscious reflection.

This dialogue between the social worker, Jim, and myself took place in the car when he was driving around trying to find Shanice, a mother who featured in Chapter 2. He had just been impolitely told to go away by an aggressive woman and responds to my question about reflecting in action by questioning whether it's possible to reflect 'while you're in it'. He distinguishes 'awareness' and 'taking in everything' from 'conscious reflection'. This social worker's analysis of the realities of reflecting in action is typical of what I have seen and heard in my research that led me to rethink some core ideas about reflection.

There is a vast literature on reflection and reflective practice, reviews of which point to the plethora of theoretical formulations, tools and techniques for reflection (Ixer, 1999; White et al, 2006, p 17; D'Cruz et al, 2007; Marshall, 2019; Tobin et al, 2024a). Despite its popularity there has been very little research into how, or indeed *if*, practitioners do actually reflect in practice (White et al, 2006, p 19; Tobin et al, 2024b). Schon's (1983) classic formulation of reflection in action and on action was intended to challenge the dominant perspective that professional practice is a technical-rational activity that merely involves the application of rules and expertise to problems. He argued that professionals use reflection to deal with the uncertainty that pervades their work, to shape their thinking and actions and learn from experience. This perspective is supported by many other researchers and writers on reflective practice (for instance, Taylor and White, 2000; Maclean, 2023). Sheppard argues (2007, p 129) that '[t]he reflexive practitioner shows a high degree of self-awareness, role awareness and awareness of assumptions underlying their practice'. Notions of reflection and 'use of self' are often used interchangeably or conflated as part of an agenda to promote 'emotional intelligence'. Howe (2008, p 185) writes that '[i]mplicit in the idea of emotional intelligence is a knowledge of the self, particularly the emotional self. The "use of self" is a key aspect of relationship-based practice'. Practitioners need to be able to acknowledge and understand their own emotional states if they are to be able to get in touch with the feelings of the service user and the potential for their emotions and experience to trigger emotional reactions in the worker (Howe, 2008, p 185). Training and supervision are seen as key to developing reflective practitioners. As Howe puts it: 'Reflective practice demands that you learn from experience. It requires you to be self-critical. It expects you to analyse what you *think*, *feel*, and *do*, and then learn from the analysis' (Howe, 2009, p 171; original emphasis).

From observing practitioners in my research, it became evident that self-awareness assisted them to be ethical and helpful. As the book has shown, social workers often manage to remain composed in moments when service users are angry or in distress, not retaliating and absorbing their sadness, shame, fears, and at times their joy. Such composure and containment are crucial to forming and sustaining what I have called holding relationships. We have also seen how sometimes practitioners do not manage to regulate their intense feelings and they end up retaliating and being punitive. Too often there is a simplicity to how reflective practice, the (use of) self and 'emotional intelligence' are written about which belies what occurs in practice. There are times and situations in which practitioners – like Jim – find that it is better *not* to reflect in the manner advocated in the literature. A significant factor in the failure to recognise the limits to reflection is how 'the self' has been conceptualised as a coherent unproblematic entity that the worker accesses by going into it to connect to themselves and their service users. Understood in this way, no limits are placed on the capacity of the self to absorb feeling, on the mind to think and on the depths of reflection that are possible and needed. The 'self' is regarded as an apparently limitless resource that the worker taps into and uses to reflect on themselves, their encounters and help service users. Similar assumptions are made about the limitless capacity of managers and supervisors to meet the emotional needs of their staff.

As I showed in Chapter 10, a core 'self' can be said to exist in the sense of a personality and identity that each individual has, albeit one that is not fixed but open to change. Ward (2018) suggests that what effective practitioners have developed (perhaps intuitively) is a personal quality which overlaps with professional skill to create an effective persona. Each person has what in Chapter 10 I referred to as a relational style that they express through the use of their 'professional self'. However, while every person has a unique persona, the 'self' that is being used by social workers is not a unified, coherent entity with a limitless capacity to be reflected upon in the manner suggested by the literature. As I have argued throughout the book, it is a self that is fractured and that splits, a *defended* self that is principally concerned with protecting itself from unbearable levels of anxiety (Hollway and Jefferson, 2000). This notion of the 'defended subject' or self (Briggs, 2005, p 23) is based on the theory that from birth the self is primarily constituted through its relationship to anxiety. Earlier chapters have shown how one manifestation of this is the ways in which unbearable ('bad') feelings are split off and projected into others, such as a past social worker, while the family's current social worker may be idealised and become a 'good' object in the minds of service users (Hollway and Jefferson, 2000, p 19). Professionals are prone to do the same kinds of psychological splitting of families into good and bad.

Reflection is too broad a term to fully capture the complexities of what occurs in practice. I argue that the internal work practitioners do on themselves is better understood as what Casement (1985) calls 'internal supervision'. This is a process that involves internal dialogue and a kind of holding of the self. Casement highlights that supervision plays a critical role in enabling practitioners to develop the capacity to reflect, self-analyse and contain themselves when working with service users. Through supervision, practitioners learn to observe both themselves and the service user, reflecting on what it might feel like to be them in their relationship with the professional. The worker silently thinks about and rehearses possible comments, interpretations and ways of posing questions.

With practice, Casement argues, practitioners can hold two perspectives simultaneously – that of the service user and their own. Internal supervision enables the practitioner to move between thinking about their own experience and that of the client (Casement, 1985, pp 34–35). As Ward (2018, p 71) puts it, the worker learns how in some respects to supervise themself. In some respects what Casement is referring to is similar to reflection in action and indeed Smith (2010, p 114) regards it and internal supervision as broadly the same thing.

In my view, Casement's concept goes further by detailing the internal work practitioners must undertake, including self-analysis and self-holding, and by emphasising the vital role of supervision and organisational support in developing these capacities. This especially applies to very challenging situations and how not only thinking but *non-thinking* occur in practice. Not being able to think happens because when anxiously defending the self, professionals are unable to think about the service user in a meaningful, potentially helpful way, and invisible, unheld children may result.

Reflective practice, in practice

Social workers generally find it challenging to explain what they were doing and feeling in the midst of doing it, in part because they are not practised at doing so. Straight after observing practice encounters I asked social workers questions such as: 'Were you reflecting in there on what was going on at the time?' The following is typical of the way many reflected out loud on the question while trying to answer it:

> Well, different bits. Obviously, depending on what she was saying, I was sort of, I would be thinking would affect I suppose the course of where I was going. So, I was obviously needing to, to absorb what she was saying and to reflect on it to some extent. I don't know. It's a good question about how much you do that at the time. And I think, I think there's a couple of things – I've forgotten what it was now – where I think, I certainly got that sense of her being a bit of a rebel; and the family have sort of said that. That was quite a quick sort of thing really. I hadn't sort of spent ages sort of thinking about it; it just occurred to me. It just popped into my head, I suppose. Whether that is what you mean I don't know?

The worker, Leon, describes how by reflecting on the spot he thinks about and to an extent revises his understanding of the service user and their needs. A great deal of what professionals do depends on what Schon (1983, p 49) calls 'tacit knowing-in-action' which involves 'knowing more than we can say' and they struggle to find the language to describe what they do. A lot of practice is performed intuitively and draws on personal and professional knowledge and experience built up over a lifetime. Knowledge of how to practice is not based on simply applying theory and technical rules and expertise to a problem but, as Schon (1983, p 49) puts it, 'our knowing is *in* our action' (emphasis added). All kinds of learning occurs in the process of enacting professional work. Understanding derives not only from what is going on in the mind but what is occurring in the body and through movement as well as stillness (Ingold, 2011, p 17). This was evident in instances I have seen where conversations with parents were difficult and workers sometimes suddenly jumped to their feet and started looking around family homes. Such improvisation sometimes occurs through the worker consciously reflecting in action, while at times it is largely instinctive and is based on tacit knowledge rather than conscious planning. This means that what practitioners are able to say about reflection and how they process what they do covers only some of the richness of their performances.

Social workers identify different levels to reflection, the most common formulation being a distinction between what is reflected upon in the moment of conducting practice – in action – and afterwards. As Amy expresses it:

> [T]he reflecting side of things I find quite important and I do quite a lot of that, almost to the point a bit, where it's like, you know, you're going to have to let it go [*laughs*]. And like you can't, you can over-analyse or worry about, you know, there's always things that you could have said differently, or missed out, or, you know, but you can't. … But no, I think I definitely do, you do do it during the visit as well, because there are times, you know, where something, and it might just sort of niggle there at the back of your head then, like a little comment or something that you don't feel you made quite clear. But then there's other stuff that they may be talking about by then that you need to talk about, and it is sort of reflecting in that sense, thinking: I'm not quite sure I said that right.

Similarly, Monica described the process of reflection and its various 'layers' as: 'It's like you're having this conversation, and yet somewhere, you're helicoptering above your conversation.' She continued:

> And it's kind of like yeah that's what we're doing as well, because it's not just reflecting afterwards, you're reflecting whilst you're, it's reflexive, I guess, you know. That you are, you know, you might feel that a certain sentence or a certain, I don't know, avenue is not going where you want it to go, so you'll, you know, rejig and so yeah, you know, there's different levels of it, aren't there. It is happening whilst you're there, in that moment, but it's also, there's another layer that continues when you've left, you know, the immediate, and then perhaps another layer, you know, when you're sat at home at night on the sofa and something comes back to you, you know.

This articulates the classic formulation of reflecting in action as a form of cognitive self-monitoring which is achieved by elevating one's mind – 'helicoptering' – above the interaction with the service user. Eraut refers to this as 'meta-cognition': 'a person's ability to be aware of what they are doing or have just done' (Eraut, 2008, p 122). This enables the worker to think about her assumptions, questioning style, actions, how the service user is responding, and the meaning and value of the encounter. Monica also vividly describes how reflection *on* action goes on after the encounter in the office, supervision and at home at night.

This social worker, Monica, was interviewed having just been observed on a home visit at which another layer of reflection – *critical reflection* – was apparent. This refers to the use of the intellect and reflective abilities to address imbalances of power between workers and service users arising from social class, gender, race, sexualities and ability (Fook and Gardner, 2007). A mother, Maggie, had complained to the police for the fourth time about her boyfriend assaulting her. The 42-minute home visit was based in the sitting room, with Maggie sat on the sofa with her 12-month-old son, Robbie, on her knee. Maggie said she is now determined to get away from her violent partner. The police had apprehended him but let him go and he has been taunting her since. Monica showed great empathy towards Maggie, assured her she was doing the right thing contacting the police and supported her analysis of men's violence and the poor response of the system to abused women:

Social worker:	Yeah, I can understand that that must feel …
Mother [*interrupting*]:	I reckon it's disgusting, to be honest.
Social worker:	Really frustrating.
Mother:	Yeah, and it's really pissed me off. Because he's had a bad past before, and the thing is, he's very clever, like I know what he was doing, he's so clever he can really turn people and make you, but I'm just really annoyed how he's, 'I've not done anything'.
Social worker:	Yeah, I think you've done exactly the right thing.

The worker practised in a critically reflective way by drawing implicitly on a feminist perspective to place abusive men's behaviour in the context of the social power and sense of entitlement men have within the patriarchy and the propensity of the criminal justice system to respond poorly to the safety needs of abused women. This is not to say that all social workers always reflect critically in this manner. What this example shows is aspects of what critical reflection involves when it does occur.

Suspended self-preservation: the limits to reflection

The foregoing discussion bears out what the literature says about reflective practice involving different levels to reflection. However, the current popular notion of reflection in action is too simplistic to capture the complexity of how social workers think, or don't. This is typified by Jenny's account:

> But you're in it; you can't do anything about it once you're in it. You kind of don't think too much about panicking and flapping, because you're supposed to be the one that's in control. You almost suspend it a little bit. It's like suspended self-preservation of: I can't be scared right now so I'm not going to be. And then later on when you're safe you can go: oh my god that was a little bit, flipping heck. But

at the time you just kind of think: I can't let myself right now, so I'm just going to think everything's fine.

While this worker is talking about dealing with frightening situations, 'suspended self-preservation' has a more general relevance to how practitioners think – or sometimes don't think – about their feelings in practice.

> [W]e don't have a lot of planning time, a lot of before time very often just because we're very busy and we don't have the time. But I generally use the time as I'm driving to a place to think about what I'm going to do. And then while I'm there if I think: okay, this isn't really working out at the moment, how can I do this differently – then I will think about it while somebody's sometimes talking back at you. … Yeah, I think I'm more critically, I more reflect back on the way I asked questions than the way this person has an impact on me. Sometimes obviously I think: God, this person's really pissing me off today and I don't want to be here, and I don't think this has been productive at all. But I do think about, I think about how I use my sessions and how I, how I ask questions and things, you know, things like that I will think about. But I won't necessarily think about how it will impact on me in the moment I'm there. That's more something I think about as soon as I leave the house and drive back to the office and drive to my next appointment. … And then as soon as I go away and have time in the office or time in the car that is when I think about how it impacts on me. And I don't think it would be productive for me, I don't know for others, productive if I would think about it while I'm there. It's basically that you don't open yourself up too much so that those projections don't have an impact or don't come onto you.

Here Angela uses meta-cognition and engages in some internal supervision that enables her to see herself in interaction with others. She allows some emotion to be felt (being 'pissed off') but closes off to the possible deeper impact of what she is experiencing and what is being projected into her. She had just been observed on a visit to a family where child neglect was a major concern and like many social workers spoke of the difficulties of shaking off the effects of the 'dirty' home conditions and unpleasant odours that attached to her nostrils and clothes. Stopping these sensory experiences and accompanying emotions like disgust from becoming overwhelming occurred through conscious and unconscious defences of the self (see also Chapter 5).

Suspension of feeling and self-preservation occur because practitioners sometimes consciously turn reflection on and off, to meet the demands of the situation. A social worker, Hannah, was shadowed on a visit where a mother refused to let her into the home and quickly became very upset, crying and shouting at Hannah and seeking assurances that she would not remove her daughter from her care. Afterwards Hannah went straight to another home visit, which I also observed. Six days later Hannah made a return visit to the woman who would not let her in and this time she did. Here, soon after that visit, is Hannah explaining aspects of how she coped with the impact of the very heated doorstep encounter:

> No, and you just turn the music up loud in the car and you forget about it, and then you focus on the next visit. But it's like if you have a lot [of difficult visits] together, then it would be draining. And that's what I was saying about, I think, like when I went, before I went on the visit today, I was sort of ranting to [colleague] about it, like, 'Oh God, you should have seen her the other day what she was like with me, and now I've got to go.' I think it's, I really draw on that, you know, being able to offload a little bit, just briefly, and her being like, 'Oh yeah.' Do you see what I mean?

This confirms the importance of practitioners having opportunities to 'offload' feelings to colleagues in the office, both informally and in supervision. It again shows how valuable 'live' supervision is for workers when they are out in the community navigating the Practice Cycle. It also confirms the vital role of the car as a potential reflective space (Ferguson, 2010; 2011). While Angela describes how she uses the transitional space of the car journey to begin thinking about the impact of the visit on her, here Hannah shows how loud music can assist by helping her *not* to reflect. Hannah used the loud music to drown out thinking about what she had experienced because to allow herself to feel her raw painful feelings would have prevented her from being resilient enough to face the next family and practice effectively. And it seemed to work, as the next visit was also very challenging and the social worker managed to overcome parental anxiety and resistance and meet her aim of seeing the child on his own.

The more emotionally and viscerally demanding and anxiety-provoking the encounter the harder practitioners find it to reflect in action, at any depth, and the less control they have over their defences and whether they reflect or not. Gary, who I observed dealing with some tense home visits that involved volatile reactions from parents, perceptively articulates a core challenge of how to adopt the position of acknowledging and monitoring feelings while suspending fully feeling them, so as to make the work possible.

> I know when I'm kind of meant to be doing it, you know, reflecting in practice. … Because say like if you walk into like a house and kind of, you know, immediately the parent starts being aggressive or something like that, then all your fight or flight response is going to kick in, but you still need to be monitoring very consciously. You know, number one: where's the exits, where's the, where's the danger, where's the risk? And number two: can I talk this person down and do the role that I came here to do? You know, if you do manage to

do that, you know, can I see the child, is it safe to see them, what's the risk to them if I ask kind of certain questions or don't? And so you can't ever be fully submerged in what you're doing because that would put you at risk as much as everybody else in that situation. So I think a certain level of splitting is absolutely fundamental to doing the job, and the more dangerous the situation, the more you've got to be able to, or the more, the more potentially volatile or dangerous the situation or the person that you're dealing with is, the more important it is to be able to do that kind of splitting, because you're going to have to be, react or respond in a very kind of considered manner to what might be some very frightening stimuli.

Through internal supervision Gary has created a split within himself whereby his mind moves between a focus on himself and the service user, between thinking and feeling. He has an internal dialogue about what he knows he needs to achieve and sizing up the demanding emotional and practical situation he is in. Some reflection is going on in the moment described in the sense of an awareness of danger and vigilance in monitoring how to get out of the house safely, while at the same time needing to defend the self from becoming flooded by anxiety.

Other workers spoke similarly of how 'mental space' is needed to reflect in action and how reflection is only possible up to a point, the cut-off being when the interaction is felt to impact on their inner self in an unbearably intrusive way. They erect what social worker Amy called an 'internal barrier' to defend their inner life from the unbearable feelings as a means to trying to get through the encounter. The irony given the importance placed in the literature on reflection is that *not* reflecting in action provides a basis for being able to act (at all) and getting through at least some of what has to be done.

Some found the challenge of being able to think and provide internal supervision for themselves on some occasions too great. This is what happened to Melissa who featured in Chapter 5 when her practice became disorganised and her thinking chaotic:

> Well, I didn't, I just didn't know what to say, I didn't know what to say, what to do, and as I was, and as I was sat there I was, I was analysing my own practice, I guess, and I'm thinking: I can't even talk to, I can't talk to the child.

This worker's inability to think arose from the anxiety caused by the father's aggression and disruptive behaviour, a very tense atmosphere and the disgust she felt at the home conditions. She was able to become aware of how ineffective her practice was while she was doing it but was so overwhelmed by anxiety and a sense of helplessness that she was unable to adjust it to achieve what she needed to. Reflecting in action does not therefore always lead to the worker being able to act there and then on the understanding gained from it. Recognising her ineffectiveness was still valuable for the worker, even if she couldn't change the outcome. If a worker leaves an encounter aware that they haven't achieved their aims, they have the opportunity to return and try again.

Serious problems arise when the self becomes completely defended, workers stop thinking and are not even aware of their non-reflection. A thoroughgoing closing down of the self occurs rather than a temporary suspension and defence of that self. It involves not only not thinking about the experience of the work but not even knowing about what is not being thought about. This is what happens in the making of avoidant patterns where children become invisible and unheld (see Chapters 4 and 5). As this chapter has shown, non-reflection can have a reflective element in how through internal supervision the worker gains momentary awareness and decides that this is so difficult it is not safe, productive or bearable to dwell on how emotionally and viscerally demanding it is. Yet at a deeper level not reflecting in action is not so much a choice practitioners make as a product of how in the moment the defended self leads them to enact the impulse not to dwell on painful feelings but to split them off. Its basis is existential and unconscious. At its most worrying, where fear of feeling becomes embedded in organisational culture, a continuous cycle of unconscious disconnection from emotional states can exist (Cooper and Lousada, 2005; O'Sullivan, 2019; Smith, 2024). This leaves practitioners and managers often unable to think clearly about the safety of service users and the well-being of staff, and alienation, burnout, blame and other toxic experiences prevail.

Towards analytical thinking

We need to think more critically about how we think about thinking and reflection. In essence, a shift is needed in our language and practice from reflection to more analytical thinking that goes below the surface into interior life, emotion and the dynamics of relationships. One form of training that research shows assists in practitioners acquiring an analytical state of mind is the experience of undertaking a period of infant observation (Hingley-Jones et al, 2016), an approach that is adopted on some social work courses and that needs to be universally implemented (Parkinson et al, 2017). This should be done alongside a focus on critical thinking about the effects of inequalities in service users' lives and the dynamics of power in practice. Freud recommended giving 'free floating attention' to the client and encounter, as a way of trying to surpass what is expected of them and the relationship and try to discover something new, unexpected or that isn't conscious (Briggs, 2017, p 103). In a similar vein, Bion (1970, p 124) argued that therapists need to achieve a 'state of patience' in being able to tolerate uncertainty.

Of course, statutory social workers are not therapists, but work in fast-moving bureaucracies where time to devote to service users and the scope for patience is severely stretched. But, if anything, this only makes the need for thinking time and calm spaces all the greater and for supervision that is not just reflective but *analytical* in the sense of going below the surface into internal life and relationships. This is why I consider the 'internal supervisor/supervision' to be a more effective concept than reflection for capturing the inner dialogue and self-analysis that occur and need to happen. As Briggs (2017) argues, practitioners and managers need to be helped to develop the capacity to 'sit with uncertainty, powerful feelings and impulses, and to treat these seriously'. This has to involve professionals learning about the complexities of the self, emotional lives (their own, colleagues and service users'), and what influences relational dynamics and patterns, thinking and non-thinking.

Conclusion

This chapter has rethought the nature of reflection in child protection, identifying significant flaws in current theories of reflection and the 'self' and in understandings of how practitioners think - and don't think - and go about their work. Developing theory that is true to what happens in the lived experience of practice is vital.

Key learning points

- Practitioners reflect in action in some ways that fit with the literature. But there are times when they limit reflection in order to defend themselves from intense emotional and sensory experiences as a way of making the work bearable and doable. Some non-reflection can therefore be healthy as a practical way of being that enables the worker to psychically protect themselves and try to meet their goals. As Smith (2010, p 115) observes, for some people some of the time 'it is necessary to move away from rather than towards their selves'.

- Crucially, however, any kind of non-reflection should only be a temporary state and needs to end with supervisors enabling critical thinking on what has been experienced and not thought about.

- The dominant theory and understanding of child protection work is based on a naive and flawed theory of the self and reflection that leads to the expectation that practitioners, even at moments of high intensity, can, and *should*, be able to reflect in action on their feelings and thinking. A key dynamic that constitutes the self is how it defends itself against unbearable anxiety. Due to the defended nature of the self there are stressful, anxiety-provoking experiences and situations where reflection in action is deeply problematic, to an extent that it may be neither possible, desirable or beneficial.

- It is crucial that the limits to reflection are fully recognised, so that workers are not misunderstood, or blamed due to expectations that they should be thinking clearly about children when this is not possible.

- Supervision is crucial in helping practitioners build the capacity for reflection, self-analysis and emotional containment when working with service users. It fosters the ability to observe both self and other, considering the service user's perspective within the professional relationship. Over time, this external process of guided reflection supports the development of an 'internal supervisor', enabling the worker to silently rehearse, evaluate and refine possible comments, interpretations and questions in practice.

- As well as through supervision, professional education and training need to help practitioners to develop their capacities to self-analyse and hold themselves. This can enable them to tolerate anxiety in difficult situations that bit more to allow vital insights about the service user and helping process to arise.

- This argument clarifies the vital importance of reflection *on* action. Staff support after practice encounters needs to be rigorous in taking fully into account the feelings and sensory experiences that may have been split off in action and not thought about. Good analytical supervision in turn supports the further development of the internal supervisor and the worker's capacity to hold themselves in the difficult circumstances that threaten to stop them from thinking and feeling what as far as is humanly possible they need to be able to.

The organisational context and nature of this supervisory support and holding work will now be explored further in the next chapter.

13

Holding environments: supervision and live organisational support for relational practice

At various points in this book, the powerful influence of organisations and their cultures in shaping child protection work has been evident. We have seen the crucial role that offices and managers play at stages 1 and 4 of the Practice Cycle in preparing practitioners to be ready to see children and families, in keeping in touch with practitioners remotely when they are out in the community and afterwards in debriefs and making sense of practice encounters. I have formulated the notion of 'bureaucratic preoccupation' to describe how audit culture and administrative demands on practitioners and managers can limit the time available for relational work with families. These demands can contribute significantly to mental and physical states that can leave children invisible and unheld and prevent families from receiving the support they need.

Yet, how this overall bureaucratic regime of desk and computer work, compliance, time scales and fast culture manifests locally in practice is complicated and nuanced. One of the most intriguing aspects of observing social workers and teams in different places is discovering how much their cultures can differ. There can be important differences between places and even *within* the same organisations and buildings. This is exemplified by a social worker who had experience in two teams with identical senior managers and systems, yet she described them as feeling as though they were from 'different continents'.

By examining child protection work in a forward-facing way that brings the experience of it to life, the book has shown just how complex and physically and emotionally demanding it is. While there can be joy, pleasure and satisfaction in the work, where there isn't any or enough of it, burnout prevails and staff leave (Hughes and Pengelly, 1997; Ravalier et al, 2021; McFadden, et al, 2024). The primary aim of this chapter is to consider the kinds of supervision and staff support that practitioners need to help them plan, reflect and process this difficult work. It develops the concept of the organisation as a 'holding environment' and addresses the kind of 'relational spaces' practitioners need if they are to feel emotionally and physically supported, or 'held'. Such holding can enable them to think as clearly as possible about the work, their relationships and develop their knowledge, self-awareness and relational styles. 'Holding' in this context refers to a cognitive, emotional and embodied process in which staff experience a supportive supervisor and/or other colleagues who help them to process their experience by listening to and validating them and their feelings and they experience a 'release' (Harrison, 2016).

Supervision has been described as 'the "pivot" upon which the integrity and excellence of social work practice can be maintained' (Bostock et al, 2019a). While this will be borne out in what follows, I also want to problematise and extend understanding of what supervision is. Staff support is typically regarded as being synonymous with supervision and is presented as a fixed activity and event that takes place periodically, every two, three or four weeks. I will argue that the vital day-to-day support that is the heart and soul of an effective supportive supervisory environment has largely been overlooked in the literature. I will refer to this as 'live supervision' and show the vital contribution it makes to workers and managers feeling held and secure. As Mark Gregory (2024) argues, supervisory interactions outside formal supervision have received scant attention. His ethnographic observations of social work offices show how staff support goes on across a diverse range of spaces and relationships. Much greater understanding is needed of what goes on in offices and teams in the minutes, hours, days and weeks before formal supervision. Only then can a comprehensive assessment be made of what the best possible support for child protection workers involves. At the heart of this is the question: where and how are staff experiences processed, emotion expressed and learning fostered in organisations?

More than formal support: 'live' supervision

Recent years have seen a growth in recognition of the importance of organisational contexts to effective child protection work and many social work agencies have strategically sought to redesign their organisational structures, culture and ways of delivering services (Sebba et al, 2017). Glisson and Hemmelgarn's (1998, p 404) pioneering work found evidence that organisational climate, by which they mean the attitudes shared by employees about their work environment, is a major predictor of the quality and outcomes of children's services. Antonopoulou et al (2017) found that low stress levels were related to workers having a sense of job clarity and control and being provided with the necessary administrative and social support by their managers and their peers to deal effectively with their daily job pressures. This led Antonopoulou et al to conceptualise organisational support as what needs to be done and provided 'to allow workers to get on with the job' (Antonopoulou et al, 2017).

The standard approach to understanding the nature and quality of organisational support is to focus on supervision in the sense of the formal meeting between worker and supervisor/manager that typically happens at least once a month. Such supervision is regarded as having three main functions: administrative, educative and supportive (Morrison, 2007; Kadushin and Harkness, 2014). Valuable research has shown how organisational priorities, cultures and supervisor styles affect the supervisory encounter. A key pattern in this is for workers' practical, emotional and developmental needs not to be met because case management and surveillance of staff are prioritised (Carpenter et al, 2013;

Davys and Beddoe, 2021). In this approach case discussions operate primarily as a mechanism for management oversight and provide limited opportunity for reflection, emotional support or critical thinking (Wilkins et al, 2017). Research observations of supervisions done like this have shown that they can often be very long (up to four hours), at worst held in confined and stuffy spaces. They are a monotonous slog as the manager sits behind their computer ticking off what the social worker has and hasn't done with each child and family. This is bureaucratic preoccupation at its worst and it is little wonder that workers find this approach soul-destroying, stressful and that they often emerge feeling more anxious and burdened than before they went in (Beddoe et al, 2022).

Group supervision is used in some places and Wilkins et al (2023) found that when supervision includes a significant focus on helping practitioners to plan their direct work, the subsequent home visit is more likely to evidence skilled practice. The feedback from parents is also more likely to be positive. Bostock et al (2019b; 2022) found that systemic supervision helped to develop practice skills and confidence and had a positive impact on the quality of direct practice with families. This is in part because systemic theory and techniques such as hypothesising offer a 'rehearsal space' for planning family conversations, enabling a richer and more analytical discussion of risk and need in supervision sessions. This is similar to the argument I made in the last chapter about the way in which one-to-one supervision sessions enable practitioners to develop a capacity for internal supervision that includes an inner dialogue that rehearses possible questions and responses to the service user.

My research observations of practice, social work organisations, office practices and relating as they are going on have enabled me to see the range of ways in which staff support is provided that go beyond and occur on top of formal supervision sessions. 'Live supervision' takes the form of discussions about families, the work and workers' thinking and feelings that occur from moment to moment during the day. As this social worker explains:

> We have monthly supervision in the office and supervision as we go along, ongoing discussion. A lot of peer mapping for cases we get stuck on. The way we're set up in the [office] you can just talk about cases all day but we do have the individual supervisions as well. … Sometimes in supervision you talk about how that person is and then you talk about the case, but you've talked that case to death all week long. So sometimes there's nothing more to add, it's an ongoing conversation, the whole team knows about our difficult cases and knows the story. Formal supervision happens monthly.

Live supervision goes on through conversations between managers and peers while sat at their desks, when completing tasks like photocopying or making tea, or while on the move when walking and in the car. This social worker's description of it as 'supervision as we go along' captures beautifully how it has a flow and rhythm to it, a fluidity that is part of the mobile nature of social work.

This is another example of how important it is to get away from fixed and static understandings of what social work is. Supervision and staff support, like practice with families, are dynamic mobile practices (Ferguson, 2008). Another striking example of this is the way that mobile phones have enabled team managers to support and advise their staff while they are out in the community, on the move (see especially Chapter 2). The last quoted social worker's experience also exemplifies how live supervision is valued just as much and by some a lot more than formal supervision. This is in part because it is often a collective experience that involves peer support and is woven into the culture and routines of the workplace. It often comes with hot drinks, treats such as chocolate, cake, hugs and other random acts of kindness that mean a lot. Friendships with colleagues are very important forms of support and pleasure for social workers that deserve greater recognition (Murphy and Bedford, 2025).

A key part of the value of live supervision lies in how it happens *in present time when the experience has just happened and even while it is happening*. As this social worker explains:

> I think the problem with the supervision is when you feel it there and then, you need to talk about it there and then. You can't save it up, you can't think, 'Right, I've got supervision in a week,' it isn't how it works. And what our team's absolutely amazing at doing is we all talk about each other's cases and listen to each other. Me, George and Caroline, who are all full-time, we know each other's cases quite well, and we're able to go back and go, 'Oh my God, this happened,' and everyone will always have time for each other. And so that's the most kind of valuable supervision.

This illustrates that a vital aspect of live supervision is the immediate debriefs that occur when workers return to the office after a home visit or a practice encounter elsewhere. These have an important role in assessing risk, need and making decisions. Their immediacy by taking place at a time when the feelings, impressions and details of the encounter are still fresh and alive within the practitioner provides a vital opportunity to help them make sense of their experience. They can gain greater clarity on the safety of the children and be helped to bring to mind what has not been thought about and offload feelings. This includes any emotions, thoughts and impressions that were suspended, put on hold, and not fully thought about during the encounter with the family because the worker practiced what I have called 'suspended self-preservation' as a way of coping with the intensity and complexity of the experience (see Chapter 12). As earlier chapters have shown, through joint visits or the use of mobile phones, live supervision also occurs in real time while work with families is being done and challenging experiences are happening.

To the frustration of some team managers, live supervision does not gain the recognition it deserves. Chantelle expressed her annoyance that so much of the support she offers isn't recognised or 'measured'. Her department did a case audit not long ago on domestic abuse cases and the feedback was that not enough reflective supervision is being done. Chantelle disagreed, feeling that this criticism leaves out all the day-to-day support she provides, when people come back to the office after a challenging visit, or off the phone after a difficult call. 'It's a live thing that goes on through the week.' I saw with my own eyes that she was quite right.

Conventional monthly supervision sessions remain crucial for ensuring formal accountability, particularly in assessing risk to children, decision-making and planning necessary actions. They also play an important role in discussing workload, performance, training needs, staff development, self-care, and personal issues and how these factors impact on work. But taking account of live supervision is crucial to understanding organisational culture and how staff support and learning occur.

Spaces for organisational support

The supportive processes and relationships between colleagues highlighted earlier can go on in all kinds of organisational arrangements. The last quoted social worker and her two colleagues, George and Caroline, had created this supportive relational space through being part of a team of eight social workers who all had their own desks and sat close to one another and whose manager was located in a separate room adjoining the team. As the worker could recognise, this traditional organisational design that separates operational ('team') managers from their staff, routinely requires the worker to hold onto their feelings and need to talk and process practice encounters for several days. This means that by the time the formal supervision comes round not only are the feelings and issues that arose on one visit likely to have passed, but experiences from many more practice encounters as well. It is *accumulated* experience and issues that formal supervision usually deals with.

As a social worker put it, if the team manager in this traditional arrangement has their door closed a lot of people would feel 'like you had to knock on the door, but you'd only knock if it was really important, because you knew that she was busy' (Beddoe et al, 2022, p 534). This does not mean that managers/supervisors who occupy a separate room from their social workers are never available to provide support in the here-and-now moment. They sometimes are, as the book has shown, including accompanying their social workers to some meetings and home visits. Or they stay in direct contact with their staff by mobile phone from the office while practitioners are out visiting children and families on their own. Yet where managers/supervisors are located separately from their staff there is a bigger risk that feelings will build, accumulate and not be sufficiently processed. Carrying the weight of accumulated emotion and responsibility over time is more likely to set staff on a path to burnout and experiencing vicarious trauma from internalising service users' distress and feelings such as anger, sadness and shame.

Highly supportive environments are those where the processing of workers' and team managers' experience occurs through multiple, often short encounters and in the moment communications that can go on in a variety of places. An office I observed had fortnightly management meetings for all the team managers that were led by the service manager. These began with a go-around where people said how they were and rated themselves on a 0–10 scale. Usually, some said they were okay, some were grumpy and not very communicative, and sometimes some were visibly upset. The senior manager who chaired the meetings would often get the brunt of their unhappiness and they'd be openly critical of her or refuse to give a self-rating. And she'd accept that and soak it up without being defensive or retaliating. This is excellent holding work because of how the senior manager positioned herself as a wise, reliable container.

Leaders have a vital role in accepting staff projections and this senior manager understood that. In Freudian terms any 'hate' towards them wasn't necessarily personal but a largely unconscious acting out of distress and uncomfortable feelings they felt the need to offload onto an authority figure, who becomes what in Chapter 2 I called a 'reliable hate object' (Winnicott, 1949). The senior managers were getting some of the anxiety, worry, anger and anguish the team managers were getting from their front-line workers and that the latter were getting from families. It wasn't expressed reasonably or rationally – it shouldn't have to be – and they were allowed to be moody and pissed off, grumpy, sad. The key point is that being held like this made at least some of the stress and painful feelings these managers were carrying bearable and freed their minds to think more clearly so that they could be more attentive to their practitioners, team and families (O'Sullivan, 2019).

The existence of these multiple spaces for the discussion of experience, anxiety and emotional expression prevent at least some unbearable feelings from building up and becoming toxic and being re-enacted through conflict or other irrational, destructive behaviours (Smith, 2024). The result: a broadly pleasant, healthy, holding environment. It is important however not to idealise it. In my research observations staff shortages, demands on the service and time restrictions meant that some of the time families did not get the help and intensive service they needed. The culture of reflection and ongoing dialogue about the work is no guarantee of consensus among colleagues, as was shown in Chapter 8, for example, by the differences of opinion within the team about whether Samantha Clarke should be reunified with her baby. But crucially these differences did not fracture relationships or escalate into conflicts or become the dominant organisational mood because of the mutual respect and emotional and practical support that was shared between colleagues.

In some organisational designs it seems easier to create supportive cultures and focus on relational practice than others. I've been helped to see this by comparing two currently popular office designs: a small team office model where two or three social workers are co-located with their team manager, an administrator and a family support worker, usually in their own small room and they all have their own allocated desks. And a hot-desking office design where several teams of six to eight social workers and an administrative worker are all accommodated together in the same large room. No one has an allocated desk and there is no on-site family support service. The social work team managers for each team are not sat with or near them as they are located all together in a completely separate room some distance away (Ferguson et al, 2020b).

At the small team office, because social workers were co-located with their team manager and family support workers and in high-risk cases could also call upon other intensive family support services, this created a shared experience of working together with families. Although it was a scarce resource, social workers knew they had the option to visit jointly with their family support colleague should they need the help. This generated a supportive culture for social workers as well as families (for a vivid example, see Chapter 8). Having a co-worker also meant that the families and the workers' experiences of working with them were regularly discussed in the small team offices, generating a culture of 'live' reflection and ongoing dialogue about the work. And because team managers also shared the small room, they were constantly engaged in discussions and giving 'live' supervisory support. All the team members knew of each other's families. A reflective culture flowed from this that enabled space for thinking, decision-making and the holding of workers and their emotions from day to day – although there may still be limits to this, as we shall see shortly. The energy in these teams was generally positive and had the 'buzz' of resonance that comes from being relational and feeling connected and the satisfaction of being able to be helpful and create change for children and families.

In the organisational design where several teams and large numbers of workers were in one room and team managers were located separately, this kind of culture of live dialogue and support was much harder to embed. In one such site I attended it was not a relational space and in general was a very unhappy place. There was a recent history of being judged 'inadequate' by the regulator Ofsted and what Murphy (2022) calls 'Ofsted Anxiety Disorder' had taken hold. Practitioners were often observed crying with frustration, feeling overburdened and unsupported. A blame culture existed, staff morale was very low and turnover so high that often existing staff did not make the effort to relate to new recruits. On her second day working there, Kate had her first research interview and became upset and cried because she said she doesn't want to be a child protection social worker any more. As the field notes recorded:

> [S]he has no one else to talk to and feels trapped. ... I finished the interview and went with her to look at her [working with children] toolbox in the car. Her boot was absolutely crammed full of paper, stickers, games, direct work tools for teens about sex, STIs, pregnancy, drugs, friendship groups etc. This has also bulged over into her back seat which had more games, jars of buttons in different colours used to communicate with children and specialist games that she told me cost her £25. I asked her if she can claim any of this money back and she laughed.

This is a compelling image that captures the core tension in contemporary child protection as it contrasts a worker's desire to be helpful to children and young people by working creatively with them and having the tools to do so, and an organisation that does little or nothing to support her or that kind of relational work. Kate's tears were a painful expression of the 'cruel optimism' that is experienced when organisations prevent workers from fulfilling their hopes and achieving their ideals (Berlant, 2011; Duschinsky et al, 2016).

Even in this soulless highly bureaucratised environment some team members managed to gel with one another and their manager (for an extended example, see Warwick et al, 2022). Overall, however, when the mood of a place is as gloomy, flat, unsafe – in a word, *alienated* – as this was, it is not surprising that the organisation could not hold onto its staff. During the 15 months of research fieldwork spent there, 42 social workers left, compared with only five who left all of the workforce housed in the small team offices. This very high turnover meant many families experienced several changes of worker. At the small team office, meanwhile, most social workers had worked there for at least five years and some for between ten and 20 years, which made continuity of care for families and relationships with the same worker much more achievable. This model of managers and practitioners being co-located in relatively small units/teams embeds the moment-to-moment discussion of experience *as it happens*. When a manager is sat beside you, or across the room, you are much less likely to have to wait and with a relatively small number of staff to support they are much more able to be attentive. The design of the office is therefore an important factor in determining whether and how this informal 'live' support and holding happens, and some workplace designs are better facilitative environments of it than others.

Regardless of spatial design, organisational culture is also heavily influenced by staff feeling safe, valued and cared about and helped to see and feel that they are having a positive impact for families (Grant and Kinman, 2018). Psychological well-being and team cohesion and identity are also sustained by sharing food, companionship and fun. As Lauren, the team manager of a referral and assessment team who are accommodated in quite a large hot-desking environment, explains:

> I have had the same team now for two years, so it is really nice, unusual in a front-line team to sustain the whole team for that period of time. … My team look forward to our office weeks [when we are on duty], really enjoy them. … We have got team lunch booked for Monday. … We have got some games in the week booked while they are on duty and stuff, so in terms of team morale it is very, very high at the moment.

Workplace defences against unbearable feelings

Where teams and organisations and formal and live supervisory practices are broadly positive and work well this does not mean that staff experiences and feelings are necessarily all adequately dealt with. In the same small team office that had a stable workforce and a palpably supportive environment, this did not easily extend to open expression of emotional distress. There was little raw emotion and conflict on display. This was partly due to what I have already argued: the routine processing of disgruntled feelings provided forms of release that prevented the toxic build-up of emotion. But there were limits to how far this went.

To make this point I want to return to the experience of team manager Olivia and the service user Roberta that was discussed in Chapter 9 and the time at a multi-agency meeting Roberta aggressively challenged everything Olivia said and 'exploded' with rage and threatened her. Immediately afterwards Olivia was very upset and cried at her desk. Many of the social workers in the team had worked closely together for several years and when observing and talking to them that day I learned that it was rare for one of them to openly cry in the office. Olivia said she was more worried about the administrative staff seeing her upset than social work colleagues and it being seen as a weakness. She was also trying to hold her emotions in so that she could undertake the several phone calls and other tasks now required to ensure Roberta's child is safe. She practised 'suspended self-preservation', where workers consciously suppress reflection on and acknowledgement of the depths of their feelings to help them get through the work they have to do and protect themselves and colleagues from their suffering and pain.

Some five days after Roberta's attack Olivia was still very upset and was observed in formal supervision with her senior manager to whom she mentioned how she was feeling. The senior manager did not pursue this, instead moving quickly on to address other high-risk cases and staff performance issues in the team Olivia managed. In a research interview straight after the supervision I asked the senior manager what they were thinking during it:

> I was thinking we'd spoken about it earlier in the week and she had got upset then and I'd heard the story, you know. So, and she, I felt, chose, and it seemed OK to come to the supervision and she didn't want in that setting to be upset and … so I sort of thought, well maybe that's OK, I don't want to press her on that. But yeah it's a hard balance between, and then you're just avoiding it and let's move on and that's not intelligent, that's just kind of colluding with shutting that sort of discussion down and that emotion down. So, yeah, it's hard and there's, you know, a limit to how much you can get involved in the in-depth of one case when you know you've got another 60 to, to make sure get covered and so on too, really. I mean, you know, there I am talking about that emotion at the beginning of the supervision, halfway through I'm talking about, 'Right, how are you going to a get a grip with this member of staff?' It's quite tough to balance.

The manager is aware of the importance of providing emotional support to staff in Olivia's situation and of the limited attention one case can get when some 60 cases are held by Olivia's team. Ultimately, however, the emotional support provided was compromised by the senior manager's regulatory role and the need they felt to address issues of staff performance and meeting timescales and targets for completing work. The opportunity for reflective, emotionally supportive supervision was sacrificed to the organisational imperative to comply with government-imposed performance indicators, audit and data collection that are also inspected by the regulatory body, Ofsted. Bureaucratic preoccupation and 'Ofsted Anxiety Disorder' (Murphy, 2022) overrode attention to what was occurring emotionally and viscerally for the workers, mother and baby and in the relationship and this contributed to social workers' relationship with the child remaining detached and avoidant (see Chapter 9).

When interviewed after the supervision, Olivia said she was hesitant about accessing her distressed feelings and reluctant to show vulnerability because she feared judgement. She felt that managerial responsibilities and accountability were what mattered most to the organisation and defended herself from accessing her unbearable feelings accordingly. Once again, suspended self-preservation was regarded as the safest course, but it only really works as a healthy coping strategy if the emotional impact of the work that is being 'suspended' is given attention as soon as possible. And it never was.

Olivia's team, like others in this organisation, were not uncaring, but kind, attentive and mutually supportive. But this must not be taken to mean they were comfortable with acknowledging the deeper, very difficult feelings the work generated. Somewhat paradoxically these were not workplaces where sadness, fear, anger, guilt, shame and other painful feelings were easily or openly expressed. There was a deep investment in not showing or fully feeling what was there deep down to be felt. The net result was an entire workforce fleeing from painful feelings. The basis for this was pragmatic in that feelings were suppressed and suspended self-preservation practised due to the need to keep going to ensure the work got done. It was also psychological, unconscious and defensive, arising from the need for organisations as well as individuals to defend the self and the group from unbearable feelings (Cooper and Lousada, 2005; Whittaker, 2011). The existence of these defensive dynamics is supported by other research, such as Menzies-Lyth's (1988) classic study of the experience of nurses. While it is an understandable reaction for social work managers to fear the shame that would come from a failed government inspection, such insistence on bureaucratic tasks and performance management involves the imposition of what Menzies-Lyth (1988, p 50) called 'ritual task performance'. This occurs when anxiety becomes 'intense and unmanageable' and attention is displaced on to what can be controlled, such as record-keeping. At times when workers' need for emotional support, holding and help to understand how they are feeling and thinking – or not thinking – and relating to children and families is particularly great, its absence makes staff feel betrayed and even worse.

The need for 'reflective supervision' and reflective consultation has gained considerable popularity in recent years (Barron et al, 2022; Williams et al, 2022; Tobin et al, 2024b). In child protection this means seeking to move away from a preoccupation with the administrative and making supervision a more educational, supportive, reflective process. This is nicely characterised by Harvey and Henderson (2014, p 344) as providing a holding experience that is 'promoted by a consistent setting and familiar person who has an available mind which is open to the emotional experiences of the practitioner'. Much depends however on what is meant by 'reflection' especially in terms of how deep it goes and the extent to which it accesses and analyses interior life. It seems important to understand the impact of emotion on two levels. The first involves difficult experiences and distressing feelings that are processed and quite quickly contained. The second operates at a deeper level and includes traumatic experiences and feelings that are internalised, build up, and lodge themselves within the self and psyche. One social worker who was shadowed in the office and on several encounters with families over a 12-month period demonstrated near the end of the study the deep emotional effects the work had on him. After some 50 minutes of sharing his experience he cried, his body shook and he sweated so profusely that his shirt became soaking wet. He was particularly distressed about a four-year-old child he had worked so hard to try and help remain with his parents but who he ended up removing and worried about whether this was the right decision. Having had a close relationship for over a year, since being removed, the child would not speak to him.

Another social worker, Geraldine, who was shadowed for several months cried during an interview and said she wants out. She had been qualified for six years and said she knew that she was at that point where many get out because it is just so painful. She had removed children from four families in recent months and she couldn't see how she was being helpful to anyone because she just didn't have time to do enough work with them. Part of Geraldine's upset was the moral distress that occurs when government policy, organisational priorities and inequalities prevent workers from applying their core values in their work (Hingley-Jones and Ruch, 2016). Knowing they have little or no time or other resources to be helpful and there being no other support and therapeutic services for individuals and families causes moral injury (Mänttäri-van der Kuip, 2016). It wasn't just the angry, hostile, grieving parents who upset her but those who don't protest or fight back she found even harder to cope with. I sensed that, as well as genuine disappointment and despair at the organisational barriers that stripped away the time and resources and self-efficacy she needed to be helpful, she had internalised these families' sense of despair and helplessness. She was carrying their trauma, loss and hopelessness, unconsciously identifying with the feelings that had been projected into her and was re-enacting them through mournful crying and a desire to escape. This is the unconscious phenomenon known as 'projective identification' (Cooper, 2018). It resulted in vicarious trauma and had exhausted her.

In her research O'Sullivan (2019) brought social workers together in work discussion groups, which take a psycho-dynamic approach, and invited participants to focus on their feelings. The discussions and group dynamics brought to the surface the deep emotional experience that child protection workers had not been helped to access through conventional supervisory approaches. They too had somatic as well as tearful reactions. These are the 'suspended' feelings social workers do not get help to deal with, that accumulate over time and that ultimately traumatise and burn them out. And because these painful feelings remain repressed, as Chapter 9 showed, they can easily be unconsciously acted out against service users in punitive, retaliatory ways.

Further insight into the heavy emotional toll can be gained from those who leave child protection. Many choose roles focused on supporting children in care and/or foster carers rather than birth families and often in the voluntary and private sectors. For their own well-being and that of their loved ones many are glad to have made the move.

> I just feel so less stressed, like before I left I was off for … months with anxiety … and before I went off I literally had … a stye in my eye every week from like being run down and stressed and I thought just last week I haven't had a stye since I started this job. (Social worker, previously long-term Child Protection, now working for an independent fostering agency). (Quoted in Ferguson et al, 2023)

Here we see how intense anxiety and relentless stress not only affects the mind but breaks out on the worker's skin. It can be seen as an expression of the bodily alienation Rosa (2019) argues can occur when the body becomes an enemy to the self and out of one's control. Salmenniemi (2022) suggests that social analysis can usefully understand the effects of how large performance-driven organisations extract as much as they can from their workers by examining the impact it has 'on the skin', 'as "rubbing up the wrong way," as something that causes itching, exhaustion, frustration, pain and snapping'. Humane holding environments are needed that can process emotion and prevent social workers feeling rubbed up the wrong way, traumatised and getting out.

Enhancing supervision and staff well-being

Creating relational spaces that enable both formal supervision and 'live' supervisory practices and cultures to thrive is very challenging. In attempting to help social work managers provide a model of supervision that could include emotional thinking Turney and Ruch (2018, p 134) found that for supervisors it was 'a significant challenge to hold thinking and feeling, process and task together' because they were so used to providing case management orientated supervision which precludes attention to detail and more open-ended conversations. One way to try to ensure difficult feelings do not build up below the surface is for the reflective, analytical aspects of formal supervisory practice ('clinical' supervision) to be provided separately from 'administrative' supervision in which managers address performance and audit issues and targets. This brings the risk, however, that Harvey and Henderson (2014) draw attention to, of a 'dichotomous view of supervision where it is regarded as either nurturing or controlling; all about feelings or all about procedure'.

At the very least, emotional and psychological support need to be freely and routinely available to staff (at all levels). There is growing recognition of the importance of psycho-dynamic and systemically informed supervision and valuable training for supervisors and supervisory resources have been developed and utilised (Williams et al, 2022). This includes the need for attention to 'parallel processes' where the supervision encounter between worker and manager unconsciously re-enacts what is occurring in the relationships between practitioners and service users and projective identification occurs (Smith, 2024). A positive parallel process can also occur where workers apply the emotional openness, listening and other skills they learn from how they themselves are contained in supervision to working with families (Tobin et al, 2024b, p 424).

Reliability, feeling safe and having a secure base are core components of relational support for both staff and service users. Learning from revelatory, 'wow moments' when insights about the self, families and relationships emerge can be applied back into practice. Group supervision and support is another valuable way to enable practitioners and managers to go below the surface to access feelings and achieve deeper understanding of relational dynamics with service users (O'Sullivan et al, 2022). The 'release' that comes from experiencing support, being heard, validated and not feeling alone occurs in the body as well as in the mind (Harrison, 2016). A weight of stress and anxiety is lifted. But as Tobin et al (2024b) argue, while insights and the 'release' of feelings may come in 'wow' 'lightbulb' moments, recovery and transformational learning can also be 'hard won', difficult and painful.

While we have seen that team support can happen spontaneously and organically in certain office settings, collective, group-oriented ways of building community and communication can be developed in more formal, structured ways. In the practice model of 'restorative practice', 'restorative circles' facilitate dialogue, address conflict and provide mutual support. Sitting together in a circle fosters a sense of equality and mutual respect and provides the opportunity for all voices to be heard. Participants engage in active listening and shared decision-making in ways that promote understanding, compassion and healing (Finnis, 2021).

Conclusion

While child protection work can be very rewarding and satisfying, it is often extremely stressful and the effects on the mental and physical well-being of workers and managers can be brutal and unforgiving.

Key learning points

- Working with risk and uncertainty, particularly with involuntary clients, and the anger, threats, intimidation, sadness, shame and loss this may bring, combined with heavy caseloads and organisational deadlines and pressures, makes the work very anxiety-provoking and demanding. Workers need to feel nurtured and held in ways that mirror the kinds of intimate practice and good authority that the book has shown is most helpful for children and parents.

- Staff support is usually only thought of and discussed in terms of formal supervision that occurs once or at most twice a month. Far more recognition needs to be given to the important supportive practices that go on outside of formal supervision meetings (Gregory, 2024). Live processing of experiences that have just happened or are still happening is a crucial form of staff support. Many regard it as more important and valuable than formal supervision. Live supervision, especially when it goes beneath the surface to support practitioners and managers in managing stress and the emotional impact of the work, helps prevent the build-up of unprocessed feelings that can lead to burnout and vicarious trauma.

- The provision of formal and live supervision is influenced by office and team designs and seems to happen more easily where supervisors are co-located with social workers, family support workers and admin staff. Staff retention and turnover are generally better in smaller teams (Antonopoulou et al, 2017, p 44). This does not mean that good supervision and support cannot be provided in larger rooms that house several teams and staff are hot-desking. The conditions for good supervision and support consist of three key things:
  1. A spatial dimension, that ensures the meeting goes on in a quiet, calm place, apart from the hubbub of busy shared spaces.
  2. A temporal dimensional, in that the time for reflective discussion needs to be protected.
  3. A relational dimension, where there is trust, respect and a sense of safety (Beddoe et al, 2022, p 528).

- The biggest problems for staff arise when painful feelings and the effects of moral injury and traumatic experiences go unprocessed, build up and become lodged deep within the self and psyche. At such times, workers experience vicarious trauma and need 'clinical' supervision and counselling/psychotherapy. While live supervision makes a vital contribution to preventing this build up, some experiences still need a deeper therapeutic response. Psychological well-being, as well as team cohesion and identity, are also nurtured through shared experiences of food, companionship and fun.

- Both live and formal supervision need to build the capacity of practitioners to tolerate anxiety and think clearly so that vital insights about relationships with children and families and their well-being and safety can arise. As O'Sullivan (2019, p 17) argues, '[i]f these overwhelming experiences can be contained and made sense of, they can be received by the worker and the family in more digestible form. This allows for the more successful toleration of ambivalence and uncertainty'. Managers, supervisors and teams need support that can help them manage uncertainty, recognise defences against anxiety and avoid ritualistic tasks that reinforce bureaucratic pressures and worker alienation. This requires not merely 'reflecting' but thinking analytically by going below the surface and addressing emotions.

- Teams where live and formal supervision are attuned to emotions and there is shared knowledge of relationships with families, including successes, are able to generate a positive, resonant energy that is grounded in relational connection and the satisfaction of contributing to meaningful change for children and families. These feel like good places to be.

Improving the quality of leadership and managers' knowledge and skills at live and formal supervision matters greatly. But ultimately, making child protection work better for staff and families requires significant structural and systemic changes and building on what works well. I will now draw together the various strands and arguments of the book to consider how child protection can be re-made in ways that will consistently make it work well.

14

Making child protection work well

The central aim of this book has been to explore how everyday child protection work is done, particularly by social workers and the interactions and relationships that are made between practitioners, children and families. The book has sought to identify and learn from how it is done in ways that keep children safe, to analyse why sometimes it isn't, and to consider how it can be made better.

When I began my research observing practitioners, I was clear that my aim was to find out what encounters between them and service users involved. On the first two home visits I shadowed, the social workers asked to see the children's bedrooms and in one of them they also checked the kitchen, including inside the fridge and cupboards. But while the social workers, children and parents moved around the home I stayed in the sitting room sat in the position I took up on arrival. I assumed that me accompanying them into bedrooms and other intimate spaces would be viewed as an intrusion too far. Then it dawned on me that I was there to learn from observing what practitioners do and how they and families interact and I was missing some key aspects of it. This included children being interviewed on their own in their bedrooms. So, I realised that I needed to shadow social workers and family members everywhere they went and thereafter I always sought their consent to do so. This enabled me to see vital experiences and aspects of how child protection is made that otherwise would have remained invisible, not just to me but in the literature.

This book has been a journey into that previously unknown and the heart and the soul of child protection and families' lives. It has argued for new ways of understanding its practices and lived experiences based on taking a forward-facing approach that, following Tim Ingold (2011), I have called 'making'. This has enabled the life to be put back into child protection, life that has always been there but that most research and commentary has left out because it has been too distant to see, smell, hear and feel. In this conclusion I will draw together the various concepts, themes, findings and arguments in the book and critically consider what is redeemable in how child protection work is made, what needs to change and how it can be made well.

Putting life and practice first

Child protection teems with life. Its vitality derives fundamentally from how it is about people: living, breathing human beings, relationships and families in all their greatness, destructiveness, vulnerability, unpredictability and complexity. Although it involves a lot of time spent in offices and at computers, it is at heart a mobile practice that involves journeys into communities, family homes, schools, walking the streets, encountering dogs, strangers, in all weathers, during daylight and darkness. All laws, policies, guidance, case reviews, theories and actions must flow from a deep appreciation of this lifeworld and how dynamic, challenging and complex it and the work are. This is only fully possible through a perspective that gets down on the ground and produces understandings of what happens and is experienced in practice as it unfolds in real time. This is the unique shift in perspective that I have called taking a forward-facing approach.

Consideration of how child protection is made (and might be re-made) must put everyday life and practice in all their richness and complexity first. This contrasts sharply with the dominant backward-facing approach which focuses on analysing events and processes that have already happened, such as why abused children who died were not protected. The dominant focus that has followed from this has been on organisations and system reforms, a current example of which in England is the setting up of Multi-Agency Child Protection Units to enhance communication and coordinated working (Child Safeguarding Practice Review Panel, 2022a; DfE, 2025). Meanwhile, limited attention is given to actual practice with children and families, how it happens and what form this relating needs to take. The absence of detailed attention to multi-agency working in this book is a limitation. However, even once initiatives like specialist multi-agency teams are implemented, and even if it turns out they help to improve some aspects of inter-agency communication and coordination, children and families still need to be engaged with and it is learning about those interactions and relationship-based practice that the book has chosen to focus on.

This forward-facing approach has enabled the book to evoke what it is like to go and see families, both when home visits are announced and unannounced. And to keep going back to see families who are welcoming, those who tolerate you and the ones who hate you. In how it is currently organised child protection needs social workers who have a range of aptitudes. An appetite for going into the unknown is required and capacity to manage the anxiety, adrenalin and risk that it gives rise to and remain composed. This is especially for duty and assessment work because it so often involves going to see families about whom little is known. It is essential that practitioners have the desire, skills and support to develop co-operative 'holding' relationships with families by being reliable, empathetic, compassionate and using good authority. In long-term work and relationships especially, the unexpected and family crises do occur, but repetition and giving disciplined attention to the day-to-day tasks of caring, relational closeness, love and going over the same ground with parents and children from week to week, month to month is a vital dimension of relationship-based work and creating change. Social workers need courage (Dickens et al, 2023), the ability to work with conflict without retaliating and an intellectual and intuitive understanding of the complexities of relationships, love and hate, rupture and repair. For families facing child protection investigations and prolonged involvement in the system it takes courage, resilience and endurance to navigate the challenges and uncertainties of the process. For some, this never brings satisfaction or gain, while for others it brings safety, help, positive change and even joy.

The Practice Cycle, presence and practising resonance

The concept of the Practice Cycle has been developed in the book to provide a framework for understanding the fluid, dynamic ways in which child protection is made. Practitioners have to navigate four key stages in the cycle: preparation, transitioning from office to family, the encounter itself, and post-encounter reflection and decision-making. Different configurations of relationships have been shown to emerge from what occurs in the cycle and the interplay of social, organisational, cultural, material and emotional factors. The diagrams depicting the Practice Cycle (Figure 1.1), and patterns of automated (Figure 4.1), disorganised (Figure 5.1) and intimate practice (Figure 6.1), and the accompanying analysis, offer a structured approach to help students, practitioners and managers to critically reflect on these stages and dynamics and make sense of their emerging or existing relationship with children and families. They may also assist teams and organisations with reflection on their working practices and culture. They can be used for supervision, or group discussion or personal reflection. You might reflect, for instance, on the feelings you carry before and after an encounter with a family, through a working day or week and how to process them. The core aim of the Practice Cycle is to ensure it is navigated in ways that enable practitioners to be fully present with children and families and engaging relationally in ways that promote connection, safety and change. There are several key things to think about at each stage.

Preparation and readiness

The aim of this beginning stage of the cycle is for social workers and managers to gather relevant information, plan and establish clear goals in preparation for interactions with children and families. Who needs to be seen, where and how? What fears, anxieties and other feelings about upcoming encounters does the practitioner have and what support from managers do they need to address them? What needs to be done to address the deadening effects of sedentary office work, screen time and bureaucracy and ensure they achieve a state of emotional readiness and are helped to feel alive, alert and able to be fully relationally present to the child and family?

Transitional space

The journey to visits, or seeing the child and family elsewhere, is another opportunity to mentally rehearse plans, manage emotions, reflect on goals and align with the needs of the encounter ahead. How can the transition be used to ensure a purposeful shift is made from being preoccupied with bureaucratic tasks and workload demands to a state of mind and body that are relationally focused and able to get physically, emotionally and energetically close to the children, parents and the family? The aim is to become energised in a way that channels arising feelings and energy in purposeful ways to achieve the required aliveness and presence.

Practice encounters

Practitioners need to be fully present, energetic and responsive during encounters. The aim is to create connections with children and parents that have relational depth and what I have called resonance. This involves being as skilful, improvisational and fully emotionally and intuitively present with children and families as it is possible to be in the time available. Practitioners must ask themselves: what impact are the adults, dogs, strangers, smells, sounds and the atmosphere (tense, hostile, welcoming?) having on me? Am I moving around wisely and as freely as I need to in order to gain a deep understanding of what it is like to be a child in this home, bedroom, community? When do I need to sit down and be still to give quality attention to the parents, to listen and observe? Or move to connect with the baby, to get close enough to make eye contact, or hold them and give voice to their experience and well-being? And how can I be alongside children by getting onto the floor to play and skilfully and enthusiastically use toys, photographs, games, electronic devices to get physically close enough to attune to them energetically and emotionally and hold them meaningfully? Am I giving off energy that communicates my delight at being with the children and desire to help the family and connect? How can I ensure young people feel such connection and are also seen outside the home, on walks, car rides and in cafes? Are the children being properly seen and held?

Post-encounter reflection and decision-making

After encounters, the reflection phase needs to incorporate not just formal supervision, but immediate debriefs and live, in the moment discussion. The key question is: what do practitioners need from managers and peers to help them process the experience they have just had, to get feedback and help with thinking and make informed decisions about further actions? This live supervision and processing of experience helps to hold the children and family in mind and provide practitioners with emotional sustenance and continuous learning about the nature of their relationship with the children, parents and family. The book has also shown how live, in the moment support while practitioners are out in the community and the work is actually going on is highly valuable. Formal supervision that is attuned to staff well-being, learning about children and families and professional development remains crucial.

The Practice Cycle framework is intended to help managers and practitioners think about what needs to be done at each stage and recognise the spaces for improvisation and creativity within the four stages that are passed through, leaving them better able to go beyond bureaucratic demands and achieve meaningful relational work that helps families.

By staying close to practice, we have seen the life draining out of practitioners after long periods at their computer screens and poor help with preparation from managers. If they do not recover by making use of the journey to the family to tune into themselves emotionally and think of strategies to deal with challenges that lie ahead, they step into the home and encounter unprepared and very anxious. Faced with parents who are fearful, distressed, angry, workers become even more anxious, are overwhelmed and unable to think about the children. The lifelessness of the worker, their flat, robotic and, as I have characterised it, 'automated' demeanour results in the children becoming invisible and unheld. Or the practitioner thinks and behaves in chaotic, disorganised ways and their relating with children is fitful and ineffective. This has shown the powerful impact of time pressures and unbearable levels of complexity and anxiety on social workers and these emotional effects require much greater recognition.

A very different use of the Practice Cycle is evident in the making of patterns of what I have called 'intimate practice'. These arise from good preparation, readiness and creative, improvisational practice that ensures relationships remain central and close. Intimate practice means practitioners having authentic, close encounters with children of the kind where they see, hear, touch and sense the truth of their experience and are able to act on it. Workers achieve a state of aliveness and move around the home and have the intent, agility and playfulness to get alongside children and down to their level. They can be graceful, still and tender when they need to be in moments when they hold babies or stand alongside a parent who is doing the holding and stroke the infant's hand or hair. They provide comforting touch for children when they sense they need to be nurtured and show relish at seeing and being with children, giving them full 'embodied attention' (Bloom, 2006, p 14). This has included the book showing how practitioners can form and sustain hands-on relationships with babies and young children.

The concepts of 'intimate practice' and 'holding' have been developed in the book to convey the need for practice that not only holds children but parents. As well as knowing when and how to move and stand in encounters, practitioners need to be still and fully attentive when listening to and holding the anxieties, shame, anger and distress of parents. We have seen how this was helpful to many of the mothers in the book, like Samantha, Maria and Shanice, when addressing the trauma they carried from when they were abused as children and the domestic abuse they experienced when they were young parents. There was also the guilt, sadness and anger they felt about their older children being placed into care and still not being allowed to have them back.

A very important insight from the book is that while social workers are not trained therapists, the relational work they do has therapeutic value and impact. I have argued that a language is needed in social work that can capture moments of connection and relationships that are meaningful, touching and therapeutic. Following Hartmut Rosa (2019), I have called this way of being and experiencing relationships 'resonance'. This concept seeks to capture the vibrating wire of connection that occurs when people feel close and are moved and changed by the experience and relationship. It speaks to the kind of energetic presence needed to make a difference. These are satisfying experiences of emotional connection that have deep meaning and, as Rosa (2019) puts it, on good days make people's hearts sing. I have been privileged as a researcher to be present at many such intimate moments and to have felt their transformative energy. As I have argued, resonance does not only apply to happy, joyful times, like when parents have been helped to provide love and good enough care for their children and they and the worker delight in them. It can be experienced at times of sadness and loss and when there is conflict, and good authority is used to work through it. The dynamic that links all experiences of resonance is a sense of connection, responsivity, and being moved and changed by the encounter and relationship. I hope that paying attention to energies and the nature of people's presence and having a concept of resonance in social work and child protection can help to ensure that what is involved in such soulful meaningful encounters and relationships is better understood, sought after and developed.

New knowledge and skills for relationship-based practice

As I have been showing, through concepts such as intimate practice, holding, hostile relationships, relational styles, good authority and resonance, the book has sought to contribute new knowledge about social work and relationship-based practice. It also contributes to knowledge of the skills that are needed.

Home visiting is so central to social work and presents such unique challenges that several skills are involved. Gaining access to the home requires negotiation skills and composure. Once inside the house the skill of what I have called 'order-making' is very important. This arises from how being suddenly immersed in family life in all its busyness, the conditions necessary to be able to gather information from parents, relate to children and observe interactions must be created. A concept of 'atmosphere' should be used to help make sense of these spaces in terms of their sounds, smells, orderliness or neglect, comfort, aggression, their *feel* and how these impact on children, families and workers. We have seen, for example, how an atmosphere of intimidation, frenetic activity, melancholy and feelings of disgust at the home conditions affected a worker's mind, resulting in chaotic thinking, disorganised practice and avoidance of the children. Empathy, openness and honesty with families are crucial in establishing trust. This is developed and maintained through humility and practitioners actively listening to service users, recognising and affirming their feelings and needs, including their criticisms of services.

How practice is thought about needs to change and the skills base needed expanded. Learning interviewing skills, rapport building, and questioning styles and techniques is essential. But as Richard Devine (2025) puts it, social work is *messy* and when the fluid ways in which the work is done are considered, the notion of a static 'interview' between practitioners and service users who are seated across from one another becomes insufficient. Significant amounts of relating is done while moving, standing, hunkering, as well as while being seated and still. Students and practitioners need to be prepared for interviewing while on the move and learn the skill of how best to flow through domestic and other spaces while holding service users' attention – and often, in the case of children, their hand. The same applies to encounters in cars and walking interviews and other forms of outdoor practice and relating with children and adults. Being skilled at virtual communication and hybrid uses of digital and in-person interactions is also now essential.

These skills apply to all forms of relationships, be they broadly co-operative 'holding relationships' or 'hostile relationships' where the family do not want a service. However, hostile relationships bring particular challenges and have received far too little attention, and intensive training on how to manage them is needed. A crucial skill is using good authority and I have outlined how it can be done through the nine steps of Practice by Negotiation. Practitioners need to have a capacity for maintaining their composure in the face of volatile risky situations and being able to calm and hold the fears and anxieties of service users, including being what I have called 'a reliable hate object'. Learning through both formal and 'live' supervision how to draw on their 'internal supervisor' can help to develop their capacity to tolerate difficult emotions and learn from their emotional experiences. Such mindful support nurtures practitioners and, along with manageable caseloads and training, gives them space and time to think and better understand their relationships with children and families (Beddoe et al, 2022; Gregory, 2024).

Workers have different relational styles and preferences in who they like to work with (babies, children, adolescents or adults). I have argued that it is crucial to adopt inclusive language that recognises infant voice and the needs of babies, children and young people and the particular knowledge and skills required to work with them. Personal characteristics, whether we call it temperament, character, traits or personality, matter. Education, training and supervision need to enable professionals to gain self-knowledge and acquire what I have called a relational vocabulary. This is essential to knowing what one is comfortable and uncomfortable doing and being able to position oneself on the relational continuum between avoidance and intimacy. Learning from infant observation and gaining hands-on experience with babies and children from across the age and developmental spectrum needs to be provided on qualifying and continuing professional development courses. Distinguishing the core self from the 'professional self' is key to being able to meet the needs of children and parents in the moment and using intimate practice in ethical, therapeutic ways. Such self-knowledge also helps to set an agenda for ongoing professional development as a relational practitioner.

Re-making systems and child protection work

At every turn in this book, it has become evident that resources, organisational rules, procedures and culture are very influential in shaping how child protection is made. Huge amounts of energy and good intentions are put into trying to improve systems. Yet the sum of what constitutes 'the child protection system' has no real vision or energy for how the work can be authentically done and should be done through human relationships. Child protection work and systems are driven by what Rosa (2023, p 149) calls 'motivational energy'. Institutions and systems can't grow, improve or innovate by themselves. They need people to make progress happen. The current system is largely driven by negative motivational energy. This is put into avoiding 'failure' and the shame of being deemed 'inadequate' by government inspections, or children known to be at risk dying (Gibson, 2019). We have seen how huge effort is directed into accountability, paperwork, compliance with procedures, timescales and 'improvement'. Regulators who make these judgements about the quality of a service do not even go near the actual practice that goes on between social workers and service users and rarely even engage with service users (Ferguson et al, 2019). It is a system of governance that is driven by information, data and what Rosa (2019) calls relation-less relating. There have been many examples in the book of the effects this has and how relation-less relating seeps into practice. A social worker doesn't get alongside a child to be involved with the game they are playing but instead rushes them to talk about very sensitive things before they are ready to so they can complete their assessment on time. A manager can see in supervision that their staff member is deeply upset about being attacked by a service user, but they overlook it and focus on staff performance issues and targets instead.

On top of bureaucratic demands, austerity and cuts to staffing and services mean that social work departments are under huge pressure to prioritise and it is not possible to provide the same level of contact and high support to all the families who need it. The social worker Miriam's comment in Chapter 8 that the therapeutic holding relationship she achieved with Samantha, Oliver and their child Louis was an exception and not the norm is a terrible indictment of how poorly the child protection system is resourced and where managers' and practitioners' energies are directed to go. This means that too often the child protection system imposes an individualised coercive response on families from diverse backgrounds, including working-class, migrant, Indigenous, and other underrepresented or marginalised communities that is based on narrow assessments of risks to children (Bywaters et al, 2022). For some critics, this means that the system is inherently oppressive and unethical, it is 'broken beyond repair' (Featherstone et al, 2021). What is needed instead is a wider framing that recognises the corrosive effects of structural inequalities and 'social suffering' (Bourdieu, 2000). Such a social model of child and family social care would be based on strengthening families by giving them the material resources, healthy neighbourhoods, social supports and therapeutic services to enable them to care well enough for their children (Parton, 2014; Featherstone et al, 2018; Hyslop and Keddell, 2018; Keddell et al, 2022; 2023). Critical, anti-oppressive practice that addresses the effects of structural inequalities based on gender, race, class, sexuality and disability is essential (Bernard, 2022).

This would also include involving families as partners and co-producers of ways to improve child well-being. Parent advocates who have lived experience of child protection can be vital allies for parents, especially mothers, who are currently forced to carry a huge burden of responsibility in families and in keeping children safe (Saar-Heiman et al, 2024). Men who are perpetrators of domestic abuse would be made accountable and fathers proactively included in all family work and helped to develop as carers where it is safe to do so (Mandel, 2024).

Foundations for change are also to be found in the increasingly prominent voices of individuals with lived experience of social work and of growing up in care (Cherry, 2022; Pierre, 2024). Such critiques are reshaping expectations of social workers and their relationships with service users. For example, Rebekah Pierre (2022) offers a powerful account of the traumas she endured, her experiences within the care system and her later return as an adult to read her case files. This revealed to her the shocking, dehumanising and reductive ways she was treated, written about, misrepresented and misunderstood. It should be impossible to engage with Rebekah's and others' experiences without feeling compelled to reflect on, and change, both practice and approaches to record-keeping (Pierre, 2023; 2024).

Child maltreatment is what Devaney and Spratt (2007) call a 'wicked problem' due to its complexity and the impossibility of simple solutions. It requires whole societal responses and long-term strategies involving earlier identification of and intervention with children who are experiencing multiple adversity. This kind of large-scale radical reset of children's social care would require a revolution in funding and provision of early family help that could include unlocking the potential of family networks to provide support for struggling parents and children (MacAlister, 2022). As Rosa (2023, p 149) puts it, we need 'to pull the energetic plug' on unbridled accountability and bureaucratisation, making the fears that drive it disappear, or at least significantly reducing them. Much greater understanding is needed of the systemic and psycho-social dynamics and complexity of relationships that this book has revealed. There needs to be greater tolerance of errors and acceptance of the limits of what it is humanly possible to achieve in protecting children. As I have argued, it is not 'perfection' but a concept of 'good enough practice' that is needed.

Child protection and a good life

Arguments for major structural reform of children's services are compelling and make a valuable contribution to reimagining child protection and 'an alternative standard for evaluating quality and performance' (Rosa, 2023, p 150). But system change has to start from where we currently are and it is vital there is knowledge and understanding of what humane and effective child protection practice looks like and can be built on. To happen, change needs to be motivated by positive energies, people need to be inspired and given hope. We need a vision of what a good life is in child protection, for children, families and professionals. In essence, this is a life based on meaningful relationships that are given the time and resources they need and that produce experiences of resonance. Even amid all today's constraints and frustrations, the book has shown that this kind of positive energy exists, that good helpful practice is achieved and I believe that learning from this can contribute a great deal to a blueprint for the future. Further evidence for this can be found in anecdotal accounts of innovative practice and the satisfaction derived from helping and being helped that are shared regularly on LinkedIn and other social media platforms by social work staff and service users.

A reformed system will always need practitioners to go out and skilfully, authoritatively and empathetically engage with children and families and we need to learn about how this can be done from the good practice that is currently going on. I'm thinking, for example, of the way practitioners like Miriam in Chapter 8 help children to be safe and parents to change through a 'holding relationship' that is made through being reliable, ethical, emotionally attuned, tactile and immersed in the family's day-to-day existence, helping them to develop care and life skills. Shelly, who featured in Chapters 3 and 7, did the same by helping Maria and Patrick keep their baby girl, Isabelle, which included Shelly having a direct relationship with the baby and regularly holding and attuning to her. Then there is the way Jessica in Chapter 6 moved so skilfully through the home and connected so quickly and intimately with Anton and Nikita. She provided material resources – beds, bedding, curtains, lightbulbs, toys – that enhanced the quality of their daily lives and created meaningful therapeutic moments for them that improved their well-being, safety and relationship with their mother. I'm thinking of Jim in Chapter 2 who would stop at nothing to try and locate children in the community and managers like Raymond who supported him so attentively and sensitively while he was doing it. I'm also thinking of Christina who, as we saw in Chapter 3, kept going back to see the James family, despite home conditions that were very difficult to be in and 16-year-old Lily often telling her how much she hated her. And Lynne in Chapter 1 and Molly in Chapter 10 who, like the others I've just mentioned, had a palpable desire to connect with and help children and families and clearly did so, with the skills and energetic presence of resonance to match. Being around these workers and managers and so close to their practice and the families they helped and listening to parents' positive accounts of their relationships and what they meant to them was inspiring. They can help us understand what is involved in child protection and a good life. My hope is that by presenting in a detailed way how such skilful, deeply humane, resonant practice is made this book can inspire others to learn from it, achieve it and even for it ultimately to become the norm.

We need to think similarly about organisational culture and support. As the book has shown, supportive working environments are those that are designed in ways that enable active communication and relational activity, formal and live supervision between practitioners and managers. There is a powerful narrative in social work that practitioners need more time to spend with families and do quality work and this is very true. But it is vital that they know how best to use that time. I hope that the book can provide learning about the kinds of relational practice and organisational settings and practices that are needed to support the adoption of intimate child protection practice and its development into the future. A cultural shift is needed that gives far more recognition to practice and outcomes that are good. In all my years of observing practitioners and managers I've been struck by how little time is spent dwelling on heartfelt achievements. Some expressions of joy for the child and family and job satisfaction can happen. Very soon, however, the worker is back at their computer, case recording, evidencing service 'improvement' and focused on all the other families they are working with.

The book has shown that the extent to which a positive culture of affirmation exists varies from place to place. In essence, the more relational social work leadership and teams are the more able they are to resist the internalisation of blame and anxiety and develop instead a humane and collegial culture. In such working environments feelings of joy and satisfaction are not only expressed but internalised individually and collectively and become embedded in the organisation and its atmosphere. It feels good to be in these environments, which vibrate with the satisfying energy of resonance. There is an underpinning shared understanding that while the work is hard and there is sadness and pain and loss for some families and moral distress for workers because they cannot help all families in ways they would like, relations of value and positive outcomes can be and are achieved. Child protection practice is most effective when it takes the form of skilful, intimate work and understands and values relationships that carry emotional resonance. The more social workers are shown compassion and given resources, space, time and support to think, learn and skilfully achieve relationship-based practice with children and families, the more able they will be to keep on making child protection work well and to make it even better.

APPENDIX

Methodology and the research studies

The book draws on research data that was gathered between 2010 and 2022 in seven research projects. The studies used ethnographic methods in various ways to closely examine social work and child protection practice, observing both direct encounters between practitioners and children and families, as well as everyday activity within social work offices. Three of the studies were funded by the UK Economic and Social Research Council (ESRC) and provided sizeable grants that enabled them to investigate practice and relationships in sustained ways over relatively lengthy periods of time. All of the studies were granted ethical approval by the universities where I worked and the agencies who took part. All participating professionals and families gave informed consent to take part. While the case materials and examples used in the book reflect actual events and findings, all names and some other details have been changed to protect the anonymity of the families, professionals and research sites.

The background to my interest in this research is that having been a social worker in child protection in the late 1970s and 1980s I became interested in researching it and why it takes the forms that it does. I did a PhD at the University of Cambridge on the history and sociology of child protection, studying its origins in the UK and Ireland from the late 19th century and tracing its development through to the 1980s (see Ferguson, 2004). I began my first lectureship in social work in 1990 and spent around 20 years researching social work and child protection by primarily using qualitative methods such as interviews with practitioners, managers and service users. I became increasingly frustrated by the limits of that approach and around 2010 it occurred to me that instead of trying to learn about practice by asking participants about their experiences I should observe them having them. While there had been important studies that observed the work of social workers and managers in their offices (Pithouse, 1987; Buckley, 2003; Broadhurst et al, 2010; Helm, 2016 Saltiel, 2016), hardly any research had taken the step of shadowing them as they worked with families. The assumption appeared to be that the work was too sensitive for a researcher to observe, as their presence might distract from the serious task of keeping children safe.

I was very fortunate to find a social work team who were willing to allow me to observe them and work with me to develop an ethnographic approach that was ethical. Then, in 2012–2013, I completed my first ESRC-funded study into what social workers do, by getting as close as possible to practice by participating in and observing social workers in their work. Senior leaders in the two local authorities where the research took place gave initial consent to allow access to their staff and individual workers could then choose whether or not they wished to be involved. It takes a lot of courage for managers and workers to allow their practice to be observed, analysed and written about, even when they know that all identifying characteristics will be changed. Twenty-four social workers took part, 19 women and five men, and three were from Black and minority ethnic backgrounds. Their length of service varied from being newly qualified to having almost 30 years' experience. I shadowed practitioners by going out with them on home visits and other places they saw children, interviewing them on the way to the visit and straight afterwards about their experience – usually in the car – and observing and audio-recording the encounters between the social workers and service users.

In total, 87 practice encounters were observed and audio-recorded, 71 of which were on home visits. The remainder took place in social work offices and schools. I conducted all the fieldwork myself over a six-month period. The key research questions were: What do social workers do in performing child protection, especially on home visits? What do they say to children and parents? How do they act? How close to children do they get? (See Ferguson (2016a) for a full account of the methodology.)

As well as ethnography, the research drew on the new interest in mobile research methods (Urry, 2007) to capture everyday movements by, for instance, conducting interviews while walking and in the car (Kusenbach, 2003; O'Neill and Roberts, 2020). The research was also informed by how ethnography had developed to take fuller account of the senses and the lived experience of the body on social practices – what Pink (2015) calls 'sensory ethnography'. These methods provided new ways for researchers to be present to capture the bodily and sensory experiences of research participants as they happen and to take fuller account of movement, atmospheres and the implications of *where* they happen, like on home visits. The psycho-social approach to the research also meant that psychoanalytic thinking influenced how I conducted observations and interviews by seeking to go 'below the surface' and understand the nature and impact of the emotional experience and internal lives of practitioners, managers, family members and entire organisations (Archard, 2020).

Social work teams at both sites were involved who did short-term duty/investigative/assessment work and longer-term work with children and families. All the access to observations of practice were negotiated through the social workers, who asked for parents' consent for the researcher to accompany them. Some families were never asked as their situations were regarded by social workers and managers as unsuitable for research visits. Some families who were asked did not wish to be involved and were never contacted or visited by the researcher. The agreement with the agencies and the families included that if there was the slightest indication that the researcher's presence was adversely affecting any family member or the social worker's practice then the researcher would leave. It was never felt necessary to do this, even though some quite dramatic and emotionally charged episodes were observed. The intention was to be as unobtrusive and invisible as possible to try and capture how the events would have happened in the same way had a researcher not been present. It is unlikely, however, that the presence of the researcher has no impact on what they are observing, but just how much and what kind of impact is debatable (Hammersley and Atkinson, 2007). Ethnographic research by many anthropologists, for instance, involves full participation in their lives and getting to know participants so well that they are regarded as friends (Miller, 2024). In my view this is not appropriate for social work research, especially if the aim is to find out what social workers do. So, my approach has always been to be as close as it is possible to get, participate as little as possible, stay quiet and observe attentively.

Observational data on the encounters was taken on the spot through handwritten notes, recording what was unfolding. Because the conversations were being audio-recorded I did not have to hurriedly try to write down what was being said. This freed me up to draw 'maps' of the room(s), noting key interactions in terms of who was seated or stood where, who moved where and when, body postures, objects (toys, ornaments, furniture, and so on) in the room and workers' use of them, or not, and the presence of dogs and other pets. This was part of the method of drawing out the nature and influence of everyday things and the material culture through which the practice went on (Miller, 2010; Ingold, 2011). Field notes were also taken afterwards, detailing further impressions of the journeys, practice encounters and what happened in the social work office involving colleagues and managers. I also gave names to the moods and tone of the encounters and atmospheres in the room(s) and their apparent impact.

All the audio data was transcribed and analysed thematically. A key finding concerned the relatively high number of young pre-school children involved. In almost a third of the cases social workers regarded the children as lacking the verbal capacity and understanding to be seen on their own (Ferguson, 2016b). This made an ethnographic approach that went beyond the analysis of conversations even more important, as observation made it possible to illuminate how workers related to children of all ages through the presence or absence of touch, the gaze, smiles, play, as well as talk. A case study method was also adopted by bringing together the social worker interview data from before and after the visit, the audio-recording of the interactions and the observation and field notes. Triangulation of that data provided for case studies of individual practice encounters in homes and elsewhere and casework over a longer period. Cross-case comparative analysis enabled the drawing out of themes, which could be illustrated by detailed case studies (Bryman, 2016). Taken together, this ethnographic approach enabled me to identify patterns of casework in how social workers reached and engaged with children and families, or did not do so. New insights were gained into social workers' embodied experiences of relating to children and parents and home visiting, enabling practice patterns to be drawn out and deeper understandings of how things did and did not go as planned.

I became increasingly aware that I needed to focus more systematically on what goes on in offices and the impact of organisational practices, culture and support on staff experiences, well-being and practice. I also wanted to dig deeper into what occurs in longer-term casework. Virtually no such research has been done into long-term social work, an absence that is even more remarkable given that in high profile cases where children have not been protected, often families were worked with over long periods and usually years. There has also been little research into how social work practitioners work with parents in order to create change and are supported by their organisations to promote children's safety and well-being over the long term (Forrester et al, 2019). I also felt I needed to hear directly from service users about their experiences. In 2016, a substantial grant was obtained for a two-year ethnographic study that incorporated all those things. I led the research team that consisted of Tarsem Singh Cooner, Jadwiga Leigh, Liz Beddoe, Lisa Warwick and Tom Disney. The research adopted a qualitative longitudinal methodology (Neale, 2019) and used participant observation to explore how social workers establish, develop and sustain long-term relationships with children and parents in child protection cases and how this is influenced by organisational life, staff support and supervision (for a comprehensive account of the study and methodology, see Ferguson et al, 2020a).

The fieldwork was conducted simultaneously in two local authorities in England and 15 months were spent based in offices and shadowing social workers at both sites (Leigh et al, 2020). The research team spent a total of 402 days in the field. The first three months of fieldwork were used to identify a sample of 30 cases that were then shadowed for as long as they were open for up to a year. We had no way of knowing at the outset how long the 30 cases (15 at each site) we sampled would be open for and in the event 12 were shadowed for the full 12 months, one for 11 and 22 were shadowed for at least eight months. A total of 271 practice encounters between social care staff and service users were observed, 146 of which were home visits. Forty-five staff supervisions were observed (Beddoe et al, 2022; Warwick et al, 2022). Fifty-four interviews took place with families, some of which involved up to three interviews with the same families over the course of the year. We also extracted data from social work case files about the total work that was done over the year. Once again, mobile research methods were used so we could travel with practitioners, interviewing them on the way to and from home visits and other places where children and families were seen (Disney et al, 2019).

The practice encounters between practitioners and service users were observed and audio-recorded. What was distinctive about this study was an approach that observed practitioners working with the same service users on multiple occasions to explore how practice was carried out as it unfolded over time. It involved repeatedly visiting the same families alongside social workers, conducting up to 21 practice observations within the same cases over the course of a year, while also gathering data from within the social work organisation. Similar close attention was given to observing and recording encounters between staff in the social work offices, soaking up atmospheres and organisational cultures. A case study method was adopted by bringing together all the data on each family/case and this provided 30 very detailed case studies of long-term social work practice. Due to the large size of each case study and the insights they gave into the detail of practice, what Wengraff (2001) calls the 'focal' or 'gold-star cases' within qualitative research samples were identified. These not only tell their own story about the family and casework but illustrate the general research findings from the study particularly well. The same approach to selection of case material has been taken in this book.

Inevitably, we grappled with many ethical issues and dilemmas about how to react to some of the things we found, such as finding men who were considered dangerous to children and women in family homes who should not have been there and the use of Facebook by some practitioners and managers as an extra form of surveillance of families (Cooner et al, 2020). We had to discover whether being embedded within social work teams for 15 months and in families and casework for up to 12 months could be done ethically and relationships with the field sites and families successfully sustained. We concluded that, on balance, it can. No participants ever told us that our presence made things worse and several social workers and family members said they found it helpful (for a full discussion, see Ferguson et al, 2020a). This supports other research that shows that involving parents is ethically important because it can do good and be to their benefit (Westlake and Forrester, 2016).

The third ESRC-funded study employed the method of 'digital ethnography', with Sarah Pink and Laura Kelly as the other research team members. Due to the COVID-19 pandemic and social distancing rules it was not possible to get close to people and practice due to the high risk of either catching or spreading COVID-19, or both. The primary research question was: How can practices that have relied on achieving closeness keep children safe and help families in a period of institutionalised social distancing? We also explored: What innovative digital methods are being adopted and how can they be most productively used during and after the pandemic? What are service users' experiences of social work during the pandemic? What is it like for staff working almost exclusively from home?

The research adopted a qualitative longitudinal approach that followed the experiences of a sample of practitioners and managers during the pandemic by interviewing them approximately every month between April and December 2020. The sample consisted of 29 social workers, ten social work managers and nine family support workers drawn from four local authority areas in England that represented a broad geographical spread. Twenty of the social workers and six operational managers worked in long-term child protection and 'child in need' teams, five social workers were in initial assessment teams, three worked with children with disabilities, two were from children in care teams, and one was in an intensive intervention team. Forty-one were women and seven men. Seven participants identified as belonging to an ethnic minority background, including Black, Asian, or other racial and ethnic groups. A core sample of social workers were interviewed seven times over the nine months of data collection. Due to how the pandemic made in-person research encounters unsafe, our data was gathered remotely on video calls, using WhatsApp video, FaceTime, Teams and Zoom. We also video-recorded interactions between social workers and families on a small number of video calls, with the aim of deepening understanding of digital communication (Pink et al, 2022). All interviews were audio-recorded, fully transcribed and were thematically analysed using NVivo 12 Plus (see Ferguson et al, 2022a).

We also interviewed 21 parents and one grandparent, most of whom (17) were involved in the longitudinal case studies. Where family support workers and social work assistants were involved with the families, they too were interviewed. This enabled us to assemble case studies that represented the experience of a range of key actors over time and to track how relationships were formed, and sustained, or not. Not being able to get physically close to practice prevented the research from being able to see, hear and sense the interactions and atmospheres of encounters and organisational cultures. However, it still helped to develop the concepts of 'intimate' and 'holding' practice and the unheld child (Ferguson et al, 2022b). Crucially, it provided the opportunity to study in-depth the use of digital technology in communicating with children and families, including 'virtual home visits' and in professional meetings and staff support (Ferguson et al, 2022a).

In between these larger studies I used similar ethnographic methods and ethical procedures to get close to practice and organisations in evaluations of children's services and child protection practice. All this research adds up to observations of over 400 practice encounters between social workers and children and families, more than 600 car journeys with social workers, lengthy periods observing in social work offices, and several hundred interviews with social work staff and many with family members.

My enthusiasm for ethnography should not be taken to mean that I regard it as a way of gaining straightforward access to the 'truth'. Knowledge produced through participant observation is not an exact reflection of what happened but a researcher's interpretation and as such is contestable (Ferguson, 2016a). The studies add up to a significant body of work but share the limitations of all qualitative research in that the amount of data gathered and the relatively small number of research sites makes generalisation across social work and child protection difficult. The aim of such research is to provide contextualised understandings of practices and cultures that can be learned from. Getting as close as it is possible to get to child protection work across a range of studies has enabled a great deal to be seen and experienced that other research methods would not have revealed and that was previously hidden.

References

Abram, J. (1996) *The Language of Winnicott*, Karnac.
Alpert, A. (2022) *The Good Enough Life*, Princeton University Press.
Andreassen, R., Nebeling Petersen, R., Harrison, K. and Raun, T. (2018) *Mediated Intimacies: Connectivities, Relationalities and Proximities*, Routledge.
Antonopoulou, V., Killian, M. and Forrester, D. (2017) 'Levels of stress and anxiety in child and family social work: Workers' perceptions of organizational structure, professional support and workplace opportunities in children's services in the UK', *Children and Youth Services Review*, 76: 42–50.
Archard, P.J. (2020) 'The psychoanalytically-informed interview in social work research', *Journal of Social Work Practice*, 35(2): 191–203.
Ash, K. and Grey, B. (2022) '"I feel … I need to defend myself": Exploring the influence of social worker's attachment history on the social worker-client relationships', *Human Systems: Therapy, Culture and Attachments*, 2(3): 125–143.
Astvik, W., Welander, J. and Larsson, R. (2020) 'Reasons for staying: A longitudinal study of social work conditions predicting social workers' willingness to stay in their organisation', *British Journal of Social Work*, 50(5): 1382–1400.
Baginsky, M. (2023) 'Parents' views on improving relationships with their social workers', *Journal of Social Work*, 23(1): 3–18.
Baginsky, M. and Manthorpe, J. (2021) 'The impact of COVID-19 on children's social care in England', *Child Abuse & Neglect*, 116(2): 104739.
Barber, J.G. (1991) *Beyond Casework*, Macmillan.
Barron, C.C., Dayton, C.J. and Goletz, J.L. (2022) 'From the voices of supervisees: What is reflective supervision and how does it support their work? (Part I)', *Infant Mental Health Journal*, 43(2): 207–225.
Bazzano, M. (2013) 'Cultivating presence', *Therapy Today*, November.
Beckett, H. and Pearce, J. eds., (2018) *Understanding and Responding to Child Sexual Exploitation*, Routledge.
Beddoe, L., Ferguson, H., Warwick, L., Disney, T., Leigh, J. and Cooner, T.S. (2022) 'Supervision in child protection: A space and place for reflection or an excruciating marathon of compliance?', *European Journal of Social Work*, 25(3): 525–537.
Beresford, P. (2005) '"Service user": Regressive or liberatory terminology?', *Disability & Society*, 20(4): 469–477.
Berlant, L. (2011) *Cruel Optimism*, Duke University Press.
Bernard, C. (2022) *Intersectionality for Social Workers*, Routledge.
Bernard, C. and Greenwood, T. (2019) '"We're giving you the sack": Social workers' perspectives of intervening in affluent families when there are concerns about child neglect', *British Journal of Social Work*, 49(8): 2266–2282.

Biggart, L., Ward, E., Cook, L. and Schofield, G. (2017) 'The team as a secure base: Promoting resilience and competence in child and family social work', *Children and Youth Services Review*, 83: 119–130.

Bilson, A. and Martin, K.E. (2016) 'Referrals and child protection in England: One in five children referred to children's services and one in nineteen investigated before the age of five', *British Journal of Social Work*, 47(3): 793–811.

Bion, W. (1962) *Learning from Experience*, Heinemann.

Bion, W. (1970) *Attention and Interpretation*, Maresfield.

Bissell, D., Straughan, E.R. and Gorman-Murray, A. (2020) 'Losing touch with people and place: Labor mobilities, desensitized bodies, disconnected lives', *Annals of the American Association of Geographers*, 110(6): 1891–1906.

Bloom, K. (2005) 'Articulating preverbal experience', in N. Totton (ed), *New Dimensions in Body Psychotherapy* (pp 56–69), Open University Press.

Bloom, K. (2006) *The Embodied Self: Movement and Psychoanalysis*, Karnac Books.

Bogue, K.S. (2025) 'For a carnal social work: A review of the body in social work literature', *British Journal of Social Work*, 55(1): 472–492.

Bostock, L. and Koprowska, J. (2022) '"I know how it sounds on paper": Risk talk, the use of documents and epistemic justice in child protection assessment home visits', *Qualitative Social Work*, 21(6): 1147–1166.

Bostock, L., Patrizo, L., Godfrey, T. and Forrester, D. (2019a) 'What is the impact of supervision on direct practice with families?', *Children and Youth Services Review*, 105: 104428.

Bostock, L., Patrizo, L., Godfrey, T., Munro, E. and Forrester, D. (2019b) 'How do we assess the quality of supervision? Developing a coding framework', *Children and Youth Services Review*, 100: 515–524.

Bostock, L., Patrizo, L., Godfrey, T. and Forrester, D. (2022) 'Why does systemic supervision support practitioners' practice more effectively with children and families?', *Children and Youth Services Review*, 142: 106652.

Bourdieu, P. (2000) *The Weight of the World: Social Suffering in Contemporary Society*, Stanford University Press.

Bower, M. (ed) (2005) *Psychoanalytic Theory for Social Work Practice*, Routledge.

Bowlby, J. (1973) *Attachment and Loss: Separation, Anxiety and Anger*, Pimlico.

Brandon, M., Belderson, P., Warren, C., Howe, D., Gardner, R., Dodsworth, J., et al (2008) *Analysing Child Deaths and Serious Injury through Abuse and Neglect: What Can We Learn? A Biennial Analysis of Serious Case Reviews 2003–2005*, Department of Children, Schools and Families.

Brandon, M., Bailey, S. and Belderson, P. (2010) *Building on the Learning from Serious Case Reviews: A Two-year Analysis of Child Protection Database Notifications 2007–2009*, Department for Education.

Briggs, S. (2005) 'Psychoanalytic research in the era of evidence-based practice', in M. Bower (ed), *Psychoanalytic Theory for Social Work Practice* (pp 15–30), Routledge.

Briggs, S. (2017) 'Working with troubled adolescents: Observation as a key skill for practitioners', in H. Hingley-Jones, C. Parkinson and L. Allain (eds), *Observation in Health and Social Care: Applications for Learning, Research and Practice with Children and Adults* (pp 101–120), Jessica Kingsley.

Broadhurst, K. and Mason, C. (2012) 'Social work beyond the VDU: Foregrounding *co-presence* in situated practice – why face-to-face practice matters', *British Journal of Social Work*, 44(3): 578–595.

Broadhurst, K., Wastell, D., White, S., Hall, C., Peckover, S., Thompson, K., et al (2010) 'Performing "initial assessment": Identifying the latent conditions for error at the front-door of local authority children's services', *British Journal of Social Work*, 40(2): 352–370.

Broadhurst, K., Alrouh, B., Yeend, E., Harwin, J., Shaw, M., Pilling, M., et al (2015) 'Connecting events in time to identify a hidden population: Birth mothers and their children in recurrent care proceedings in England', *British Journal of Social Work*, 45(8): 2241–2260.

Broadhurst, K., Mason, C. and Ward, H. (2022) 'Urgent care proceedings for new-born babies in England and Wales: Time for a fundamental review', *International Journal of Law, Policy and the Family*, 36(1): ebac008.

Bryan, A., Hingley-Jones, H., and Ruch, G. (2016) 'Relationship-based practice revisited', *Journal of Social Work Practice*, 30(3): 229–223.

Bryman, A. (2016) *Social Research Methods*, Oxford University Press.

Buckley, H. (2003) *Child Protection Work: Beyond the Rhetoric*, Jessica Kingsley.

Bull, R. (2018) 'The investigative interviewing of children and other vulnerable witnesses: Psychological research and working/professional practice', in *Investigating the Truth: Selected Works of Ray Bull* (pp 126–146), Routledge.

Bülow, C.v. and Simpson, P. (2022) *Negative Capacity in Leadership Practice*, Palgrave Macmillan.

Burns, K., Christie, A. and O'Sullivan, S. (2020) 'Findings from a longitudinal qualitative study of child protection social workers' retention: Job embeddedness, professional confidence and staying narratives', *British Journal of Social Work*, 50(5): 1363–1381.

Burton, V. and Revell, L. (2018) 'Professional curiosity in child protection: Thinking the unthinkable in a neo-liberal world', *British Journal of Social Work*, 48(6): 1508–1523.

Bywaters, P., Brady, G., Sparks, T. and Bos, E. (2016) 'Inequalities in child welfare intervention rates: The intersection of deprivation and identity', *Child and Family Social Work*, 21(4): 452–463.

Bywaters, P., Skinner, G., Cooper, A., Kennedy, E. and Malik, A. (2022) *The Nuffield Foundation, Final Report – The Relationship Between Poverty and Child Abuse and Neglect: New Evidence*. Available at: https://www.nuffieldfoundation.org/wp-content/uploads/2022/03/Full-reportrelationship-between-poverty-child-abuse-and-neglect.pdf (Accessed 2 January 2023).

Calder, M.C. (ed) (2008) *The Carrot or the Stick? Towards Effective Practice with Involuntary Clients in Safeguarding Children Work*, Russell House Publishing.

Cameron, C. and McDermott, F. (2007) 'Social work and the body', *British Journal of Social Work*, 37(1): 41–56.

Carpenter, J., Webb, C.M. and Bostock, L. (2013) 'The surprisingly weak evidence base for supervision: Findings from a systematic review of research in child welfare practice (2000–2012)', *Children and Youth Services Review*, 35(11): 1843–1853.

Casement, P. (1985) *On Learning from the Patient*, Tavistock.

Casement, P. (2006) *Learning from Life*, Routledge.

Cellan-Jones, R. (2021) *Always On: Hope and Fear in the Social Smartphone Era*, Bloomsbury.

Cherry, L. (ed) (2022) *The Brightness of Stars: Stories from Care Experienced Adults to Inspire Change*, Routledge.

Child Safeguarding Practice Review Panel (2022a) *National Review into the Murders of Arthur Labinjo-Hughes and Star Hobson*, OGL, Crown copyright.

Child Safeguarding Practice Review Panel (2022b) *Bruising in Non-mobile Infants*, OGL, Crown copyright.

Child Safeguarding Practice Review Panel (2024) *Annual Report, 2022–23*, OGL, Crown copyright. Available at: https://assets.publishing.service.gov.uk/media/65b90b75ee7d4900139849c3/Child_Safeguarding_Review_Panel_annual_report_2022_to_2023.pdf (Accessed 21 June 2024).

Collins, S. (2008) 'Statutory social workers: Stress, job satisfaction, coping, social support and individual differences', *British Journal of Social Work*, 38: 1173–1193.

Cook, L. (2020) 'The home visit in child protection social work: Emotion as resource and risk for professional judgement and practice', *Child & Family Social Work*, 25(1): 18–26.

Cook, L. and Zschomler, D. (2020) 'Virtual home visits during the COVID-19 pandemic: Social workers' perspectives', *Practice*, 32(5): 401–408.

Cook, L., Zschomler, D., Biggart, L. and Carder, S. (2020) 'The team as a secure base revisited: Remote working and resilience among child and family social workers during COVID-19', *Journal of Children's Services*, 15(4): 259–266.

Cooner, T.S., Beddoe, L., Ferguson, H. and Joy, E. (2020) 'The use of Facebook in social work practice with children and families: Exploring complexity in an emerging practice', *Journal of Technology in Human Services*, 38(2): 137–158.

Cooper, A. (2005) 'Surface and depth in the Victoria Climbié Inquiry Report', *Child and Family Social Work*, 10(1): 1–9.

Cooper, A. (2018) *Conjunctions: Social Work, Psychoanalysis and Society*, Routledge.

Cooper, A. and Lousada, J. (2005) *Borderline Welfare: Feeling and Fear of Feeling in Modern Welfare*, Karnac.

Copson, R., Murphy, A.M., Cook, L., Neil, E. and Sorensen, P. (2022) 'Relationship-based practice and digital technology in child and family social work: Learning from practice during the COVID-19 pandemic', *Developmental Child Welfare*, 4(1): 3–19.

Coulter, S., Houston, S., Mooney, S., Devaney, J. and Davidson, G. (2020) 'Attaining theoretical coherence within relationship-based practice in child and family social work: The systemic perspective', *British Journal of Social Work*, 50(4): 1219–1237.

Coventry LCSB (2013) *Serious Case Review into the Experience of Daniel Pelka*, Coventry Children's Safeguarding Board.

Cozolino, L. (2004) *The Making of a Therapist*, Norton.

Critchley, A. (2020) '"The lion's den": Social workers' understandings of risk to infants', *Child and Family Social Work*, 25: 895–903.

Critchley, A., Grant, A., Brown, A. and Morriss, L. (2022) 'Breastfeeding, social work and the rights of infants who have been removed', *Qualitative Social Work*, 21(1): 3–14.

Davys, A. and Beddoe, L. (2021) *Best Practice in Professional Supervision: A Guide for the Helping Professions*, Jessica Kingsley.

DCSF (Department for Children, Schools and Families) (2009) *Safeguarding Children and Young People from Sexual Exploitation: Supplementary Guidance to Working Together to Safeguard Children*, HM Government.

DCSF (2010) *Working Together to Safeguard Children: A Guide to Interagency Working to Safeguard and Promote the Welfare of Children*, HM Government.

D'Cruz, H., Gillingham, P. and Melendez, S. (2007) 'Reflexivity, its meanings and relevance for social work: A critical review of the literature', *British Journal of Social Work*, 37(1): 73–90.

Deleuze, G. and Guattari, F. (1987) *A Thousand Plateaus: Capitalism and Schizophrenia*, University of Minnesota Press.

Department of Health (2000) *Framework for the Assessment of Children in Need and Their Families*, The Stationery Office.

Department of Health and Social Care (2024) *Reflecting on Parent-Infant Relationships: A Practitioner's Guide to Starting Conversations*, HM Government.

Department of Health and Social Security (1974) *Report of the Committee of Inquiry into the Care and Supervision Provided in Relation to Maria Colwell*, HMSO.

Derby and Derbyshire Local Safeguarding Practice Review (2024) *Theo*, https://www.ddscp.org.uk/media/derby-scb/content-assets/documents/serious-case-reviews/ddscp_tds20_lcspr_final(2)_14.03.24.pdf (Accessed 23 June 2024).

Devaney, J. and Spratt, T. (2007) 'Child abuse as a complex and wicked problem: Reflecting on policy developments in the United Kingdom in working with children and families with multiple problems', *Children and Youth Services Review*, 31(6): 635–641.

Devaney, J., Hayes, D. and Spratt, T. (2017) 'The influences of training and experience in removal and reunification decisions involving children at risk of maltreatment: Detecting a "beginner dip"', *British Journal of Social Work*, 47(8): 2364–2383.

Devine, R. (2025) *Messy Social Work*, Jessica Kingsley.

DfE (Department for Education) (2013) *Working Together to Safeguard Children*, HM Government.

DfE (2018) *Working Together to Safeguard Children*, HM Government.

DfE (2023) *Working Together to Safeguard Children*, HM Government.
DfE (2024) *Characteristics of Children in Need, Reporting Year 2023*, HM Government.
DfE (2025) *Families First Partnership Programme*, HM Government.
Diaz, C. (2020) *Decision Making in Child and Family Social Work: Perspectives on Children's Participation*, Policy Press.
Dickens, J., Taylor, J., Cook, L., Cossar, J., Garstang, J., Hallett, N., et al (2022a) *Learning for the Future: Final Analysis of Serious Case Reviews 2017–19*, Department for Education.
Dickens, J., Taylor, J., Cook, L., Cossar, J., Garstang, J. and Rimmer, J. (2022b) *Serious Case Reviews 1998–2019: Continuities, Changes and Challenges*, Department for Education.
Dickens, J., Cook, L., Cossar, J., Okpokiri, C., Taylor, J. and Garstang, J. (2023) 'Re-envisaging professional curiosity and challenge: Messages for child protection practice from reviews of serious cases in England', *Children and Youth Services Review*, 152: 107081.
Dillon, J. (2021) '"Wishes and feelings": Misunderstandings and missed opportunities for participation in child protection proceedings', *Child and Family Social Work*, 26(4): 664–676.
Dingwall, R., Eekelaar, J. and Murray, T. (1983) *The Protection of Children: State Intervention and Family Life*, Basil Blackwell.
Disney, T., Warwick, L., Ferguson, H., Leigh, J., Cooner, T.S. and Beddoe, L. (2019) '"Isn't it funny the children that are further away we don't think about as much?": Using GPS to explore the mobilities and geographies of social work and child protection practice', *Children and Youth Services Review*, 100: 39–49.
Douglas, M. (1966) *Purity and Danger: An Analysis of the Concepts of Pollution and Taboo*, Routledge.
Dunk-West, P. (2018) *How to be a Social Worker* (2nd edn), Bloomsbury.
Duschinsky, R., Lampitt, S. and Bell, S. (2016) *Sustaining Social Work: Between Power and Powerlessness*, Palgrave.
Edwards, S. and Turnell, A. (1999) *Signs of Safety: A Solution and Safety Oriented Approach to Child Protection Casework*, Norton.
Elwick, S., Bradley, B. and Sumsion, J. (2014) 'Infants as others: Uncertainties, difficulties, and (im)possibilities in researching infants' lives', *International Journal of Qualitative Studies in Education*, 27: 196–213.
Eraut, M. (2008) 'Knowledge creation and knowledge use in professional contexts', *Studies in Higher Education*, 10(2): 117–133.
Featherstone, B., Gupta, A., Morris, K. and White, S. (2018) *Protecting Children: A Social Model*, Policy Press.
Featherstone, B., Morris, K., Daniel, B., Bywaters, P., Brady, G., Bunting, L., et al (2019) 'Poverty, inequality, child abuse and neglect: Changing the conversation across the UK in child protection?', *Children and Youth Services*, 97: 127–133.
Featherstone, B., Gupta, A. and Morris, K. (2021) 'Post-pandemic: Moving on from "child protection"', *Critical and Radical Social Work*, 9(2): 151–165.

Ferguson, G., Featherstone, B. and Morris, K. (2020) 'Framed to fit? Challenging the domestic abuse "story" in child protection', *Critical and Radical Social Work*, 8(1): 25–40.

Ferguson, H. (2004) *Protecting Children in Time: Child Abuse, Child Protection and the Consequences of Modernity*, Palgrave Macmillan.

Ferguson, H. (2005) 'Working with violence, the emotions and the psycho-social dynamics of child protection: Reflections on the Victoria Climbié case', *Social Work Education*, 24(7): 781–795.

Ferguson, H. (2008) 'Liquid social work: Rethinking welfare interventions as mobile practices', *British Journal of Social Work*, 38(3): 561–579.

Ferguson, H. (2010) 'Therapeutic journeys: The car as a vehicle for working with children and families and theorizing practice', *Journal of Social Work Practice*, 24(2): 121–138.

Ferguson, H. (2011) *Child Protection Practice*, Palgrave.

Ferguson, H. (2016a) 'Researching social work practice close up: Using ethnographic and mobile methods to understand encounters between social workers, children and families', *British Journal of Social Work*, 46(1): 153–168.

Ferguson, H. (2016b) 'What social workers do in performing child protection work: Evidence from research into face-to-face practice', *Child and Family Social Work*, 21(3): 283–294.

Ferguson, H. (2016c) 'Professional helping as negotiation in motion: Social work as work on the move', *Applied Mobilities*, 1(2): 193–206.

Ferguson, H. (2016d) 'Patterns of engagement and non-engagement of young fathers in early intervention and safeguarding work', *Social Policy and Society*, 15(1): 99–111.

Ferguson, H. (2017) 'How children become invisible in child protection work: Evidence from day-to-day social work practice', *British Journal of Social Work*, 47(4): 1007–1023.

Ferguson, H. (2018a) 'How social workers reflect in action and when and why they don't: The possibilities and limits to reflective practice in social work', *Social Work Education*, 37(4): 415–427.

Ferguson, H. (2018b) 'Making home visits: Creativity and the embodied practices of home visiting in social work and child protection', *Qualitative Social Work*, 17(1): 65–80.

Ferguson, H., Gibson, M. and Plumbridge, G. (2019) 'Independent evaluation of the implementation of Ofsted's framework for inspection of local authority services (ILACS)', in Ofsted, *Inspection of Local Authority Children's Services Framework Implementation Review* (pp 41–75), Ofsted.

Ferguson, H., Leigh, L., Cooner, T.S., Beddoe, L., Disney, T., Warwick, L., et al (2020a) 'From snapshots of practice to a movie: Researching long-term social work and child protection by getting as close as possible to practice and organisational life', *British Journal of Social Work*, 50(6): 1706–1723.

Ferguson, H., Warwick, L., Cooner, T.S., Leigh, J., Beddoe, E., Disney, T., et al (2020b) 'The nature and culture of social work with children and families in long-term casework: Findings from a qualitative longitudinal study', *Child & Family Social Work*, 25(3): 694–703.

Ferguson, H., Disney, T., Warwick, L., Leigh, J., Cooner, T.S. and Beddoe, L. (2020c) 'Hostile relationships in social work practice: Anxiety, hate and conflict in long-term work with involuntary service users', *Journal of Social Work Practice*, 35(1): 19–37.

Ferguson, H., Warwick, L., Disney, T., Leigh, J., Cooner, T.S. and Beddoe, L. (2020d) 'Relationship-based practice and the creation of therapeutic change in long-term work: Social work as a holding relationship', *Social Work Education*, 41(2): 209–227.

Ferguson, H., Kelly, L. and Pink, S. (2022a) 'Social work and child protection for a post-pandemic world: The re-making of practice during COVID-19 and its renewal beyond it', *Journal of Social Work Practice*, 36(1): 5–24.

Ferguson, H., Pink, S. and Kelly, L. (2022b) 'The unheld child: Social work, social distancing and the possibilities and limits to child protection during the COVID-19 pandemic', *British Journal of Social Work*, 52(4): 2403–2421.

Ferguson, H., Kelly, L. and Gilsenan, A. (2023) *Social Work and Child Protection Beyond the COVID-19 Pandemic: Key Challenges and Good Practice*, Research in Practice.

Finnis, M. (2021) *Restorative Practice*, Independent Thinking Press.

Fiorentino, V., Romakkaniemi, M., Harrikari, T., Saraniemi, S. and Tiitinen, L. (2023) 'Towards digitally mediated social work: The impact of the COVID-19 pandemic on encountering clients in social work', *Qualitative Social Work*, 22(3): 448–464.

Firmin, C. (2020) *Contextual Safeguarding and Child Protection: Rewriting the Rules*, Routledge.

Firmin, C., Lefevre, M., Huegler, N. and Peace, D. (2022) *Safeguarding Young People Beyond the Family Home: Responding to Extra-Familial Risks and Harms*, Policy Press.

Fook, J. and Gardner, F. (2007) *Practicing Critical Reflection*, Open University Press.

Forrester, D. (2024) *The Enlightened Social Worker: An introduction to Rights-Focused Practice*, Policy Press.

Forrester, D., Westlake, D., Killian, M., Antonopolou, V., McCann, M., Thurnham, A., et al (2019) 'What is the relationship between worker skills and outcomes for families in child and family social work?', *British Journal of Social Work*, 49(8): 2148–2167.

Forrester, D., Wilkins, D. and Whittaker, C. (2021) *Motivational Interviewing for Working with Children and Families: A Practical Guide for Early Intervention and Child Protection*, Jennifer Kingsley.

Forrester, J. (2017) 'On holding as metaphor: Winnicott and the figure of St Christopher', in J. Forrester, *Thinking in Cases* (pp 89–104), Polity.

Foster, S. and Duschinsky, R. (2025) '"In practice we don't use that much theory": Questioning claims of the dominance of attachment theory in children's safeguarding social work', *British Journal of Social Work*, 55(6): 2716–2733.

Froggett, L. (2002) *Love, Hate and Welfare: Psychosocial Approaches to Policy and Practice*, Policy Press.

Gibson, M. (2019) *Pride and Shame in Child and Family Social Work: Emotions and the Search for Humane Practice*, Policy Press.

Gill, A.K. and Harrison, K. (2015) 'Child grooming and sexual exploitation: Are South Asian men the UK media's new folk devils?', *International Journal for Crime, Justice and Social Democracy*, 4(2): 34–49.

Glisson, C. and Hemmelgarn, A. (1998) 'The effects of organizational climate and inter organizational coordination on the quality and outcomes of children's service systems', *Child Abuse and Neglect*, 22(5): 401–421.

Gohir, S. (2013) *Unheard Voices: The Sexual Exploitation of Asian Girls and Young Women*, Muslim Women's Network UK.

Goldberg, P. (2018) 'Reconfiguring the frame as a dynamic structure', in I. Tylim and A. Harris (eds) *Reconsidering the Moveable Frame in Psychoanalysis: Its Function and Structure in Contemporary Psychoanalytic Theory* (pp 92–110), Routledge.

Gottlieb, A. (2000) 'Where have all the babies gone? Towards an anthropology of infants and their caretakers', *Anthropological Quarterly*, 73(3): 121–132.

Grant, L. and Kinman, G. (2018) *Developing Resilience for Social Work Practice*, Bloomsbury.

Green, L. (2017) 'The trouble with touch? New insights and observations on touch for social work and social care', *British Journal of Social Work*, 47(3): 773–792.

Gregory, M. (2024) 'Supervision as a dispersed practice: Exploring the creation of supervisory spaces in day-to-day social work practice', *Child and Family Social Work*, early view, https://doi.org/10.1111/cfs.13191

Guard, C. (2023) '"It's the little bits that you have enabled me to see": Reconceptualising the voices of babies using the video interaction dialogue model with early years educators', *Early Years*, 43(3): 606–625.

Gupta, A. (2017) 'Poverty and child neglect: The elephant in the room?', *Families, Relationships and Societies*, 6(1): 21–36.

Gupta, A. and Blumhardt, H. (2017) 'Poverty, exclusion and child protection practice: The contribution of "the politics of recognition and respect"', *European Journal of Social Work*, 21(2): 247–259.

Hallett, S. (2017) *Making Sense of Child Sexual Exploitation: Exchange, Abuse and Young People*, Policy Press.

Hammersley, M. and Atkinson, P. (2007) *Ethnography: Principles in Practice* (3rd edn), Routledge.

Handley, G. and Doyle, C. (2014) 'Ascertaining the wishes and feelings of young children: Social workers' perspectives on skills and training', *Child & Family Social Work*, 19(4): 443–454.

Harker, L. and Ryan, P. (2022) 'Remote hearings in family courts in England and Wales during Covid-19: Insights and lessons', *Family Court Review*, 60(2): 207–219.

Harrison, M. (2016) 'Release, reframe, refocus, and respond: A practitioner transformation process in a reflective consultation program', *Infant Mental Health Journal*, 37(6): 670–683.

Harvey, A. and Henderson, F. (2014) 'Reflective supervision for child protection practice: Reaching beneath the surface', *Journal of Social Work Practice*, 28(3): 343–356.

Helm, D. (2016) 'Sense-making in a social work office: An ethnographic study of safeguarding judgements', *Child and Family Social Work*, 21(1): 26–35.

Henderson, F. (2018) 'Difficult conversations on the frontline: Observations of home visits to talk about neglect', in M. Bower and R. Solomon (eds), *What Social Workers Need to Know* (pp 31–47), Routledge.

Herman, J. (1992) *Trauma and Recovery*, Pandora.

Hicks, S. (2020) '"The feel of the place": Investigating atmosphere with the residents of a modernist housing estate', *Qualitative Social Work*, 19(3): 460–480.

Hingley-Jones, H. and Ruch, G. (2016) '"Stumbling through"? Relationship-based social work practice in austere times', *Journal of Social Work Practice*, 30(3), 235–248.

Hingley-Jones, H., Parkinson, C. and Allain, L. (2016) 'Back to our roots? Revisiting psychoanalytically-informed baby and young child observation in the education of student social workers', *Journal of Social Work Practice*, 30(3): 249–265.

Hogg, S. (2021) 'Including infants in children and young people's mental health', NHS Confederation. Available at: https://www.nhsconfed.org/articles/including-infants-children-and-young-peoples-mental-health (Accessed 25 October 2024).

Hollway, W. (2015) *Knowing Mothers: Researching Maternal Identity Change*, Palgrave.

Hollway, W. and Jefferson, T. (2000) *Doing Qualitative Research Differently: Free Association, Narrative and the Interview Method*, Sage.

Home Office (2020) *Characteristics of Group-based Child Sexual Exploitation in the Community: Literature Review*, Home Office.

Hood, R. (2018) *Complexity in Social Work*, Sage.

Hood, R. and Goldacre, A. (2021) 'Exploring the impact of Ofsted inspections on performance in children's social care', *Children and Youth Services Review*, 129: 106188.

Hood, R., Brent, M., Abbott, S. and Sartori, D. (2019) 'A study of practitioner–service user relationships in social work', *British Journal of Social Work*, 49(3): 787–805.

Horwath, J. and Platt, D. (2018) *The Child's World: The Essential Guide to Assessing Vulnerable Children, Young People and their Families* (3rd edn), Jessica Kingsley.

Howe, D. (1998) 'Relationship-based thinking and practice in social work', *Journal of Social Work Practice*, 12(1): 45–56.

Howe, D. (2008) *The Emotionally Intelligent Social Worker*, Palgrave.
Howe, D. (2009) *A Brief Introduction to Social Work*, Palgrave.
Hughes, L. and Pengelly, P. (1997) *Staff Supervision in a Turbulent Environment: Managing Process and Task in Front-Line Services*, Jessica Kingsley.
Hunt, S., Goddard, C., Cooper, J., Littlechild, B. and Wild, J. (2016) 'If I feel like this, how does the child feel? Child protection workers, supervision, management and organisational responses to parental violence', *Journal of Social Work Practice*, 30(1): 5–24.
Hyslop, I. and Keddell, E. (2018) 'Outing the elephants: Exploring a new paradigm for child protection social work', *Social Sciences*, 7(7): 105.
Ingold, T. (2011) *Being Alive: Essays on Movement, Knowledge and Description*, Routledge.
Ingold, T. and Hallam, E. (2007) 'Creativity and cultural improvisation: An introduction', in E. Hallam and T. Ingold (eds), *Creativity and Cultural Improvisation* (pp 1–24), Berg.
Ingram, R. (2013) 'Emotions, social work practice and supervision: An uneasy alliance?', *Journal of Social Work Practice*, 27(1): 5–19.
Ingram, R. and Smith, M. (2018) 'Relationship-based practice: Emergent themes in social work literature', *IRISS Insights* (no. 41), Institute for Research and Innovation in Social Services.
Ixer, G. (1999) 'There's no such thing as reflection', *British Journal of Social Work*, 29(4): 513–527.
Jaeggi, R. (2014) *Alienation*, Columbia University Press.
Jeyasingham, D. (2014) 'The production of space in children's social work: Insights from Henri Lefebvre's spatial dialectics', *British Journal of Social Work*, 44(7): 1879–1894.
Jeyasingham, D. (2018) 'Place and the uncanny in child protection social work: Exploring findings from an ethnographic study', *Qualitative Social Work*, 17(1): 81–95.
Jeyasingham, D. and Devlin, J. (2024) 'Hybrid and digitally mediated practice in child and family social work: Impacts on more or less experienced practitioners' communication, relationships sense-making and experience at work', *British Journal of Social Work*, 54(5): 2163–2180.
Jones, D. (2003) *Communicating with Vulnerable Children*, London.
Jones, R. (2014) *The Story of Baby P: Setting the Record Straight*, Policy Press.
Kadushin, A. and Harkness, D. (2014) *Supervision in Social Work* (5th edn), Columbia University Press.
Kahr, B. (2020) *Bombs in the Consulting Room: Surviving Psychological Shrapnel*, Routledge.
Kanter, J. (2004) *Face-to-Face with Children: The Life and Work of Clare Winnicott*, Karnac.
Keddell, E. (2020) 'The case for an inequalities perspective in child protection', *Policy Quarterly*, 16(1): 36–38.
Keddell, E. (2022) 'Mechanisms of inequity: The impact of instrumental biases in the child protection system', *Societies*, 12(2): 83.

Keddell, E., Fitzmaurice, L., Cleaver, K. and Exeter, D. (2022) 'A fight for legitimacy: Reflections on child protection reform, the reduction of baby removals, and child protection decision-making in Aotearoa New Zealand', *Kōtuitui*, 17(3): 378–404.

Keddell, E., Cleaver, K. and Fitzmaurice, L. (2023) 'Experiences of baby removal prevention: A collective case study of mothers and community-based workers', *Qualitative Social Work*, 22(2): 266–285.

Kennedy, S. (2020) *Seeing the Child in Child Protection Social Work*, Red Globe Books.

Kinman, G., Grant, L. and Kelly, S. (2020) '"It's my secret space": The benefits of mindfulness for social workers', *British Journal of Social Work*, 50(3): 758–777.

Klein, M. (1946) 'Notes on some schizoid mechanisms', *International Journal of Psycho-Analysis*, 27: 99–110.

Kohli, R.K.S. and Dutton, J. (2018) 'Brief encounters: Working in complex, short-term relationships', in G. Ruch, D. Turney and A. Ward (eds), *Relationship-based Social Work: Getting to the Heart of Practice* (2nd edn, pp 77–94), Jessica Kingsley.

Kong, S.-T., Noone, C. and Shears, J. (2022) 'Social workers' sensual bodies during COVID-19: The suspended, displaced and reconstituted body in social work practice', *British Journal of Social Work*, 52(5): 2834–2853.

Koprowska, J. (2020) *Communication and Interpersonal Skills in Social Work*, Sage.

Kristeva, J. (1982) *Powers of Horror: An Essay on Abjection*, Columbia University Press.

Kusenbach, S. (2003) 'Street phenomenology: The go-along as ethnographic research tool', *Ethnography*, 4(3): 455–485.

Laird, S.E. (2013) *Child Protection: Managing Conflict, Hostility and Aggression*, Policy Press.

Laming, H. (2003) *The Victoria Climbié Inquiry*, The Stationery Office.

Laming, H. (2009) *The Protection of Children in England: A Progress Report*, The Stationery Office.

Leedham, M. (2022) '"Social workers failed to heed warnings": A text-based study of how a profession is portrayed in UK newspapers', *British Journal of Social Work*, 52(2): 1110–1128.

Lefevre, M. (2018) *Communicating with Children and Young People: Making a Difference*, Policy Press.

Leigh, J., Beddoe, E. and Keddell, E. (2019) 'Disguised compliance or undisguised nonsense: A critical discourse analysis of compliance and resistance in social work practice', *Families, Relationships and Societies*, 9(2): 269–285.

Leigh, J., Disney, T., Warwick, L., Ferguson, H., Beddoe, L. and Cooner, T.S. (2020) 'Revealing the hidden performances of social work practice: The ethnographic process of gaining access, getting into place and impression management', *Qualitative Social Work*, 20(4): 1078–1095.

Littlechild, B. (2005) 'The nature and effects of violence against child protection social workers: Providing effective support', *British Journal of Social Work*, 35(3): 387–401.

Luckock, B., Lefevre, M. and Tanner, K. (2006) 'Teaching and learning communication with children and young people', *Child and Family Social Work*, 12(2): 192–201.

Lundberg, B. (2013) *Serious Case Review in Respect of the Death of Keanu Williams*, Birmingham Children's Safeguarding Board.

Lundy, L. (2007) '"Voice" is not enough: Conceptualising Article 12 of the United Nations Convention on the Rights of the Child', *British Educational Research Journal*, 33(6): 927–942.

MacAlister, J. (2022) *Independent Review of Children's Social Care*, Department for Education.

Maclean, S. (2023) *The Reflective Social Worker*, Kirwin Maclean Associates.

Mandel, D. (2024) *Stop Blaming Mothers and Ignoring Fathers: How to Transform the Way We Keep Children Safe from Domestic Violence*, Legitimus Media.

Mänttäri-van der Kuip, M. (2016) 'Moral distress among social workers: The role of insufficient resources', *International Journal of Social Welfare*, 25(1): 86–97.

Marshall, T. (2019) 'The concept of reflection: A systematic review and thematic synthesis across professional contexts', *Reflective Practice*, 20(3): 396–415.

Mason, P., Ferguson, H., Morris, K., Monton, T. and Sen, R. (2017) *Leeds Family Valued: Evaluation Report*, Department for Education.

Masson, J. and Dickens, J. (2015) 'Protecting unborn and newborn babies', *Child Abuse Review*, 24(2): 107–119.

McFadden, P., Maclochlainn, J., Manthorpe, J., Naylor, R., Schroder, H., McGrory, S. et al (2024) 'Perceptions of safe staffing, self-reported mental well-being and intentions to leave the profession among UK social workers: A mixed methods study', *British Journal of Social Work*, 54(5): 1965–1987.

McFadyen, A., Gray Armstrong, V., Masterson, K. and Anderson, B. (2022) 'The voice of the infant', *Infant Observation*, 25(2): 104–122.

McLaughlin, H. (2009) 'What's in a name: "Client", "Patient", "Customer", "Consumer", "Expert by Experience", "Service User" – what's next?', *British Journal of Social Work*, 39(6): 1101–1117.

Menzies-Lyth, I. (1988) *Containing Anxiety in Institutions: Selected Essays, Volume One*, Free Association Books.

Miller, D. (2008) *The Comfort of Things*, Polity.

Miller, D. (2010) *Stuff*, Polity.

Miller, D. (2024) *The Good Enough Life*, Polity.

Miller, D., Rabho, L.A., Awondo, P., de Vries, M., Duque, M., Garvey, P., et al (2022) *The Global Smartphone: Beyond a Youth Technology*, UCL Press.

Miron, D., Bisaillon, C., Jordan, B., Bryce, G., Gauthier, Y., St-Andre, M., et al (2013) 'Whose rights count? Negotiating practice, policy, and legal dilemmas regarding infant–parent contact when infants are in out-of-home care', *Infant Mental Health Journal*, 34: 177–188.

Mishna, F., Milne, B., Sanders, J., and Greenblatt, A. (2021) 'Social work practice during COVID-19: Client needs and boundary challenges', *Global Social Welfare*, 9: 113–120.

Morris, K. (2013) 'Troubled families: Vulnerable families' experiences of multiple service use', *Child & Family Social Work*, 18(2): 198–206.

Morrison, T. (2007) 'Emotional intelligence, emotion and social work: Context, characteristics, complications and contribution', *British Journal of Social Work*, 37(2): 245–263.

Munro, E. (1999) 'Common errors of reasoning in child protection work', *Child Abuse and Neglect*, 23(8): 745–758.

Munro, E. (2005) 'Improving practice: Child protection as a systems problem', *Children and Youth Services Review*, 27: 375–391.

Munro, E. (2011) *The Munro Review of Child Protection: Final Report*, The Stationery Office.

Murphy, C. (2022) 'If it's not on the system, then it hasn't been done: "Ofsted anxiety disorder" as a barrier to social worker discretion', *Child Abuse Review*, 31(1): 78–90.

Murphy, C. (2023a) 'From "intimate-insider" to "relative-outsider": An autoethnographic account of undertaking social work research in one's own "backyard"', *Journal of Children's Services*, 18(3/4): 195–206.

Murphy, C. (2023b) '"Rising demand and decreasing resources": Theorising the "cost of austerity" as a barrier to social worker discretion', *Journal of Social Policy*, 52(1): 197–214.

Murphy, C. and Bedford, A. (2025) 'What is the nature and impact of workplace friendships within child protection social work? Implications for emotional support, professional learning, job satisfaction and worker wellbeing', *British Journal of Social Work*, 55(3): 1121–1140.

Murphy, D. (2012) 'Mutuality and relational depth in counselling and psychotherapy', in R. Knox, D. Murphy, S. Wiggins and M. Cooper (eds), *Relational Depth: Contemporary Perspectives and Developments* (pp 61–74), Palgrave.

Murphy, D., Duggan, M. and Joseph, S. (2013) 'Relationship-based social work and its compatibility with the person-centred approach: Principled versus instrumental perspectives', *British Journal of Social Work*, 43(4): 703–719.

Murray, J. (2023) *Three Steps for Baby Safety*, Derby and Derbyshire Integrated Care Board.

Music, G. (2019) *Nurturing Children*, Routledge.

Neale, B. (2019) *What is Qualitative Longitudinal Research?*, Bloomsbury.

Noyes, C. (2018) 'Written on the body', in M. Bower and R. Solomon (eds), *What Social Workers Need to Know* (pp 48–70), Routledge.

O'Connor, L. (2022) 'Agile emotion practices: Findings from an ethnographic study of children and families social work', *British Journal of Social Work*, 52(7): 4149–4170.

O'Keefe, R. and MacClean, S. (2023) *Case Recording in Social Work with Children and Families: A Straightforward Guide*, Kirwin MacClean.

O'Keefe, R., Geddes, E., Vincent, S. and Davies, P. (2025) 'Enabling child-centred case recording in children's social work: The voice of practitioners', *Child and Family Social Work*, https://doi.org/10.111/cfs.13288

O'Neill, M. and Roberts, B. (2020) *Walking Methods: Research on the Move*, Routledge.

Osei-Buapim, C. (2021) 'Transition to teletherapy with adolescents in the wake of the COVID-19 pandemic: The holding environment approach', in C. Tosone (ed), *Shared Trauma, Shared Resilience during a Pandemic: Social Work in the Time of COVID-19* (pp 145–156), Springer.

O'Sullivan, N. (2019) 'Creating space to think and feel in child protection social work: A psychodynamic intervention', *Journal of Social Work Practice*, 33(1): 15–25.

O'Sullivan, N., Patterson, D. and Kennedy, A. (2022) 'Anchoring social care and social work practice in structured reflection: Introducing a model of group reflective practice', *Journal of Social Work Practice*, 36(2): 179–193.

Page, D. (2021) 'Atmospheres, spaces and job crafting: home visits in Alternative Provision', *Research Papers in Education*, 38(1): 102–120.

Page, J. (2018) 'Characterising the principles of professional love in early childhood care and education', *International Journal of Early Years Education*, 26(2): 1–17.

Pappas, G., Harrell, S. and Wahab, S. (2024) 'Nuance as praxis for teaching about mandated reporting: Classroom activities', *Journal of Teaching in Social Work*, 45(1): 93–104.

Parent-Infant Foundation (2023) *An Introduction to the Parent-Infant Teams Network*. Available at: https://parentinfantfoundation.org.uk/wp-content/uploads/2022/06/220621-Introduction-to-the-Parent-Infant-Network.pdf (Accessed 1 October 2024).

Parkinson, C. (2018) 'Sustaining relationships: Working with strong feelings: Part II: Hopelessness, depression and despair', in G. Ruch, D. Turney and A. Ward (eds), *Relationship-based Social Work: Getting to the Heart of Practice* (2nd edn, pp 113–128), Jessica Kingsley.

Parkinson, C., Allain, L. and Hingley-Jones, H. (2017) 'Observations for our times', in H. Hingley-Jones, C. Parkinson and L. Allain (eds), *Observation in Health and Social Care: Applications for Learning, Research and Practice with Children and Adults* (pp 9–20), Jessica Kingsley.

Parton, N. (2014) *The Politics of Child Protection: Contemporary Developments and Future Directions*, Palgrave.

Pascoe, K.M., Waterhouse-Bradley, B. and McGinn, T. (2023) 'Social workers' experiences of bureaucracy: A systematic synthesis of qualitative studies', *British Journal of Social Work*, 53(1): 513–533.

Pearce, J. (2014) 'What's going on to safeguard children and young people from child sexual exploitation: A review of local safeguarding children boards' work to protect children from sexual exploitation', *Child Abuse Review*, 23(3): 159–170.

Pérez-Rojas, A.E., González, J.M. and Fuertes, J.N. (2019) 'The bond of the working alliance', in J.N. Fuertes (ed), *Working Alliance Skills for Mental Health Professionals* (pp 11–44), Oxford University Press.

Pierre, R. (2022) 'An open letter to the social worker who wrote my case files', *BASW*, 21 October. Available at: https://basw.co.uk/articles/open-letter-social-worker-who-wrote-my-case-files (Accessed 25 January 2023).

Pierre, R. (2023) 'The dos and don'ts of case recording', *Children and Young People Now*, 26 September.

Pierre, R. (ed) (2024) *Free Loaves on Fridays: The Care System As Told By People Who Actually Get It*, Unbound.

Pink, S. (2015). *Doing Sensory Ethnography*, Sage.

Pink, S., Morgan, A. and Dainty, A. (2015) 'Other people's homes as sites of uncertainty: Ways of knowing and being safe', *Environment and Planning A*, 47(2): 450–464.

Pink, S., Ferguson, H. and Kelly, L. (2022) 'Digital social work: Conceptualising a hybrid anticipatory practice', *Qualitative Social Work*, 21(2): 413–430.

Pithouse, A. (1987) *Social Work: The Social Organisation of an Invisible Trade*, Ashgate.

Ravalier, J.M., McFadden, P., Boichat, C., Clabburn, O. and Moriarty, J. (2021) 'Social worker well-being: A large mixed-methods study', *British Journal of Social Work*, 51(1): 297–317.

Reder, P., Duncan, S. and Gray, M. (1993) *Beyond Blame: Child Abuse Tragedies Revisited*, Routledge.

Redmond, B. (2006) *Reflection in Action*, Ashgate.

Reith-Hall, E. and Montgomery, P. (2022) 'The teaching and learning of communication skills in social work education', *Research on Social Work Practice*, 32(7): 793–813.

Robson, A., Cossar, J. and Quayle, E. (2014) 'The impact of work-related violence towards social workers in children and family services', *The British Journal of Social Work*, 44(4): 924–936.

Rogers, C.R. (1961) *On Becoming a Person: A Psychotherapist's View of Psychotherapy*, Houghton Mifflin.

Rooney, R. (ed) (2018) *Strategies for Working with Involuntary Clients* (3rd edn), Columbia University Press.

Rosa, H. (2015) *Social Acceleration: A New Theory of Modernity*, Columbia University Press.

Rosa, H. (2019) *Resonance: A Sociology of Our Relationship to the World*, Polity.

Rosa, H. (2023) 'Dynamic stabilization and the expansion of our share of the world: An analysis of the modern social formation', in A. Reckwitz and H. Rosa, *Late Modernity in Crisis: Why We Need a Theory of Society* (pp 114–126), Polity.

Ruch, G. (2007) 'Reflective practice in contemporary child care social work: The role of containment', *British Journal of Social Work*, 37(4): 659–680.

Ruch, G. (2013) '"Helping children is a human process": Researching the challenges social workers face in communicating with children', *British Journal of Social Work*, 44(8): 2145–2162.

Ruch, G. (2018) 'The contemporary context of relationship-based practice', in G. Ruch, D. Turney and A. Ward (eds), *Relationship-based Social Work: Getting to the Heart of Practice* (2nd edn, pp 19–36), Jessica Kingsley.

Ruch, G., Winter, K., Cree, V., Hallett, S. and Hadfield, M. (2017) 'Making meaningful connections: Using insights from social pedagogy in statutory child and family social work practice', *Child and Family Social Work*, 22(2): 1015–1023.

Ruch, G., Turney, D. and Ward, A. (eds) (2018) *Relationship-based Social Work: Getting to the Heart of Practice*, 2nd edn, Jessica Kingsley.

Ryan, M., Harker, L., and Rothera, S. (2020) *Remote Hearings in the Family Justice System: Reflections and Experiences (September 2020)*, Nuffield Family Justice Observatory.

Saar-Heiman, Y., Damman, J.L., Lalayants, M. and Gupta, A. (2024) 'Parent peer advocacy, mentoring, and support in child protection: A scoping review of programs and services', *Psychosocial Intervention*, 33(2): 73–88.

Sachs, B. (2020) *The Good Enough Therapist*, Routledge.

Salmenniemi, S. (2022) *Affect, Alienation, and Politics in Therapeutic Culture: Capitalism on the Skin*, Palgrave Macmillan.

Saltiel, D. (2016) 'Observing front line decision making in child protection', *British Journal of Social Work*, 46(7): 2104–2119.

Salzberger-Wittenberg, I. (1970) *Psycho-Analytic Insights and Relationships: A Kleinian Approach*, Routledge.

Scholar, H. (2017) 'The neglected paraphernalia of practice? Objects and artefacts in social work identity, practice and research', *Qualitative Social Work*, 16(5): 631–648.

Schon, D. (1983) *The Reflective Practitioner: How Professionals Think in Action*, Basic Books.

Sebba, J., Luke, N., McNeish, D. and Rees, A. (2017) *Children's Social Care Innovation Programme Final Evaluation Report*, Department for Education.

Sennett, R. (2008) *The Craftsman*, Yale University Press.

Sheppard, M. (2007) 'Assessment: From reflexivity to process knowledge', in J. Lishman (ed), *Handbook for Practice Learning in Social Work and Social Care* (pp 128–137), Jessica Kingsley.

Shoesmith, S. (2016) *Learning from Baby P: The Politics of Blame, Fear and Denial*, Jessica Kingsley.

Simpson, J. (2017) 'Staying in touch in the digital era: New social work practice', *Journal of Technology in Human Services*, 35(1): 86–98.

Smith, H. (2024) 'Too hot to handle? Unthought anxiety and parallel process in social work supervision', *Journal of Social Work Practice*, 38(3): 273–286.

Smith, M. (2010) 'Sustaining relationships: Working with strong feelings 1, anger, aggression and hostility', in G. Ruch, D. Turney and A. Ward (eds), *Relationship-based Social Work* (1st edn, pp 102–117), Jessica Kingsley.

Smith, M. (2018) 'Sustaining relationships: Working with strong feelings: Part I: Anger, aggression and hostility', in G. Ruch, D. Turney and A. Ward (eds), *Relationship-based Social Work: Getting to the Heart of Practice* (2nd edn, pp 95–112), Jessica Kingsley.

Smith, M., Gallagher, M., Wosu, H., Stewart, J., Cree, V., Hunter, S., et al (2012) 'Engaging with involuntary service users in social work: Findings from a knowledge exchange project', *British Journal of Social Work*, 42(8): 1460–1477.

Stanley, J. and Goddard, C. (2002) *In the Firing Line: Violence and Power in Child Protection Work*, Wiley.

Steggall, D. and Scollen, R. (2024) 'Clown-based social work as dissent in child protection practice', *British Journal of Social Work*, 54(5): 2124–2141.

Stern, D.N. (2004) *The Present Moment in Psychotherapy and Everyday Life*, W.W. Norton & Company.

Stevenson, O. (ed) (1989) *Child Abuse: Professional Practice and Public Policy*, Harvester Wheatsheaf.

Sudland, C. (2020) 'Challenges and dilemmas working with high-conflict families in child protection casework', *Child & Family Social Work*, 25: 248–255.

Taylor, C. and White, S. (2000) *Practising Reflexivity in Health and Welfare: Making Knowledge*, Open University Press.

Thomas, R. and Darcy, M. (2017) 'Child sexual exploitation: A review of the literature', *British Journal of Social Work*, 47(1): 1–19.

Tobias, D. (2013) *From Pariahs to Partners: How Parents and their Allies Changed New York City's Child Welfare System*, Oxford University Press.

Tobin, M., Carney, S. and Rogers, E. (2024a) 'Reflective supervision and reflective practice in infant mental health: A scoping review of a diverse body of literature', *Infant Mental Health Journal*, 45(1): 79–117.

Tobin, M., O'Sullivan, N. and Rogers, E. (2024b) '"You go in heavy and you come out light": An interpretative phenomenological analysis of reflective practice experiences in an Irish infant mental health setting', *Infant Mental Health Journal*, 45(4): 411–437.

Trevithick, P. (2003) 'Effective relationship-based practice: A theoretical exploration', *Journal of Social Work Practice*, 17(2): 163–176.

Trevithick, P. (2011) 'Understanding defences and defensiveness in social work', *Journal of Social Work Practice*, 25(4): 389–412.

Trevithick, P. (2012) *Social Work Skills and Knowledge*, Open University Press.

Trevithick, P., Richards, S., Ruch, G. and Moss, B. (2004) *Teaching and Learning Communication Skills in Social Work Education*, Policy Press.

Triggs, S. (2024) 'Becoming a "social work coach": How practicing coaching creates beneficial agility in social work identity', *British Journal of Social Work*, 54(1): 286–304.

Tronick, E., Adamson, L.B., Als, H. and Brazelton, T.B. (1978) 'The infant's response to entrapment between contradictory messages in face-to-face interaction', *Journal of the American Academy of Child Psychiatry*, 17(1): 1–13.

Trotter, C. (2015) *Working with Involuntary Clients: A Guide to Practice* (2nd edn), Allen Lane.

Tuck, V. (2013) 'Resistant parents and child protection: Knowledge base, pointers for practice and implications for policy', *Child Abuse Review*, 22(1): 5–19.

Turnell, A. and Essex, S. (2006) *Working with Denied Child Abuse: The Resolutions Approach*, Open University Press.

Turner, D. (2025) '"We're not professionals when it comes to dogs": Social work encounters with dogs and their implications for education and practice', *British Journal of Social Work*, 55(5): 2464–2481.

Turney, D. (2012) 'A relationship-based approach to engaging involuntary clients: The contribution of recognition theory', *Child and Family Social Work*, 17: 149–159.

Turney, D. (2018) 'Sustaining relationships: Working with strong feelings: Part III: Love and positive feelings', in G. Ruch, D. Turney and A. Ward (eds), *Relationship-based Social Work: Getting to the Heart of Practice* (2nd edn, pp 129–146), Jessica Kingsley.

Turney, D. and Ruch, G. (2018) 'What makes it so hard to look and to listen? Exploring the use of the Cognitive and Affective Supervisory Approach with children's social work managers', *Journal of Social Work Practice*, 32(2): 125–138.

Tyler, I. (2013) *Revolting Subjects: Social Abjection and Resistance in Neoliberal Britain*, Zed Books.

Tylim, I. and Harris, A. (2018) *Reconsidering the Moveable Frame in Psychoanalysis: Its Function and Structure in Contemporary Psychoanalytic Theory*, Routledge.

Urry, J. (2007) *Mobilities*, Polity.

Valentine, M. (1994) 'The social worker as "bad object"', *British Journal of Social Work*, 24(1): 71–86.

van Rhyn, B., Barwick, A. and Donelly, M. (2020) 'Embodiment as an instrument for empathy in social work', *Australian Social Work*, 74(2): 146–158.

Wall, K., Cassidy, C., Robinson, C., Hall, E., Beaton, M., Kanyal, M., et al (2019) 'Look who's talking: Factors for considering the facilitation of very young children's voices', *Journal of Early Childhood Research*, 17(4): 263–278.

Walsh, J. (2018) 'Being alongside: Working with complexity and ambiguity in caring relationships', in G. Ruch, D. Turney and A. Ward (eds), *Relationship-based Social Work: Getting to the Heart of Practice* (2nd edn, pp 203–220), Jessica Kingsley.

Ward, A. (2018) 'The use of self in relationship-based practice', in G. Ruch, D. Turney and A. Ward (eds), *Relationship-based Social Work: Getting to the Heart of Practice* (2nd edn, pp 55–76), Jessica Kingsley.

Ward, H., Brown, R. and Westlake, D. (2012) *Safeguarding Babies and Very Young Children from Abuse and Neglect*, Jessica Kingsley.

Warner, J. (2015) *The Emotional Politics of Child Protection*, Policy Press.

Warwick, L. (2021) '"Depends who it is": Towards a relational understanding of the use of adult-child touch in residential child care', *Qualitative Social Work*, 21(1): 18–36.

Warwick, L., Beddoe, L., Leigh, J., Disney, T., Ferguson, H. and Cooner, T.S. (2022) 'The power of relationship-based supervision in supporting social work retention: A case study from long-term ethnographic research in child protection', *Qualitative Social Work*, 22(5): 879–898.

Wengraff, T. (2001) *Qualitative Research Interviewing: Biographic Narrative and Semi-Structured Methods*, Sage.

Westlake, D. and Forrester, D. (2016) 'Adding evidence to the ethics debate: Investigating parents' experiences of their participation in research', *British Journal of Social Work*, 46(6): 1537–1552.

Whincup, H. (2017) 'What do social workers and children do when they are together? A typology of direct work', *Child and Family Social Work*, 22(2): 972–980.

White, S., Fook, J. and Gardner, F. (2006) *Critical Reflection in Health and Social Care*, Open University Press.

White, S., Gibson, M., Wastell, D. and Walsh, P. (2020) *Reassessing Attachment Theory in Child Welfare*, Policy Press.

Whittaker, A. (2011) 'Social defences and organisational culture in a local authority child protection setting: Challenges for the Munro Review?', *Journal of Social Work Practice*, 25(4): 481–495.

Whittaker, A. (2018) 'How do child-protection practitioners make decisions in real-life situations? Lessons from the psychology of decision making', *British Journal of Social Work*, 48(7): 1967–1984.

Whittaker, A. and Havard, T. (2016) 'Defensive practice as fear-based practice: Social work's open secret?', *British Journal of Social Work*, 46(5): 1158–1174.

Wilkins, D. and Whittaker, C. (2018) 'Doing child-protection social work with parents: What are the barriers in practice?', *British Journal of Social Work*, 48(7): 2003–2019.

Wilkins, D., Forrester, D. and Grant, L. (2017) 'What happens in child and family social work supervision?', *Child & Family Social Work*, 22(2): 942–951.

Wilkins, D., Pitt, C. and Addis, S. (2023) 'What do child protection social workers talk about when they talk about helping children and families? An observational study of supervision', *Practice*, 35(2): 169–187.

Williams, J. (2022) 'Supervision as a secure base: The role of attachment theory within the emotional and psycho-social landscape of social work supervision', *Journal of Social Work Practice*, 37(3): 1–15.

Williams, J., Ruch, G. and Jennings, S. (2022) 'Creating the conditions for collective curiosity and containment: Insights from developing and delivering reflective groups with social work supervisors', *Journal of Social Work Practice*, 36(2): 195–207.

Winnicott, C. (1963) *Child Care and Social Work*, Bookstall Publications.

Winnicott, D.W. (1949) 'Hate in the counter-transference', *International Journal of Psycho-Analysis*, 30: 69–74.

Winnicott, D.W. (1957) *The Child and the Outside World*, Tavistock.

Winnicott, D.W. (1965) *The Maturational Processes and the Facilitating Environment: Studies in the Theory of Emotional Development*, Hogarth Press.

Winnicott, D.W. (1971) *Playing and Reality*, Tavistock Publications.
Winter, K. (2011) *Building Relationships and Communicating with Young Children*, Routledge.
Winter, K., Cree, V., Hallett, S., Hadfield, M., Ruch, G., Morrison, F., et al (2017) 'Exploring communication between social workers, children and young people', *British Journal of Social Work*, 47(5): 1427–1444.
Wuori, D. (2024) *The Daycare Myth: What We Get Wrong About Early Care and Education (and What We Should Do About It)*, Teachers College Press.
Yang, M.Y. (2015) 'The effect of material hardship on child protective service involvement', *Child Abuse and Neglect*, 41: 113–125.
Young, I. (2005) *On Female Body Experience: 'Throwing Like a Girl' and Other Essays*, Oxford University Press.
Yuill, C. (2018) 'Social workers and alienation: The compassionate self and the disappointed juggler', *Critical and Radical Social Work*, 6(3): 275–289.

Index

References to figures appear in *italic* type.

A
abjection 67, 74–76, 78, 87
accountability 17–19, 47, 206–207; *see also* Ofsted
addiction *see* alcohol abuse; drug abuse
aggression towards social workers 125, 132, 135, 177–178; *see also* hostile relationships
alcohol abuse 34, 68, 136
alienation 148–150, 154
aliveness 5–6, 24, 61, 63, 76, 92–93, 118, 134, 202; *see also* energy of social workers; relational styles
analytical thinking 179–180
Antonopoulou, V. 184
anxiety 64–66, 68, 72–74, 76–79, 194, 203
  defended self 170, 172, 177–179, 180
  for service users 135, 138
  support and processing 192, 197
  see also emotional strain
Ash, K. 141
assessment visits 27–32, 57–60, 81, 200
  drama and risk 33–38
atmosphere during home visits 57, 58–59, 61, 64, 66, 70–74, 133–134, 204
attachment 9, 102, 107, 141–142, 143
austerity 206
automated avoidant practice 55, 60–61, 65–66, 138, 179, 203
  Practice Cycle 61–64, *62*
  see also disorganised practice
avoidant/detached relational style 143, 144–145, 148, 152, 153

B
babies and young children 108–109
#babyblindspot 100
baby blind spot 4, 97–101, 131–132
  caring for 41–42, 46
  case study 113–117
  developing relationships 30, 101–104
  digital intimacy 159–161
  hands-on practice and training 104–107, 120–121, 136, 205
  relational styles 144–147
backward-facing approach 7–9, 200
'bad' social workers/service users 48–50, 130, 137, 172
Barber, J.G. 135
Bateson, Karen 100
Bazzano, M. 6
Beckford, Jasmine 7
bedrooms of children 29–30, 58–59, 89, 165, 199
  in cases of neglect 50–51, 72, 73–74, 83
Bell, S. 19
Beresford, P. 125
Berlant, L. 19
Bion, Wilfred 9, 42, 179
blame culture 7–8, 18, 47, 149, 189, 206–207
Bloom, K. 6, 43, 82, 143
bodies of social workers 4–5, 60, 73, 75, 79, 173–174, 194; *see also* embodied self
bodily alienation 194
Bostock, L. 185
Brandon, M. 56
Briggs, S. 180
Broadhurst, Karen 98
Bülow, C.v. 21
bureaucratic preoccupation 3, 14–20, 25, 32, 56, 63, 146, 185, 206
  in long-term practice 43, 121–122
  staff well-being 183, 192–193, 197

239

burnout 149, 154, 193–194
Burns, K. 141

C

car journeys to practice encounters *see* transitions
car journeys with children 163, 164
care, living in 113, 116, 156, 207
career coaching 152
case reviews 7–8, 45, 55, 66, 135, 170
Casement, P. 81, 88, 172–173
child abuse, definition and scope 4, 10, 15
child development 97, 102, 107, 108
child protection and a good life 207–209
Child Protection Plans 15–16, 44, 46, 98, 137
child protection system 15–16, 206–207
Child Safeguarding Practice Review Panel 98, 99, 135; *see also* case reviews
child sexual exploitation 4, 90–91, 105, 156, 163, 164
Children Act, 1989 15
Children in Need plans 15, 44
choice for service users 136–137, 138, 164
cleanliness *see* living conditions
Climbié, Victoria 7, 170
colleagues *see* peer support
Colwell, Maria 7
communication breakdowns 56
compassion 47–50
composure 37–39, 171, 205
confidentiality 164–165
Connelly, Peter 7, 18
consistency 47–50
containment 42, 43, 88, 112, 171, 188
contextual safeguarding 4, 156
Cooper, A. 130
core self 142, 150–151, 152, 153, 172, 205
courage 37–39
court proceedings 43, 113, 159
COVID-19 pandemic 158–160, 162
Cozolino, L. 47
Critchley, A. 33, 98–99

critical reflection 175, 179
cruel optimismc 19, 190
cultural awareness 166–167

D

dangerous situations 33–39
deaths of children and babies 4, 7–8, 18, 33–34, 47, 55, 66, 99, 135, 166, 170
decision-making after assessment 35–36, 64, 91–92, 202
defended self 143, 170, 172, 177–179, 180
demoralisation 149–150
depression 14, 149
detachment *see* automated avoidant practice; avoidant/detached relational style; disorganised practice
Devaney, J. 151, 207
development *see* child development
Devine, Richard 205
digital intimacy 158, 160–161, 164, 165, 166
digital spaces 92, 158–162, 165–166
disguised compliance 113, 119, 130
disgust 67, 73–76, 78, 87, 145, 176
disorganised practice 67, 78–79, 138, 178–179, 203
  case study 67–72
  disgust and abjection 73–76
  Practice Cycle 76–78, 77
  see also automated avoidant practice
diversity awareness 166–167, 206
domestic abuse 22–23, 37–38, 47, 103, 113, 117, 175
Douglas, Mary 67, 74
drug abuse 34, 35–36, 44, 45, 136
Duschinsky, R. 19

E

embodied attention 155, 173–174, 203
embodied self 4–5, 142–144, 157–158
Emergency Duty Teams 36
emotional child abuse 4
emotional distress 191–194
emotional holding 120–121, 122
emotional intelligence 171

emotional readiness of social workers 20, 21, 33, 63, 92–93, 201–202, 203
emotional strain 37–39, 60–61, 64, 65–66, 76–79, 113, 132
  hostile relationships 136, 137–138
  support and processing 190–197
  see also anxiety
empathy 4–5, 47–50
endurance 47–50, 51–52
energetic attunement 6, 114, 121
energy of social workers 20–24, 32, 78, 86–87, 103, 115, 123; *see also* aliveness; relational styles
Eraut, M. 174
Essex, S. 135, 136
ethical holding 113–114, 119
ethics 90–91, 104–105, 144, 164
ethnographic methods 9, 184, 211–216
excitement of social work 33–34
extra-familial child abuse 4, 156

F
family group meetings 137
family support services 114–115, 116, 189
fathers 45, 117, 136, 144, 155, 156, 167, 207
female social workers 38
feminism 175
financial support for families 116
Firmin, C. 4, 156
Forrester, Donald 125, 138–139
Forrester, John 42, 43
forward-facing approach 8–10, 13, 56, 112, 138, 183, 199–200
foster care 98
frame for social care work 155–156, 159, 164
frequency of visits 43
Freud, Sigmund 9, 179
funding for social work 206–207

G
gender inequalities 10, 155, 156, 167
Glisson, C. 184

good authority 41, 45, 53, 88, 93, 120, 134–139, 147, 205
good enough parenting 41–42, 46, 136
good enough practice 46–47, 53, 121, 207–209
'good' social workers/service users 48–50, 130, 172
Gottlieb, A. 99
government guidance 15, 109
Gregory, Mark 184
Grey, B. 141
grooming 90–91, 105
group supervision 185, 195
Guard, Caroline 99, 108

H
Hallett, Sophie 90
Harvey, A. 193, 195
hate in relational dynamics 126, 128, 130, 132–133, 137, 139; *see also* reliable hate objects
Hemmelgarn, A. 184
Henderson, F. 193, 195
Hicks, S. 28, 89
Hobson, Star 7–8
Hogg, Sally 99
holding environments 9, 115, 120, 183–184, 196–197, 208–209
  emotional support and staff well-being 190–195
  'live' supervision 184–187
  spaces for support 187–190
  see also managers, support of; supervision
holding practice 9–10, 41–43, 46, 49–50, 52–53, 61–62, 64, 202, 203
  babies and young children 101–107
  digital 161
  see also intimate practice
holding relationships 4, 111, 122–123, 171
  case study 113–117
  components of 118–122
  parental perspectives 117–118
  Practice Cycle and seasons 112
  relational styles 145–147

home as space for improvisation and mobile practice 155–158, 165–167; *see also* movement
home conditions *see* living conditions
home visits 155–158, 204; *see also* practice encounters
homophobia 143
honesty 134–135
hostile relationships 4, 125–126, 138–139, 205
   good authority and negotiation 134–138
   involuntary relationships 126–128
   long-term 128–132
   relational dynamics 132–134
   see also reliable hate objects
hostile responses to social workers 29, 34, 38, 48, 58–60, 64, 77, 113, 117–118
   and reflective practice 176–179
Howe, D. 171
Huegler, N. 156
hybrid approach (digital and in-person) 160–161, 166, 205
hygiene *see* living conditions

I
immersion in children's lives 89–90, 121
improvisation 24, 29, 48, 86, 93, 157–158, 162, 173–174
inequalities 10, 119, 175, 179, 206–207
infant observation 107, 108, 179, 205
infant voice 98–100, 108, 136, 205; *see also* babies and young children
Ingold, Tim 9, 199
injuries sustained by children 7, 99
inquisitiveness 33
internal supervision 172–173, 176, 178–179, 180, 181, 185, 205
intimate practice 81, 94–95
   babies and young children 101–107
   ethics 90–91
   immersion in children's lives 89–90
   initial encounter case study 82–86
   meeting children's needs 86–89
   older children and teenagers 92
   Practice Cycle 92–93, *93*, 203
   relational styles 145–147, 152, 153

investigative approach 27, 36
invisible children 10, 55–57, 60–61, 65–66
   babies and young children 97–101, 131–132
   case study 57–60
   see also automated avoidant practice; disorganised practice
involuntary relationships 125–128; *see also* hostile relationships

J
Jeyasingham, D. 34
job satisfaction 208–209

K
Kahr, Brett 133
Klein, Melanie 9
Kong, S.-T. 160
Kristeva, Julia 67, 75

L
Labinjo-Hughes, Arthur 7
Laming, H. 125, 170
Lampitt, S. 19
Lefevre, M. 91, 156
life and practice 9, 199–201
LinkedIn 208
lived experience of child protection 199, 207
living conditions 67–76, 83, 157, 176
location for encounters with children 28–32, 39, 136, 162–165; *see also* bedrooms of children; out and about practice
long-term practice 16, 34, 43–46, 53, 200
   empathy, compassion, endurance 47–50
   reliable hate object 50–52
   see also holding relationships; intimate practice
Loving, Alice 142

M

making child protection work 2–3, 8–10, 13, 22–25, 56, 62, 76–78, 92–93, 101, 112, 142, 158, 169, 179, 199–201, 203, 209
male social workers 30, 90, 105, 143–144
managers, support of 27, 36, 39, 46, 62–63, 64
    for disorganised and avoidant workers 76, 78–79
    facilitating holding relationships 113, 121–122
    facilitating intimate practice 92–95
    hostile relationships 129–130, 132, 134, 137–138, 139
    relational styles 152–153, 154
    during visits 35, 77, 186
    see also holding environments; supervision
masculinity 143–144
MASH (Multi-Agency Safeguarding Hubs) 16
Mason, Clare 98
McFadyen, A. 99
media coverage 4, 7, 33 34, 47, 76, 105
men, violent and abusive 37–38, 99, 117, 175, 207
Menzies-Lyth, I. 192
meta-cognition 174, 176
Miller, D. 89
mobile practice see movement; out and about practice; Practice Cycle
modelling 90–91, 107
monitoring of social workers 17–19, 47, 206–207;
    see also Ofsted
morale 32, 189–190, 193–194
Morton, Lucy 107
motherhood and the home 10, 155, 156, 167, 207
mothers 10, 45, 98, 102, 123, 135, 137, 139, 144, 155, 167, 203, 207
motivational energy 18, 32, 141, 206
movement 103, 115, 155, 157–158, 173–174, 202, 205; see also embodied attention; embodied self; walking interviews

Multi-Agency Child Protection Units 8, 200
multi-agency coordination 8, 12, 15–16, 44, 159, 200
Multi-Agency Safeguarding Hubs (MASH) 16
Murphy, C. 189

N

negative outcomes 47
neglect 7, 14, 19, 68, 73–74, 98, 176
negotiation see Practice by Negotiation
non-physical touch 62, 82, 94, 101, 102, 121, 147, 161; see also digital intimacy
non-reflection and non-thinking practice 170, 173, 179, 180

O

objects, importance of 89–90, 92
O'Connor, L. 20
office work 14–15, 16–21, 27–28, 62–63, 153; see also bureaucratic preoccupation; organisational arrangements and practices; organisational culture
Ofsted 16, 18, 47, 189, 192
older children 92, 121; see also teenagers
optimism, rule of 8, 56, 66
order-making 29, 204
organisational arrangements and practices 16–19, 187–190, 196
organisational culture 44, 49, 61–63, 66, 106, 121–122, 123, 208–209
    reflective practice 179
    relational styles 142, 152–153
    staff well-being 193–197
    see also holding environments; managers, support of; peer support; supervision
O'Sullivan, N. 194, 197
out and about practice 92, 162–165, 166–167, 205

P

Page, J. 91
parallel processes 195

parent advocates 207
parental perspectives 117–118, 126–127, 207
parental power 136–137, 138
Parent-Infant Foundation 106–107
parenting assessments 113
Peace, D. 156
peer support 177, 186, 187–190, 191, 194, 195
Pelka, Daniel 7, 55
personal preferences of social workers 78; *see also* relational styles
physical child abuse 4, 7, 19, 98, 128; *see also* deaths of children and babies
physical contact and touch 23, 43, 56, 61–62, 81, 83–86, 87–89, 94–95
   babies and young children 98–100, 101–107, 114–115, 120–121, 131–132
   digital intimacy 159–161
   ethics 90–91
   older children and teenagers 92
   relational styles 142–143, 144–147, 152
   see also holding relationships; intimate practice; non-physical touch; relational styles
Pierre, Rebekah 207
Pink, S. 212
play 23, 58, 60, 89, 92, 107, 117, 142, 151, 153, 164, 202
playfulness 2, 32, 47, 58, 87, 94, 143
positive impacts and outcomes 46, 208–209
poverty 74, 75–76, 121; *see also* inequalities
power dynamics 10, 119, 126, 133–134, 136–137, 139, 145, 175, 179
Practice by Negotiation 134–139, 147, 205
Practice Cycle 6, 20–24, *20*, 25, 32, 39, 155, 201–203
   automated avoidant 55, 61–64, *62*
   disorganised and avoidant 76–79, *77*
   hostile relationships 134, 138
   intimate relational 92–93, *93*
   in long-term practice 46, 112, 121–122
practice encounters 1–2, 21–24, 28–32, 202

pre-birth assessments 98, 130, 160
prejudice of social workers 75–76, 119, 129–130, 132; *see also* power dynamics
preparation for practice encounters 20–22, 24, 27–28, 63, 76, 83, 92–93, 185, 201, 203; *see also* Practice Cycle
pre-school children *see* babies and young children
pressurised situations 37–39
privacy 164–165
professional curiosity 8, 45
professional development 142, 149, 150–152, 154, 204–205; *see also* training for social workers
professional self 142, 150–154, 172, 205
projective identification 193, 195
psychoanalysis 9, 3, 118, 133, 152
psycho-social approach 9, 120, 170
psychotherapy 6, 9, 46–47, 115, 120, 133, 152, 155–156, 179
punitive measures 128, 132, 137

R
racism 76, 88, 105, 119
referrals 15; *see also* assessment visits
reflection 35–36, 64, 73–74; *see also* reflective practice; self-awareness in social work
reflection in action 169, 172, 173–175
reflection on action 169, 174, 181
reflective practice 169–170, 180–181, 189, 202
   analytical thinking 179–180
   levels of reflection and self-preservation 175–179
   in practice 173–175
   supervision 193
   theories of 170–173
relational continuum 144–147, 150, 152, 154, 205
relational spaces 165–167
   digital 158–162
   homes 155–158
   walking and outings 162–165
   see also holding environments

relational styles 78, 94, 141–142, 153–154, 205
   core self and professional self 150–153
   embodied self and relational vocabularies 142–144
   relational continuum 144–147
   resonance and alienation 148–150
   see also automated avoidant practice; disorganised practice; holding practice; holding relationships; intimate practice
relational vocabularies 142–144, 152–153, 154, 205
relation-less relating 149, 206
relationship-based practice 3–5, 19, 43–46, 204–205; see also holding relationships; intimate practice; long-term practice
relationship-building with children 30–32, 38–39; see also babies and young children: developing relationships; relational styles
relationships to the world 148–150, 152
reliability 41, 42, 48, 53, 118, 121, 123, 152
reliable hate objects 50–52, 53, 112, 120, 188, 205
repulsion 149; see also disgust
research methods and aims 2–3, 9, 11–12, 113, 128–129, 211–216
resonance 6, 24, 45–46, 91, 103, 118, 148–149, 153, 161, 204, 208–209
resources for social work 206–207
respectful uncertainty 125
responsivity 148
restorative practice 125–126, 195
retaliation by social workers 128, 132, 137
risk assessing 27–28, 33–34, 37–38
ritual task performance 192
Rogers, Carl 91, 120
role modelling 90–91, 107
Rosa, Hartmut 18, 207
   alienation 60, 73, 148, 149, 194
   motivational energy 18, 206
   resonance 6, 10, 103, 118, 142, 144, 148, 204
Ruch, Gillian 3, 30, 194

S

Sachs, B. 47
Salmenniemi, S. 194
Salzberger-Wittenberg, I. 48, 52
Schon, D. 169, 171, 173
schools 13, 14, 34, 85, 164
Scollen, R. 47
seasons of social work 112, 128
self see core self; defended self; embodied self; professional self; suspended self-preservation
self, use of 171–172
self-awareness in social work 56–57, 60, 61, 73–74, 143, 171, 205; see also reflective practice; relational styles
self-preservation see suspended self-preservation
sensory experiences 4–5, 67, 76, 79, 176, 180–181, 212
sexual abuse allegations against social workers 30, 90, 105
sexual abuse of children 7, 82, 91, 164; see also child sexual exploitation
Sharif, Sara 7
Shedler, Jonathan 111
Sheppard, M. 171
Shoesmith, Sharon 18
short-term practice 16, 27, 38–39, 200; see also assessment visits
Signs of Safety 125
Simpson, J. 158
Simpson, P. 21
skills required of social workers 13–14, 29, 32, 38–39, 45, 61, 204–205; see also professional development; relational styles; training for social workers
sleep safety 99, 109
Smith, M. 172, 180
social acceleration 18
social class 75–76; see also inequalities; power dynamics
social media 99, 100, 158, 208
social model of child protection 156, 206, 207
spaces for support 187–190
splitting into 'good' and 'bad' objects 48–50, 130, 134, 172

Spratt, T. 207
staff morale 32, 189–190, 193–194
staff recruitment and retention 49, 189, 193–194, 196
statutory visits 165
Steggall, D. 47
Stern, D.N. 13
Stevenson, Olive 106
stillness 158, 202
stress 37–38, 60, 184, 194; *see also* anxiety; emotional strain
supervision
    emotional support and staff well-being 184, 191–192, 194–195, 196–197
    formal 184–185, 187
    internal 172–173, 176, 178, 180, 181, 205
    'live' 177, 184–187, 188, 189–190, 196
    reflective practice 171, 181, 202
    during visits 35, 77, 186
    see also holding environments; managers, support of
suspended self-preservation 170, 175–179, 180, 186, 191, 192
systemic change 139, 200, 206–207

T

teenagers 4, 92, 121, 153, 164, 165
therapeutic practice 9, 52, 81, 88, 93, 104, 120, 203–204
therapy *see* psychotherapy
time management and pressures 16–19, 24, 56, 61–63, 121–122, 137–138; *see also* bureaucratic preoccupation
timescales 15–16, 31–32
Tobin, M. 195
touch *see* physical contact and touch
training for social workers 139, 143, 144, 154, 166, 204–205
    babies and young children 97, 106–109
    reflective practice 171, 179, 181
    see also professional development
transitions 21–22, 63, 68, 74, 76, 93, 122, 134, 177, 201–203; *see also* Practice Cycle
trauma 193–194, 196–197, 207
Triggs, Suzanne 152

trust 44–46, 53, 91, 118, 119
Turnell, A. 135, 136
Turney, D. 194
Tyler, I. 75

U

unannounced home visits 28, 29, 33–36, 116, 135, 147
unborn babies 98, 128–130
unheld children 10, 55–57, 60–61, 65–66
    babies and young children 97–101, 131–132
    case study 57–60
    see also automated avoidant practice; disorganised practice

V

van Rhyn, B. 4–5
video calls 159–160

W

walking interviews 162–165, 166–167, 205
Walsh, J. 121
Ward, A. 150, 172
Ward, H. 98
Warner, Jo 76
Warwick, Lisa 92
well-being of staff 190–197; *see also* holding environments
Wengraff, T. 214
WhatsApp 160–161, 164, 165
Wilkins, D. 185
Williams, J. 141–142
Williams, Keanu 55
Winnicott, Clare 9, 41–42, 43, 48, 49, 112
Winnicott, Donald 9, 41–42, 46, 50, 112, 118, 119, 128, 133, 152
Winter, K. 30, 98
women in the home 155, 156, 167
Wuori, Dan 99

Y

Young, Iris Marion 156
young children *see* babies and young children

www.ingramcontent.com/pod-product-compliance
Lightning Source LLC
Chambersburg PA
CBHW051350070526
44584CB00025B/3710